HIGHER CALLING

HIGHER CALLING

CYCLING'S OBSESSION WITH MOUNTAINS

MAX LEONARD

PEGASUS BOOKS
NEW YORK LONDON

HIGHER CALLING

Pegasus Books Ltd
148 West 37th Street, 13th Floor
New York, NY 10018

First Pegasus Books hardcover edition January 2018

ISBN: 978-1-68177-618-7

10 9 8 7 6 5 4 3 2 1

Printed in the United States of America
Distributed by W. W. Norton & Company, Inc.

CONTENTS

Great things are done when Men & Mountains meet;
This is not Done by Jostling in the Street.
                                        William Blake

I suppose we really amounted to nothing more significant than a gang of overgrown children delighting in the conquest of altitude by the force of our own muscles. Yet to see a companion arrive for the first time on a sunlit crest, his eyes full of happiness, seemed in itself an adequate recompense. Tomorrow he might return to the valley and be swallowed up by all the mediocrity of life, but for one day at least he had looked full at the sky.
                        ***Conquistadors of the Useless*, Lionel Terray**

Camp des **FOURCHES**

Hameau **DU PRA**

Saint ETIENNE de TINÉE

ISOLA

NICE

Prologue

AIN'T NO MOUNTAIN HIGH ENOUGH

Stop me if you've heard this one, but I want to tell you about a man called George Mallory. George Mallory loves climbing mountains. He's good at it. His grandfather used to love climbing mountains too, but unlike his grandfather (who was also very good at it and was also called George Mallory) our George prefers to do it on a bicycle.

Oh, you thought I meant *that* George Mallory. Sorry.

George Christopher Leigh Mallory (the grandson) is the inventor of the concept of Everesting. Everesting is diabolically simple: pick a hill, any hill, and ride your bike up and down it until the cumulative elevation gain equals or surpasses the height of Mount Everest itself (8,848 metres, or 29,028 feet, above sea level). George Christopher Leigh Mallory completed the first known Everesting in 1994 by riding eight times up a 1,100-metre road climb on a peak called Mount Donna Buang near Melbourne. He was training for an expedition to the summit of the real Everest via the mountain's North Ridge, and his cycling feat, only achieved after several unsuccessful attempts, seemed to exist in a dialogue with his ancestor. George Herbert Leigh Mallory was, of course, the dashing, brave British mountaineer who was tragically lost on Mount Everest in 1924, as he attempted to become the first man to reach the top. Before that expedition, the *New York Times* interviewed him and asked: 'Why did you want to climb Everest?'

1

'Because it's there,' he famously replied.

Whereas a more appropriate answer for those wishing to Everest on a bicycle (who are therefore contemplating scaling a mountain that exists only in their head) might be: because it's not there.

Without the internet, George Mallory II's cycling achievement might have remained undiscovered by the wider world, and he would have continued life as just another cyclist who loved riding uphill. (In mountaineering circles, on the great scroll of people who have climbed Mount Everest, he's known as George Mallory II, and, as a way of distinguishing between the two Mallories in writing, it works for me.) But the internet came, Everesting became a thing and we would be destined to meet. Not before, however, the internet convinces me to give Everesting a try, and I find myself on top of a hill in Sussex slightly before dawn, pulling my bike out of the back of the car as a weak sun struggles to rise through the sea mist. As is helpful with any foolish and borderline unhealthy activity, I have an enabler. Jimmy is a guy I have met thanks to Strava, the online community for cyclists, and he will pedal the day next to me. We have met once before, at a cycling event, and now are planning to ride a stretch of asphalt that is 1.3 kilometres long and a 10 per cent average gradient 68 times.

Not long into our ordeal, a couple of Jimmy's friends arrive as moral support, to share the road with us for a short while before they go to work. On about their second ascent, one of them says something along the lines of, 'You must be mad, mate. Why are you doing this?'

And Jimmy just looks right back at him and says: 'You know why.'

᠕

That 'why' is really the question of this whole book: why do we have this obsession with cycling up mountains?

As kids, we all love going down things. First on a slide, perhaps, or in a buggy, and then for many of us on a bike. When we're adults, bicycles return us to the freedom we had as children – the freedom seemingly to go anywhere and do anything, to whizz downhill with our feet off the pedals sticking straight out in the air, almost like flying. But for a few of us, when we take up road cycling, some kind of switch flicks in our heads and we start to love going uphill instead. It's not a straight swap: I still like the downhills too, but the reward of the downhill (which lots of non-cyclists assume to be the 'point' of all that uphill) never factors into my thinking about why I want to ride in the mountains. This a book more about going up, not down. Why do we choose there, and choose that? If the downhill is not the point, what is? Why do we love doing something that's so *hard*?

As a cyclist, it's always been about the mountains for me. I'm naturally a skinny person, so as a bike rider I'm never going to win a sprint and I'm not built for the cobbled Classics of northern France and Belgium. But that doesn't mean I was a born mountain goat. I was actually born in London, a good way from any actual mountains, and didn't show any early signs of unnatural uphill tendencies. I didn't start cycling seriously (whatever that means) until my early twenties, and didn't ride a proper mountain until a few years after that, but when I did, something just clicked. Something was right, and I was hooked.

Some years ago – never mind how long precisely – having little or no money in my purse, and nothing particular to interest me in town, I thought I would cycle about a little and see the mountainous part of the world. It is a way I have of driving off the spleen, and regulating the circulation. Whenever I find myself growing grim about the mouth; whenever it is a damp, drizzly November in my soul; whenever I find myself involuntarily pausing before coffin warehouses, and bringing up the rear of every funeral I meet; and especially whenever my hypos get such an upper hand of me, that it requires a strong moral principle to prevent me from deliberately stepping into the street, and methodically knocking people's hats off – then, I account it high time to get to altitude as soon as I can. This is my substitute for pistol and ball. With a philosophical flourish Cato throws himself upon his sword; I quietly take to the bicycle. There is nothing surprising in this. If they but knew it, almost all men in their degree, some time or other, cherish very nearly the same feelings towards the mountains with me.

It is, however, definitely a minority interest. If I meet someone at a party, say, and tell them that I like riding my bicycle in the mountains – that I regularly embark on uncertain, self-propelled journeys 20 kilometres or more up exhaustingly steep slopes, from the safety and warmth of the valleys to the storm-threatened, cold and inhuman peaks (and, moreover, that I often base my holidays around them and pay hundreds, maybe even thousands, of pounds for the privilege) – I usually meet one of two responses. One: a disbelieving laugh and a nervous stare, and then a look over my shoulder, a scan of the room for someone else to talk to. And less often, two: a hint of kinship, or jealousy, in my interlocutor, and their eyes mist over as their thoughts travel somewhere beyond the horizon, to deeper wonders than the waves. Closely followed by an inquiry as to where, and a long conversation about routes and gradients, often concluding in a request to come along too.

OK, that's a slight exaggeration, but it really is polarising. Some people get it, and some people don't. Ditto if we talk about the Tour de France or the Giro d'Italia and their excursions into the high peaks. Take, for example, Irishman Stephen Roche's superhuman effort climbing to the La Plagne ski station in 1987. On that crucial stage of the Tour de France he hauled himself back towards race leader Pedro Delgado, weaving and bobbing through the follow cars behind the Spaniard, limiting his losses to stay in contention for the yellow jersey he would eventually win. It was a gloomy day, the finish line was in a total whiteout and, when a lone figure emerged from the mists, nobody, least of all TV commentator Phil Liggett, could believe it was Roche. He had pushed himself so far beyond his limits that he collapsed on the finish line and was administered oxygen for half an hour after the stage. I watch it on YouTube now, 30 years distant, and feel a tingle down my spine. Many cyclists will feel the same shiver. They just get it.

But even if you do 'get it', it's not all that clear what you actually 'get'.

Everesting does, after all, look very much like extreme and inexplicable behaviour. I've not always been the type of person who wants to spend all the daylight hours (and a few of the night-time ones too) riding up and down an imaginary mountain. Several times on that Everesting day, the question 'How did I get here?' passed through my mind. Literally speaking, I drove down to the coast the night before from London and stayed at a pub in Peacehaven, which was good for cheap steak, chips and beer, but which I cannot recommend wholeheartedly on other fronts. Zoom up a level and you could say that George Mallory II is directly to blame for me being on top of a hill in Sussex with a man called Jimmy whom I hardly know. More cosmically, George's granddad is equally a part of it – he seems to have felt something like the same pull of the mountains that many people feel, and his story of doomed endeavour has undoubtedly added to the romance of the high peaks. Why is the fight against gravity so appealing? Why are mountains so important to pro racing? Why do we amateurs go up there too, and what do we see and feel when we do?

There is a mystique here that needs, erm, demystifying. Cycling is a simple activity, and a lot of the pleasures you get from it while riding in the mountains – fresh air, beautiful views – are simple too. But the 'why' is not a simple question. At times, trying to formulate it, let alone answer it, has been like nailing jelly to a wall. Like a nailed jelly, this book shoots off in many different directions, but they can be grouped into a few main strands.

Pro cycling. We're in Andorra and it's July 2009: Bradley Wiggins – not at this point known as a climber – has surprised the world by placing 12th on the Tour de France's first mountain stage, keeping pace with renowned *grimpeurs* including Andy Schleck, Cadel Evans and Lance Armstrong. Later in this Tour he will finish tenth on the legendary Mont Ventoux, helping him to fourth place overall.[1] This achievement equals the previous highest-ever British Tour finish (Robert Millar, a climber, in 1984) but, more significantly, it is the first step in his transformation into the Tour winner he will later become. And there, in Andorra, a mountaintop kingdom in between France and Spain, he is jubilant. This is real cycling, he tells TV presenter Ned Boulting, at the top of the 10.6-kilometre finishing slope: it's not about the velodrome (where Wiggins has been world champion in multiple disciplines and already has five Olympic medals to his name); nor time-trialling (where he holds British records); nor road racing on the flat (where he's pretty handy too). *This* is real cycling. This is where the glory is and where the dreams come true, he tells Ned. Wiggins reveres the exploits of tiny featherweight climbers such as Marco Pantani. He knows his cycling history – and he's right. All of road cycling's most enduring legends and breathtaking rivalries have been

---

1 Years later, when Lance Armstrong was stripped of all his Tour de France titles and results, Bradley Wiggins was bumped up to third place. But this is what we all thought happened at the time.

forged in the mountains. Every rider, from Chris Froome to Mark Cavendish to the greenest amateur, wishes they could climb better. Climbing a mountain gracefully – and beating your competitors up the slope – represents the pinnacle of cycling achievement. How did the mountains become so important to professional cycling? Who are the characters whose endeavours have ignited our love for them, and why are they so appealing? How come I, a 30-something guy from a major metropolis whose early experiences of sublime infinitude and awe-inspiring wilderness were pretty much limited to Hackney City Farm, knows and loves (and sometimes hates) such a remote and alien place as the Col du Galibier? Some of these founding myths may be familiar in outline, but the real details are surprising. There is a fascinating story behind why the Alps are cycling's Colosseum, the Dolomites its Wembley.

Psychology. It has long seemed to me that much of what we seek to know about the mountains – the wheres, the how-highs and how-fars – is fairly easy to discover. You can find those things in Stanfords map and travel bookshop in Covent Garden in London, in the books section at big bike shops, or on computer screens pretty much anywhere. And there are countless articles on how to train for a sportive in the mountains, or how to pace yourself up an Alpine climb. But all these facts presuppose one thing: that you want to be there in the first place.

There is no map for what goes on inside your head.

In 1984 the famously uncompromising mountaineer Rheinhold Messner journeyed into the Karakoram region of the Himalaya, to climb Gasherbrum I and Gasherbrum II. Messner had been one half of the duo (the other was Peter Habeler) that first scaled Everest without oxygen, and, if the new expedition was successful, he and his new partner Hans Kammerlander would become the first climbers ever to traverse between two 8,000-metre summits, carrying on their backs everything they needed to survive, and with no returning to a fixed camp in between. If they were unsuccessful, then the most likely outcome was freezing or starvation. Bitter, lonely deaths . . . which might have been part of what attracted the German filmmaker Werner Herzog to document their attempt in *The Dark Glow of the Mountains*. He followed the pair to base camp, and in the resulting film, as the camera pans across the shining peaks where their uncertain future lies, he ponders: 'What goes on inside mountain climbers who undertake such extreme endeavours? What is the fascination that drives them up to the peaks like addicts? Aren't these mountains and peaks like something deep down inside us all?' Herzog disdained the 'accountant's truth' – his description of the banal external realities of life – and dug into people's psyches to reveal (sometimes made-up) 'ecstatic' truths. Hopefully, this book will uncover a few ecstatic truths of its own about the mental challenges we face – and seek – in the hills.

How is that even possible (part I)? There's no point honing the mind if the body is going to give up on you when the going gets tough, so next to psychology is physiology. One of the big draws of cycling in the mountains is the physical exertions it demands, and watching pro racers attack, up 10 per cent slopes and at altitudes where the air is thin, speeding in a way that normal riders would find tough on the flat, is an amazing and humbling sight. How do humans push themselves like this? What does it feel like, and what is actually happening when they do? But it's not all about pros: physical training, effort, suffering, pain, are a huge part of everyone's experience of road riding in the mountains, and, without going into 'training manual' territory, this book will explore the personal and emotional landscapes we encounter.

How is that even possible (part II)? This might be the most neglected of all the strands. What is it that road cyclists wishing to ride in the mountains simply cannot do without? Mountains, yes; and bikes. But the real conundrum here is the roads. They seem like a road cyclist's playground, like they were made for cyclists, even. Of course they were not – but what on earth are they doing up in these inhospitable, lonely places? Ribbons of tarmac that lead from nowhere special to nowhere else, whose tortuous routes are a mediation between some of humankind's greatest civil engineers and the immense geological forces that millions of years ago created the topography the roads now climb. Yet if one considers that these forbidding peaks have for centuries formed a natural – yet contested – barrier between European nations, the roads begin to make more sense. Far from being remote and insignificant regions, the mountain ranges of the Alps are key strategic areas in the struggles that have shaped the continent. Napoleon, the Archduke Franz Ferdinand and Mussolini will all play a part in our story, though if we're going back to first principles we could even look to Hannibal and his elephants (around 38 of which survived a march over the Alps in 218 BC). How does this relate to cycling? Simple: without this hidden history, the Alpine roads – and our sport as we know it – would not exist.

But it's more than geopolitics that have shaped human life in the mountains. You can ride past glaciers tumbling in supercooled slow motion, past abandoned refuges and watermills, or on roads overlooked by Second World War-era concrete bunkers on one side and 19th-century barracks on the other. Road cycling is not just competition, it's exploration. It's about seeing what's around the corner, in the next valley along and in the one after that – or looking back into the past. After many years pedalling slowly uphill, I started to question what had shaped everything I saw. I got to thinking that if you do not appreciate what has created the views you see, the very ground beneath your feet, then you may as well be on an exercise bike in a gym.

This part of the journey will range far and wide. Just as

we'll head behind the scenes of a Grand Tour, we'll also go behind the scenes on a mountain, to listen to the stories told by mountaineers, shepherds, road workers and other mountain people (and cyclists), whose presence and work can, in the rush for the top, sometimes go unnoticed. We'll search for what is unique to cycling in the mountains, but enrich that with their stories, since there is probably something in all of our experiences that is common, that will help us understand the mountain better. What does it take to live, work, ride among peaks . . . and what do we take from the mountains in return?

If the big question I'm asking is 'why', then each chapter contains at least one 'because . . .', even if it's not spelled out as such. One of the main characters I've enlisted to help is a young pro rider called Joe Dombrowski. He agreed to meet and chat, over the course of a year or more, and help me capture something of the life of a pro climber, the experience of training and racing in the mountains. For this I can't thank him enough. The other main character is the Col de la Bonette, a mountain pass in southern France. Many of the rewards of being in the mountains are no doubt similar if you're riding in Colorado, the Victorian Alps, the Atlas mountains or Montenegro, but much of what is particular to the history of cycle sport is distilled in the sweat spilt on the roads of the French and Italian Alps, so it made sense to me to remain there. There are plenty of climbs more famous than the Bonette, cycling-wise, but it is a place I knew well and kept returning to. It has the mystique of being the 'highest road in Europe' (which may not actually be true, as we'll see), which draws cyclists like moths to a flame, and it also became important in so many other ways: I found drama and war in its history, beauty and struggle in its natural environment, and people there who helped me understand the mountain more deeply. So, while the cycling stories roam far and wide across the Alps and the Pyrenees, the book also became a portrait of one mountain, built up over several years of riding and visiting it. It is a worthy stand-in, I think, for the iconic mountains of the Grand Tours, and the stories I found there will, I hope, resonate widely. There are a few other writers in here too, and you'll find a list of their books in the back pages of this one.

I'll be honest: I don't have a ready answer to any of this (that old thing of 'If I could tell you what this book was about, there wouldn't be any point in writing it'). At some points I'll be the White Rabbit leading you tumbling down the rabbit hole. But I hope there is enough common ground, bizarre adventures and amazing characters to carry all of us – those who 'get it' and those who don't – through. This is the story of an obsession, or rather several: we'll be travelling by the side of some mountain addicts, and some of the most remarkable sportspeople and explorers; across the world and back in time, to the earliest geological eras, the edges of civilisation and the cutting edge of scientific progress. The aim is to build an overall picture of the sensations, emotions, natural, physical and historical things, people and cultures you find in the mountains. If, by the end, we've clarified even something of what pushes people to ride their bikes in the mountains and keeps us coming back to see the wonderful things you can see there, then I'll have succeeded.

This is my whale. Call me Ishmael.

Chapter 1
SETTING THE STAGE

Or, Jean-Marie's feeling for snow and digging for the
'highest paved road' in Europe

I am drinking a coffee made for me in a Ricard glass by a man called Didier, and we are higher than the sun. I would go so far as to say nobody drinking coffee in Europe is higher than us right now. It is just past eight o'clock in the morning and we are in a blue portacabin placed slap bang in the middle of a road near a mountain peak north of Nice. To the south the road slopes downhill all the way to the Mediterranean Sea 115 kilometres away, and below us the surface is already warm in the morning light, but the asphalt here is covered by sheet ice. Behind us is a wall of snow some two or three metres high that – temporarily at least – forces a dead end, and to our left a narrow gap in the rocky ridge, where the road passes over the Col de la Bonette and down towards the Ubaye valley to the north.

The sun, which is literally below us, has just appeared between two other peaks some miles off in the gentle remote air, and is broadcasting silver darts across all creation, save for where the still-proud snow dunes around us cast deep dark shadows.

We are in a blue portacabin – HQ, lunchroom, sanctuary when the 100 km/h winds blow and the unpredictable blizzards come – emblazoned with fierce zebra stripes from the metal grilles at the windows, and Didier, a short man in sports sunglasses who in physical appearance owes much to both boulders and snowmen, is looking gnomic. On the picnic table in front of him are more Ricard glasses, Nestlé powdered instant coffee presented for our delectation in sugar-style sachets, and some actual sugar. He is leaning on a worktop with a small kitchen sink, and a gas bottle underneath it; to one side, a 25-litre plastic jerrycan half full with water, from which Didier earlier filled a saucepan to set on the stove for coffee.

It had taken a long time to heat. We're at 2,715 metres and although that means water will boil at lower temperatures (around 90°C at these heights), the altitude means the gas pressure is low and the stove's flame weak. There is barely any air up here, and Didier's colleague, Éric, is currently making sure there is less: he is slouched against the doorway watching, through sports sunglasses, the sheet ice melt at the bottom of the portacabin steps while he rolls a cigarette, one of many high-altitude gaspers he will smoke today.

We are in a blue portacabin and Aurelien, a young man with a deep tan and an air of perpetual surprise thanks to the white circles around his eyes, the negative image of the sports sunglasses he habitually wears, is outside taking his work boots and an avalanche transceiver from the back of a Citroën Berlingo 4 × 4, which is decked out in the jaunty white and yellow livery of the local authority's roads department. It is Wednesday 20 April and they have already been working for almost three weeks.

We drink our coffees, chat; then, once Éric finishes his cigarette, we walk out into the glare without bothering to lock the cabin (there's nobody around for miles) and drive off to clear snow from the roof of Europe.

ᐱ

It is an obvious and yet rarely considered fact that many of the roads that are central to cycling's mystique exist on the very margins of reality. They are places that can be said only properly to be there for four or five months of the year. In Europe's high mountains, if a climb doesn't lead somewhere important, like a ski resort, then most of the time, typically between early October and late May, it is shut. It is often covered with snow: at best, a lazy blue run; at worst, buried without a trace. Galibier, Croix de Fer, Tourmalet, Aubisque, Stelvio, Gavia: out of sight, but not out of mind – their names live on in our memories of the races we have watched and the rides we have done, or in our daydreams of sunny days to come.

In the summer, they are alive, busy with cyclists, hikers, motorbikes and even coach parties. Then, towards the end of each year, they revert from being a torture chamber or paradise (delete as applicable) for cyclists back to the harsh, untamed wilderness they otherwise are. And then, at the start of each following year, they need to be dug out so that we can enjoy them again. The responsibility for that lies with municipal authorities and so, propelled by an obscure conviction that significant things must happen there when cyclists are not around, I sought permission to go up the Bonette with the road-clearing crew. That meant arranging a meeting with Aurelien, Didier, Bernard (we'll come to Bernard later) and Éric's boss. His office was at the municipal depot in Saint Étienne de Tinée, the pretty village at the southern foot of Bonette. There, above the garages housing the salting lorries and the snowploughs, subdivision head Jean-Marie-André Fabron (soft pinstriped red shirt with the sleeves rolled up, three buttons loose, gold necklace not quite big enough to be termed a medallion nestling in a bed of grey chest hair), who talked me through the work and explained the schedule: that the *département* administration was obliged to secure the Bonette road as far as the little hamlet of Bousiéyas by 20 April, so people could get back into their houses and check what damage had occurred over the winter, and that was when they would begin the snow-clearing work in earnest; given good weather they should be hitting the top of the col around 20 days after that; and, since the local authority on the other side didn't have much money, the annual agreement was for the southern crew then to head down the northern road and clear that, even though it wasn't really in their jurisdiction. If the other side was not, strictly speaking, their responsibility, it was definitely in their interest: once the road opens, Jean-Marie said, the cyclists, motorcyclists and hikers come – 100,000 to 120,000 motor vehicles in the four peak months of summer – and the economy in both valleys is boosted by 25 per cent. On top of that, I thought, it must get boring living at the end of a col-de-sac, mustn't it? For seven months a year only to have one route to the outside world. To be able to turn left as well as right, and go to Jausiers for your shopping instead of Nice; that must be nice for locals too.

Jean-Marie's office was finished in light varnished slatted wood, in a ski chalet style, though the cheap lino floors and ringing telephones were a reminder of the council business at hand. On the walls were maps of the region and a few small photos of himself and others at the top of the mountain, dwarfed between white walls of snow, with huge road-clearing machinery behind them. He showed me more photos on his computer: guys in sports sunglasses and big coats with thermos cups in hand, posing smiling year after year behind the diggers, as if the magic of the thing, of the journey through the wardrobe to Narnia, never quite wore off.

It looked like quite a party. And the mountain man in him bristled when I cautiously inquired whether it was – although clearly good fun – risky in any way, shape or form. 'Not dangerous!' he scoffed, took stock a second, and finished up: '*Bon*. There is still that sheer weight of snow . . .'

Jean-Marie was the boss of the whole of the Tinée valley, named after the tiny river that wells up just under the summit of the mountain and which runs 75 kilometres down to join the Var river not far from Nice. His beat included five ski stations, 14 villages and at least one other high mountain pass. But it all paled in front of the Bonette: 'Bonette is a special mission,' he said. 'For me, for my teams of guys . . . it's a source of pride for us to do it.' Even in summer he sent a road-sweeping lorry up there almost every day. From Saint Étienne's position of relative shelter at 1,100 metres you could never quite know what the weather was doing up there, and the friable rocks at the top were prone to rockfalls or even landslides in freak summer storms. 'We don't want cyclists hitting stones,' he said.

Once I explained what I wanted to do, Jean-Marie was almost extravagantly unconcerned about letting me loose in the pristine wildernesses above, with the avalanches and the ice sheets and all that heavy machinery. But this was October. I wouldn't be able to hitch a lift on a snowplough until April or May next. Jean-Marie said he'd drop me a line when the work was in progress, and I left.

The Col de la Bonette closed just a couple of days after my visit, on 13 October. It is often called the 'highest paved road' in Europe, and it is always one of the first to be surrendered to the winter snows. But, if we're being honest, it is not really Europe's highest paved road. That accolade is usually given to the Cime de la Bonette road, above the col. We commonly think of cols as high places, but col is the French word for a mountain pass, and a pass is usually, relatively speaking, the opposite of a high place: it is the lowest or the most easily accessible way of crossing a shoulder of land between two peaks, from one valley into another. The Col de la

Bonette-Restefond, to give it its full title is, at 2,715 metres high, superseded by several roads in Europe, including the Col de l'Iséran (2,770 metres) behind Val d'Isère in the French Alps and the Passo dello Stelvio (2,757 metres) near the Italian border with Switzerland. Cime, on the other hand, means 'summit', and the Cime road, at 2,802 metres, is widely proclaimed to be the highest paved road on the continent. It is a loop that lassos the Cime de la Bonette itself, the dark, very regular pyramid-shaped peak which has a viewpoint and a panorama on top. However, the Cime is actually not the highest paved road either. The Ötztal Glacier road in Sölden, Austria, is surfaced higher, but it's a toll road and a dead end; the Pico de Veleta in Spain's Sierra Nevada is higher too, but that's also a dead end and vehicle access is restricted.

And so the Cime de la Bonette may conceivably be the highest inter-valley road in Europe, which is, if you dig into the history a bit, pretty much what it was built to be.

Though there had long been a mule track over the mountain, the road was not built on the northern side until the end of the 19th century, and even then it did not connect with the villages in the south. It rose, via a slightly different route called the Col de Restefond, to link two military barracks, and did not go further. The two sides weren't truly connected until 1950, when the junction was made with the existing road on the south side. Previously, that had only reached as far as Bousiéyas which, at 1,880 metres above sea level, was about halfway up. Quickly the new route, the first proper link between the *départements* on either side, became popular with tourists, but the road at the top was in a terrible state. It was now strategically useless so the army had no interest in maintaining it. But given that it was perilous, remote and extremely high (and also partly belonged to the army), the regional authorities on either side weren't keen on spending any money either. Finally, the prefect ruled that the state wouldn't give any funds unless it became a 'prestige' road. What better way to do that than to abandon the old Restefond col and build a new road along the top of the ridge, add a little loop around the peak and go for the altitude record? So that's what they did, and the road as we now know it opened in 1961.

But even this 'highest road' is problematic. It's only the highest inter-valley road if you ignore the fact that the Cime's start and end are within metres of each other, across a narrow ridge above a perfectly usable col, and that the loop is therefore completely pointless. It is a 'long-cut' built simply for the glory, a treacherous circle of tourist road, two kilometres long, with steep drops and 15 per cent gradients on all sides.

I wouldn't, however, bother expending much energy debating the case. Ever tried arguing with the French? It's a losing game. And besides, the factoid is announced on signposts everywhere, and written in books and everything. The French are nothing if not masters of branding. In fact – think Bordeaux, think Champagne, think Camembert, hell, think cycling

itself – they practically invented branding. So Bonette may not be the highest paved road, but since they've said it is so, that's what it's known as.

Approached from the villages of Jausiers to the north and Saint Étienne de Tinée to the south, it's a beautiful, fairly regular climb of around 25 kilometres. In summer, above Bousiéyas, that last outpost of civilisation, shepherds wander the pastures with their flocks in the time-honoured way of the *transhumances*, while even further up the deserted barracks still forlornly survey the landscape. Like all the very highest roads in the Alps, the climb seems to take you from one landscape to another, one season and one mood to another, as you ascend from valley to ridge and into valley again, up until there are no more valleys, to where all earthly lines converge at the peak. You can be in 30°C summer at the bottom and by the top be surrounded by stormy winter, or start off in a heavy mood and 25 kilometres later have been lifted out of it – having, thanks to the twin analgesics of the scenery and hard physical work, left your troubles on the road far behind.

There may be longer climbs elsewhere, and ones more brutal, and ones with more Tour de France history, but this is the highest point ever to have been ridden in a Grand Tour, and it is really something to be able to say I have ridden up the highest road in Europe (and show pictures of the signposts that prove it).

However, none of this works without a road.

The journey to the blue portacabin started at sparrow's-fart o'clock on Wednesday 20 April in Saint Étienne. The previous Friday, the road-clearing crew had reached and passed the col in their machines, and they were already engaged on the descent. We had travelled from Nice in the dead of night to catch them before their drive up the mountain and I was keen to know why they were so far along so early in the year. The first of the crew to arrive, Bernard, was no help. He was unsure of who we were, how the work was progressing, what would be happening for the rest of the day, or, equally possibly it seemed, how he had arrived at that place, at that time, why he was not in his bed. He seemed cheerful about it all, however, and in that moment, fresh from a late flight from the UK, a 4 a.m. alarm bell and two shots of bad black coffee, I envied him his eternal present and the equanimity – nay, dry humour – with which he was able to confront all things that crossed his path.

Aurelien arrived on a mountain bike, then Didier, and then Éric, and the situation became clearer: it was because of the Giro d'Italia.

By lucky coincidence (both for my snowblowing visit and, it would turn out, this whole book), it had been announced only a week before my visit to Jean-Marie that the 2016 Giro would be passing over the Col de la Bonette. It was the first time the Giro was to cross the Bonette, and it was to take place on 28 May, the penultimate stage before the grand finale in Turin. The race would enter France the day before, and having overnighted in Risoul to the north, would climb the 2,111-metre Col de Vars before attacking the 24-kilometre climb of the Bonette from Jausiers. Then it would head down the other side and take a left turn at Isola, where the riders would face another 20 kilometres or so of uphill – through Isola 2000, a ski resort, and over the 2,350-metre Col de la Lombarde. There, it would re-enter its homeland and continue via a short, technical descent and a steep uphill to the finish line at the holy shrine of Sant'Anna di Vinadio.

That opened up some interesting prospects.

Most excitingly, it might very well happen that these French climbs – the Vars, the Bonette and the Lombarde – would prove decisive in the battle for the overall leader's pink jersey (the *maglia rosa*) or the mountains classification jersey (currently a very Italian shade of blue). Equally, they might very well not. It was also totally possible that the Italian favourite, Vincenzo 'The Shark' Nibali, or another contender could have built an unassailable lead in the nineteen stages before then. However, given that the Giro's last day is traditionally just a celebratory procession (and in this particular edition's case, almost all downhill), the Bonette stage would be the last chance for any real racing. This would be the last place any of the climbers would be able to show themselves or make their mark on the race. I could already imagine hordes of thin-limbed cyclists hurling themselves in a sort of reverse-lemming manoeuvre at the flanks of these formidable mountains in a kamikaze final lunge for glory, victory or self-immolation on the bonfire of best-laid plans and dashed hopes. Either way, it was certain that my favourite corner of the Alps, one that seemed often criminally overlooked by the big races, would be the scene of a right rip-roaring Grand Tour battle.

Or was it?

The thing about the Giro is that the weather can be, well, interesting. Italy is a long, thin place, and while the south can be sweltering, even in May, the north can offer an entirely different climate. One of the reasons sometimes proffered for why the Tour de France is a bigger and more prestigious race than the Giro (aside from its seniority and that branding thing the French do) is that the Tour de France occupies a prime position in July. There is a logic to this: people are on holiday, the sun is reliably shining almost everywhere in France, and consequently the race has a *laissez-passer* to go anywhere: the highest, most picturesque climbs and the most breathtaking roads in France. The whole thing screams summer and good times. The Giro's position in May makes all that less certain, and the race has often famously run into difficulties in the high mountains. Think, for example, of the celebrated pictures of Andy Hampsten climbing the Passo di Gavia in a blizzard in 1988. That year, in preparation for the stage, the 7-Eleven team riders covered themselves from head to foot in lanolin and team *soigneurs* raided the local ski shops to keep their riders warm.[1] Or, more recently, the Passo dello Stelvio, the Giro's iconic climb close to the Gavia in the Ortler Alps: in 2014 it was the scene of some confusion when, in a freezing, dank near-whiteout, the racing on Stelvio's long, looped-spaghetti descent was neutralised, on safety grounds. And then it wasn't. Or maybe it was. Whatever the race orders (it is still not 100 per cent clear what actually happened), the Colombian Nairo Quintana raced down the hill regardless, winning the stage and putting himself in the *maglia rosa* – which he would eventually win.

You've spotted the flaw in this line of thinking, haven't you. The Bonette is clearly not in Italy. It is very near Italy, yes, but it's also pretty near the Côte d'Azur and should be more blessed by sun than the Italian Alps to the east, where the climate is much more Mitteleuropean. Nevertheless, the basic point remains. Any high European climb can be hit by bad weather in any season (I took a drive up the Stelvio once, in mid-August, and looked pretty silly wandering around in espadrilles in the few centimetres of snow at the top) and there is always an element of playing chicken with the forecasts. But the bottom line is, taking a race over 2,000 metres in

---

1 Lanolin is an oily substance produced by sheep which helps waterproof their woolly coats. It is used in beauty products but not, to my knowledge, by cyclists at any time other than this. A *soigneur* is the name given to the cycling team's masseur. It means 'carer', and *soigneurs* are very often asked to do other tasks, like handing out food in the feed zones or fetching supplies. (There is a glossary at the back of this book of some common cycling terms.)

May is definitely a more risky business than in July, and the 2016 Giro wasn't planning to do it just once, but 10 times. (By contrast, the always-more-conservative Tour was programming four 2,000-metre-plus highs in 2016.)

We'll leave the question of 'why go so high?' until a bit later: for now, let's just concentrate on the final two climbs, the Bonette and the Lombarde, which were the ones on Jean-Marie Fabron's turf. The decision to include them was surely the result of a detailed feasibility study, risk assessment, long consultation with stakeholders and serious high-level debate. *Non?*

'I've no idea whose initiative it was . . . So far I've only heard about it in the newspaper,' Jean-Marie told me that day we met.

Oh. Right.

Bonette can suffer serious snowfall and is not reliably open until May, so the decision not to consult the man in charge seemed, from the vantage point of his office at least, slightly flawed. The previous winter there hadn't been much snow, so the road had opened on 11 May. The year before that, however, had been a snowy one, and it hadn't happened until 31 May.

'In May, we're not certain of having made the link. I . . . Listen. If the Giro comes through, that's great. Great for the valley and for everyone. But nevertheless, there's two cols to open, the Lombarde and the Bonette. When that's done, it could very well come through. But so far, nobody's asked my advice, whatever that is, on any of it.'

Jean-Marie was a little miffed. The mention of the Giro was the only time in our conversation that he seemed discomfited, not king of his castle. Miffed, but was he worried? No: 'Let's be clear: we've got what we need, we know what we're doing. It'll be a great experience for the valley, for the col. It's a great advert. I'm very happy, proud even.'

The Giro has never been over the Bonette before, but the Tour de France has taken it on four times, in 1962, 1964, 1993 and, most recently, 2008. Jean-Marie had been in charge for that one – a memorable Tour stage where the race passed over the Cime and the first man over, South African Barloworld rider John-Lee Augustyn, overshot a corner on the descent and tumbled down the mountain. Remarkably, Augustyn was OK, and even managed to finish the stage in 35th place, but for Jean-Marie there was more to regret that day: 'For me that was a bit of a missed opportunity. The Tour de France is magnificent, but when you see it elsewhere it's always so crowded, and here . . . I shouldn't go on about it, and we're in the middle of the Park, for sure, but I think that not everything was done to make people come, you know, and that's a shame.'

His phone begins to play a cha-cha-cha, which he ignores.

'It's clear that when people come there's always cleaning up afterwards, but we could have organised that and shown off this mythical col to cycling fans. I hope that for the Giro there can be an agreement to accommodate people at the side of the road. We can sort out patrols . . . there will be cleaning to be done for sure.'

The unspoken context of all of this is that the Bonette is in the middle of a national park, the Parc National du Mercantour. It's one of the wildest and most deserted parts of Western Europe, complete with roaming packs of wolves, Bronze Age remains and vultures wheeling overhead. It had been implied to me more than once (when speaking to other people in the area and not, I should stress, Jean-Marie) that the park rangers would prefer nothing else happening in the park at all. No cars, no roads, no bicycles, no people, nothing – and that they were militant about getting their way. So this was Jean-Marie's situation: he was a man. A man who loved a mountain. A man who loved a mountain and wanted to share it. A man who loved a mountain, with a big job to do. 'It's great that people can come to these mythical high cols to watch the riders pass. If not, what's the use? All the interest is lost.'

This is the backstory, then, to the accelerated schedule that Aurelien and gang are following – the pressure of the prospect of the passage of Italy's greatest race – and we are driving in convoy behind their jaunty Citroën as the sky lightens above the black cliffs on either side of us. It's a hell of a commute, up a road traversed by rivulets of meltwater that have refrozen overnight. A breakneck drive made safer by the more-or-less-certain knowledge that no vehicles will be coming down – though there may be newly fallen rocks, or large chamois or curly-horned ibexes around any corner, still sure that the mountain is theirs. We barrel past the tumbledown buildings of Le Pra with their rusty corrugated iron roofs, steam through Bousiéyas, and finally see banks of snow just below the Camp des Fourches, the roofless, abandoned collection of 19th-century huts that had once housed hundreds of soldiers defending the valleys against Italy. Two weeks ago, Didier explains, the drifts in this particularly gusty corner were up to six metres deep. 'The wind takes it from some places and dumps it somewhere else,' he says. Now, where it was six metres it is three, and where it was three it is only one. Once the snow's mantle is broken and the road dug out, the newly uncovered blacktop absorbs the sun's heat and accelerates the melting. This radiator effect is another good reason to get clearing early – the extra days will melt more snow, and make it safer and easier when race day arrives for the hoped-for multitudes of roadside spectators.

Above us, now, all is white, and you can trace a line of disruption, like animal tracks, high on the mountainside kilometres ahead, a rumple and a ripple and a ruff of tumbledown snow boulders that show where the mechanical shovelling has taken place. It must be a very satisfying job, I think, mixing as it does public service and breathtaking surroundings, and something childlike with high doses of risk and testosterone. It is not abstract and modern, like human resources or social media, say, or management consultancy (all fine choices in themselves). Or much like writing, save for the fact that most days the only thing a writer can do is dig down into the white page on screen to find the black words below that will offer him or her a way forward.

For the road-clearing crew there must be a tangible sense of achievement. We get in our machines and we move snow. We cut and we blow and we dig and we tip. Our progress is measured in metres advanced every day, and at the end we all sleep well because we've worked hard and we've helped. How many metres? Up to a kilometre on good days where there isn't too much snow banked up, says Aurelien. On other days, progress into this pristine backcountry of chamois, marmots and wolves slows to a crawl. The view, magnificent in macro, monotone in micro, barely changes, and only rock 'n' roll at full volume, through earbuds jammed into ear holes in an attempt to cut out the infernal racket of the machines, can make the time pass at a satisfactory pace.

Around three kilometres from the top we reach a wooden barrier swung across the road. The cars stop. It is secured with a padlock and two large bolts, which Aurelien, who is weighed down with a large bunch of keys and a hefty socket wrench, undoes. He hefts it open, we pass through and he locks it again behind us, and even just doing this is ticking off a life goal, albeit a fairly minor one: riding past a 'Road Closed' sign is a primal thrill. These barriers exist on almost all the climbs that shut annually, and they're padlocked open in summer, but which cyclist hasn't ridden past them and thought fleetingly about the secret playgrounds that must, in the off-season, exist above? The private stretch of blacktop all to yourself, with no cars and no people, and just the sun and the wind and the snow all around ... I am quickly disabused of this romanticism by Aurelien, who says the barriers aren't generally needed in winter: the avalanche risks are so great that the roads are closed much further down, usually by placing a few signs and dumping a large pile of the white stuff right in the middle. Instead, they are mainly used in spring-time, when the thaw has advanced and the road-clearing crews are working up top – both to stop unwelcome drivers and, it turns out, diesel thieves. There is enough slow-moving, thirsty machinery up there to need a smaller snowplough to service them; one which has sufficient diesel in the big tank behind the cab, apparently, to tempt thieves to drive up a steep, narrow, icy dead-end road in the cold black night to siphon it off. Good luck to you, boys, I think, and shudder inwardly.

From here our path is increasingly covered with hard-packed, dirty ice and large rocks, which appear from under the moving

Citroën without warning and force us to swerve. Sheer, high white walls rise up to three metres on either side, which in cross-section show the winter's different snowfalls like geological ages or *millefeuille* pastry. With blue above and white all elsewhere, the shadows are an icy aquamarine, like driving through a Fox's Glacier mint. Maybe a kilometre from the top our convoy stops by a dormant machine and Bernard gets out of the car, climbs into it and starts the engine. It is what any three-year-old might call a digger, with the tiny cab and oversized wheels and bucket of a child's toy, but weighing multiple tons and on a gigantic scale. (Frankly, it's what I would have called a digger too, though I have now learnt better and will call it a wheel loader.) Today, Bernard will be widening the channel and tidying the road we have just driven up, to make it perfectly passable. After the unnerving cannon-ball ascent, I find it reassuring that it will be in a better condition for our escape from the rapid chill of the high-altitude evening. We leave Bernard to it and then we're there, at the top, at the portacabin, and the coffee's on. And when that's drunk and gaspers gasped we head out over the col to where the machines are waiting.

Jean-Marie had promised to give me fair warning of progress, so I could visit for the most interesting bit of the work, and he hadn't disappointed. It would be difficult to overestimate the amount of snow up here and, even though I am told that clearing downhill is easier than up, it looks like the team is tackling the hardest bit. The north side of the mountain gets less sun and the road, after sloping gently for about a kilometre around the cirque of the Restefond valley, plunges sharply. I know from my summer visits that this is a steep scree slope, but now it is just a smooth white blanket punctuated here and there by tall wooden poles, poking skywards.

Somewhere under there is a road. They'd traced it

successfully over the top and around the cirque. The question is, where is it now?

Didier scrambles up into the driving seat of another wheel loader, and Aurelien gets into the snowblower – a Mercedes Unimog truck with a metre-high roller mounted across the front, and above that two curved, swivelling chimneys that lend it something of the look of a giant beetle with protruding antennae. The rotating drum is powered by an 11-litre turbo diesel engine that sits on the flatbed behind the cab. As it spins, the grooved surface chews into the snow, which is inhaled and then spat out in a plume in whichever direction the chimneys are pointing. Aurelien invites me to sit in the passenger seat, a dirty, metal-framed contraption surrounded by oily levers and gauges. He starts engine number one, then engine number two, and the snowblower belches out smoke from its snorkel exhausts – even engines lack oxygen up here and spit black fumes because of the half-combusted diesel. Then he engages first gear and we roll towards the snow bank where the road ends. The MO is that Aurelien's *fraise* (as the French call the machine, which for some reason is the same word as 'strawberry') cuts a first passage through the snow, exactly the rolling drum's width, and then Didier in the loader comes along behind to dig down to the asphalt, and clean it up and widen it until there is something you could, more or less, cycle along. It's not very scientific, and questions present themselves to me almost immediately

One: even with the snow poles, how do you know where to go? The markers we can see poking upwards are positioned on the downhill edge of the road, and the idea seems to be that you aim just above the poles and hope for the best. The rest of it is down to memory (of the landscape and roadway in summer) and, well, luck. 'Better to be too high than too low,' Aurelien tells me, and his understatement is not lost. The second is Newtonian: how do you stop the Unimog from just

tumbling sideways? Gravitationally speaking, that seems far and away the most likely outcome of all this hoo-ha. In other parts of France the *fraises* have caterpillar tracks, which are more sure-footed and stable in deep snow. Indeed, they did here too until quite recently, but there are relatively few roads this far south that benefit from it, and wheeled vehicles can be used elsewhere in better conditions, so a €300,000 investment is difficult to justify. Very quickly our Unimog, sallying forth on a bed of snow of unknown depth and constitution, seems right on the edge of tipping over to the left and into the depths of the valley below. I find myself bracing against the seat frame and leaning hard right, like a bubble in a spirit level bobbing upwards, as the horizontal underneath me see-saws left. Although he seems to be controlling the juddering, jolting machine with little more than gritted teeth and determination, Aurelien does not appear worried. He steers into the cool snow wall on the uphill side, and hopes the snow chains will bite. There are controls to keep the rolling drum level, thus creating a horizontal track for us to follow, and that's really all we can do: cut a level path and stay above the road.

Another problem quickly becomes apparent. The snow-blower can only deal with about 1.5 metres of drift, so if the snow is deeper, the snowblower must be lifted from the roadway where it is parked up to a height where the snow will not simply overwhelm the drum, fall into the blowers and get backed up. When this happens, Aurelien stops the engine, gets out and stands on the bonnet to dig both chimneys clear with a shovel. We attempt to begin again, but the wall is just too high and we are stuck, unable to move forward or backwards, staring through the Unimog's windows at a blank wall of snow on two sides. Aurelien gets out – this time through a roof hatch, as we are boxed in by snow and his door will not open – and unhooks one end of the tow chain from the back, walks over to Didier's loader, attaches it, gets back in. The gigantic digger takes up the slack and, barely straining, jerks us out. I reach out of the window and grab some snow from the vertical wall sliding past, and eat it.

The difficulty, Aurelien explains, was that the slope up to cutting position was too steep. We couldn't get high enough to get going, and we chat as we wait for Didier to landscape us a new ramp up. It's Aurelien's first full year as a member of the snow-clearing crew, but he's a mountain man through and through, having moved from his native Pyrenees to this valley of the southern Alps to be with his wife, whose family have a restaurant in one of the ski resorts. In the summer he works as a builder, and part time with the roads department, maintaining bridges and retaining walls, and mowing. 'Lots of mowing,' he says wearily. In the Pyrenees he'd also done what he calls acrobatic building work – abseiling down dams and cliffs, laying irrigation pipes for shepherds, that sort of thing – and I can see that trimming brambles is an anticlimax

after any of that. He explains the controls and the gear dif-
ferentials, and the different types of snow (icy is better for
snowblowers, slushy for loaders, powder for nobody at all,
and there's never a Goldilocks – 'just right' – situation); where
to find the best mountain bike trails in the area and how the
département is training up younger guys to clear snow on the
mountains as a lot of the older guys are retiring.

While we wait, I climb up and out and take a wander
around. In the UK, health and safety would be having kittens,
but nobody here worries about sharing their 'workplace' with
a city dweller who, though having frequently passed through
on two wheels, proves himself embarrassingly inept at walking
on the crusty snow above the road, and several times almost
slips down the slope. It's warm and sunny, and though the
journey up was hairy, now we're here, under a big sky and an
almost 360° view of peaks, there is a meditative tranquillity,
only broken by the tinkling of snow chains as Didier trundles
back and forth. Surrounded by the sea of white, the possibility
of a bicycle race passing here in five weeks – *five weeks* –
seems very remote. Finally, the snow slope that Didier has
fashioned is ready. Aurelien advances and we ride up, tip
backwards, backwards, and there is a precarious moment of
teetering, like a rollercoaster at the zenith of its climb, with
the entire windscreen full of blank blue sky sliding up and
away. Then we tip forward, the cutting motor engages, the
drum bites and fountains of white crystals stream from the
two chimneys and we are biting, chewing, spitting, motoring
on our way again.

It's not fast. One engine pushes us forward into the wall,
the other scoops the wall away so we can advance. The whole
shebang vibrates and shivers, the wheels slip, snow chains grip,
and centimetre by centimetre we carve a channel. Behind us
is Didier. He is a metre or more below us, just about un-
covering the road on which they will be racing in five weeks'

time, and he is demolishing the false floor we have created, scooping it up and tipping it over the side, then reversing and starting anew, advancing in a two-steps-forward-one-step-backwards Y formation. If Didier strays too far from the median he starts scraping at the dirt verge, pushing streaks of brown mud through the white, and he has to be vigilant: as the loader pushes snow sideways and off the edge, he is in danger of creating a snow platform, a false impression of flat ground where there isn't any. Even at this stage it's guesswork as to where the tarmac actually is, but with a bit of trial and error, the black emerges from underneath its white coat. With each tip of the loader's bucket, snow chunks the size of white goods – kitchen appliances, I mean – roll down the mountain and, contrary to popular belief, do not snowball and gather more weight, but instead eventually break up and explode into a million tiny snowflakes. Or they slow and sit in large, dirty chunks as a reminder of the heavy lifting that has cleared this road for cyclists.

We chug along for a hundred metres, maybe more, and then Aurelien shuts the engine off. It is a truism that at one o'clock each day half of France stops working and is served food by the other half, but it's also a valid insight into the national character. And the only difference that working since 7 a.m., being 25 kilometres up a mountain and surrounded by avalanches makes is that this great national pause happens a bit earlier. We get back in the car and drive up to the portacabin. Before eating, Didier puts the water on the stove to start its slow transformation into coffee for afters, and everyone compares notes on the morning. Not quite everyone. Bernard is not there. Why not, I ask. We can see his machine from afar, engine still running, but not moving or engaged in much work. In the distance, down the road, a solitary figure moves towards us, lean and rangy on a bike, navigating between the rocks and the ice patches on deep carbon rims. Decidedly, it is not Bernard. The man arrives at the portacabin and shakes Aurelien's hand. He's a local, a physiotherapist from Saint Étienne de Tinée at the foot of the mountain, and he clearly knows his way around it. In fact, he says, it's his fourth ride up this year. Last year he made it up 59 times – but he's in competition with a friend who beat him, with 60, so a few reps before the road is officially open is standing him in good stead. He hopes. Why do it, I ask, why this one? 'It's the most beautiful road in the Alps,' he says.

The physio also brings news of Bernard. Bernard was, as he rode past, sleeping in the cab of his loader. No lunch for Bernard. Just sweet oblivion in front of one of the best office views in the world. As for me, I have done no work whatsoever, but I am starving. I savour that irony keenly as I savour the taste of my Pret A Manger avocado sandwich. (This obviously compounds and multiplies said irony by a million, though in my defence, given the late nights and early starts, Gatwick Airport was the only viable option for me to buy the day's lunch.)

The afternoon's work passes quickly. Now we are in position we chug forward steadily and meet no more problems. The drop becomes less steep and the transverse cut of the road across the gradient less deep, and so less snow blocks our path. As the snowblower and the loader perform their synchronised dance the newly cut tarmac behind them becomes a slushy trickle and then a rushing stream. All too quickly, it seems, the noise and the shuddering stop, and Aurelien is hitching the snowblower to the loader and we are being pulled back down to earth. It's barely a quarter to three, but the machines have to be brushed down and refilled with diesel, and then it's almost an hour back down to the depot. It's not just the French functionaries' love of a short working day that's taking us down now: the afternoon heat brings softening snow, and with that come avalanches. Nobody here has ever been killed in one, and they employ geologists to survey the work when the risks are highest, but it's important to get out when the going is good.

Right at this moment Jean-Marie arrives, slaloming with insouciance down the stream in a two-wheel-drive hatchback. He is wearing a polo shirt, open at the collar, and cowboy boots and Ray-Ban Aviators, not sports sunglasses. He surveys

the work done, approves, gazes out over the unbroken white below. 'We'll be at the barracks by Friday,' he says, gesturing expansively towards the top of a long stone wall a few hundred metres distant, the remains of the large, squat Caserne de Restefond, the barracks that guarded the pass in the 19th century. Even though it's in plain view, the road serpents gently around the contours of the mountain so it's still a fair way off, but Jean-Marie can see far past it, down the hill to where the air is warm and the snow peters out, to where his crews will make the junction with the tarmac of the northern side; at which point they will take their machines back up and drive down in the Citroën to Jausiers, where the mayor will buy them all dinner. 'Opening this col, it's magic, you know,' he says.

There may well be more snowfall. But once the channel is cut the battle is won, and teams will just keep on going. 'We had 40 centimetres of fresh snow two days ago, and look at it now,' he says jubilantly, gesturing at the streams of meltwater glistening in the sun, wearing away at the snow walls by the side of the road. The only potential problem would be a big storm on the day of the stage itself, which would leave no time for clearing the road anew. And so, for Jean-Marie, the stage is set. Even the Lombarde (the Giro's other major climb in his jurisdiction, which is narrow and tricky in its upper reaches) will be ready. 'Our side will be OK,' says Serge, Jean-Marie's deputy, indicating that their snowblowers and ploughs will only attend to the road this side of the French–Italian border. 'The other side is their business.'

And, with that, we shake hands and they're gone, securing the barrier behind them so that we can enjoy the end of the afternoon alone. For my friends who came along for the ride (and who brought their bikes), it is time to realise that dream of cycling along an empty *route barrée*, the road winding between banks of snow like newly discovered buried treasure.

I, without a bike, am left with some time to think. Let's say we advanced 250 metres today and cut a 3-metre wide channel with an average depth of 2.5 metres. Light powdery snow weighs (so Google now tells me) around 5–7 pounds per cubic foot. Let's take six as a good figure, which makes it around 210 pounds or around 95 kilos per cubic metre. The loader's bucket has a volume of four cubic metres, which means that each of those overflowing loads tipped down the side of the mountain weighed approximately 400 kilos. So, at a rough guess, that means 1,875 cubic metres of snow in total, weighing around 178 tons, was cleared today alone. Can that really be right? The mind boggles at the effort put in so that we cyclists, walkers, mountain lovers, can indulge our passion and share these wild, remote places, these roads on which cycling legends were built and now exist almost solely for us.

I walk back up to the top and surprise two walkers in the loader's bucket, which is nicely bathed in the setting sun and affords a marvellous view . . . and privacy. They have laid out a camping mat within and appear to be preparing to have sex, and there is a good chance that this is – would have been – the highest sex in Europe; but clearly, with my arrival, the moment passes and they corral their two dogs and clear off.

So I sit, instead, alone, and watch the light soften, turning the snow on the distant mountains a delicate buttery gold. I think back to Aurelien: he was a mountain lover too, just like us. Why did he keep coming back, I asked. Exploring, he said – and though the answer was not surprising I was some-how surprised that someone so at home in the bright thin air was motivated by the same impulses as the rest of us, or that he found anything here left to explore. He was a skier and a mountain biker and a climber (and had a fat bike to ride in the snow), but he did a bit of road riding as well. Every year, he said, he would set off with a couple of friends on their road bikes over the Bonette down to Jausiers, then over the Col de Larche into Italy and back to the start via the Col de la Lombarde – a loop of three 2,000-metre-plus cols that would make a formidable Grand Tour stage and a grand day out for anyone else.

I asked him if, when he passed over the Bonette on a road bike in the summer, he felt proud of the work he'd done, and proud that he was responsible for giving us this experience. 'Yes, when there's still snow around,' he said. 'But when it's all gone people don't understand.' He continued: 'It's like the snow was never there. And then you have to start all over again the next year.'

It's a funny kind of work, then.

Hard and physical and with a certain pleasure, but ultimately intangible, ephemeral, a bit like cycling up a mountain itself.

Chapter 2
HORS CATÉGORIE

Or, how we attempted to drive a Citroën 2CV up the
Bonette, followed a brave adventurer into a crevasse and
neither proved nor disproved how the high mountains
came to the Tour de France

For reasons that, looking back on it, I am not now adequately able to explain, my friend Rémi and I once tried to drive a Citroën 2CV to the top of the Col de la Bonette. Or rather, I can still discern our motivations but, in hindsight, they seem threadbare and unable to justify such a bizarre undertaking.

To say that we were both at a moment in our lives in which piloting an old, underpowered car up a mountain made sense was true, and not even simply a metaphor. Some days before I had finished a period working as a journalist in France, and thanks to an extended amount of time away from home and long sojourns in the mountains I found myself without anchor or goal. My only aim was to enjoy the warm light and soft colours of the Riviera autumn, since heading back to England would be to admit that summer was over and to concede defeat for another year. Thus, in the 2CV escapade, I had no defined role: I was simply joining in for the ride, wherever that might take us. As for Rémi, he was head of a company in Nice that made cycling apparel – bib shorts, jerseys and the like – with a twist of French style; he needed to shoot his winter collection, and reasoned that only by getting high, high above the sparkling blue sea (still warm enough to swim in) would he find the weather to suit his clothes. However, aside from his professional obligations, I suspected he had private reasons for embarking on this strange mission: we were both perhaps open to something reckless and futile, which might fail, or even, somehow, obscurely succeed only in its own failure.

> In England – where there has to be a product – they ask: 'Is it for charity?' In Flanders, Italy, Spain or rural France, where lunacy is celebrated, they say: 'What beautiful madness!'[1]

I was all in for some beautiful madness. Whether you're the legendary climber Rheinhold Messner, two men in a 2CV or simply an average Joe on a bike, climbing a mountain always contains something of it, and the motivations that push you to climb are rarely sufficient to rationally explain the endeavour.

Rémi had decided that a 2CV, that quintessential Gallic motor, should be enlisted to add character to the photo shoot, and also as a platform from which the photographer might shoot. But there was of course only one way to get it up there: driving. The rest of the crew and the models were already in the mountains, so it was only Rémi and I who collected the car. The man who rented it to us kept a garage full of the bug-eyed Citroëns, on a street outside central Nice whose steepness seemed to me at least a minor reassurance that the nags in his stable were up to the job. He was interested that we were doing a photo shoot in the backcountry, and even gave us a magnetic sign advertising his business to place on the car door at an opportune moment. Frankly, being a mobile billboard was not in our game plan; neither was telling him

---

1 This maxim is printed on the route directions for the Dunwich Dynamo – an overnight ride of around 120 miles from London to the Suffolk coast every July. It's a kind of beautiful madness that, in fine-weather years, appeals to hundreds or even thousands of cyclists in a region where there are no lofty peaks they might pit themselves against.

that we would be pointing his antique up the highest road in Europe. And, more importantly, driving it safely back down again too. We did not feel we could fully disclose to him our plans for fear that he would take fright and forbid us from taking it on to those high distant roads of sharp turns flanked by crevasses, dangers that surely might provoke cheap and geriatric car parts to fail catastrophically.

After all, climbing mountains was not what the 2CV was meant to do. The car was the product of Citroën's search to provide 'an umbrella on four wheels' for France's large, poor rural population in the 1930s, and the initial brief stipulated the resultant car must be driveable in clogs, and be able to take four farmers and 50 kilograms of goods to market at 50 kilometres per hour. Most famously, it had to be able to drive a tray of eggs across a ploughed field without them breaking. Its development was hampered by the Second World War, and when the production model finally appeared in 1948, although it was something of a marvel of engineering it wasn't anywhere near the forefront of technology. Almost 70 years later, it had slipped even further behind the times.

The one that we were hiring was the 'Fourgonnette' variation, the little delivery van version of the familiar classic. It had a standard front half, but the back seats and curved rear had been hacksawed off and replaced with a raised ceiling and boxy load-carrying compartment that looked like a small shed (and anyone who has ridden in the French countryside can testify that thousands of Fourgonnette rear ends did indeed end their days as sheep shelters, chicken coops and the like), which may as well have been made of corrugated tin foil, for all the rigidity and protection it afforded. It was one of the last off the production line in the late 1970s, we were proudly told, but even this late model had four drum brakes rather than discs. (Drum brakes have enough stopping power for a tandem, but not much else.) Passenger ventilation consisted of two metal flaps under the windscreen that you could open or close, depending on how much wind you wanted around your armpits, and door windows that folded upwards along a horizontal axis and attached with a fiddly little catch to the door frame – an arrangement that seemed designed both to whack you painfully, were you to chance your arm for a little forearm tanning session, and to smash the glass when it inevitably jolted loose and fell. Door handles were little straps, and the front seats a metal-framed bench sofa with a few springs sticking out to snare unwary under-carriages. It had square headlights, not round ones, and in colour was somewhere between Dijon mustard and *crème anglaise*.

It was perfect.

After breezily signing a few waivers, we waved goodbye and nonchalantly sped off before the owner changed his mind. Or rather, with a bit of gearbox crunching we managed to point our Fourgonnette down the hill towards Nice's cauldron of traffic and roll away. It took a bit of getting used to. Every gear change was like plunging a bent umbrella pole into a bucket full of rusty washers and rummaging around to find the precise point that didn't cause the small engine to howl like a scalded donkey. Every roundabout presented the poten-tial for capsize as the vanette tipped and listed on its suspension; every junction an opportunity to test your body weight against the brakes, which seemed completely ineffect-ive unless you braced your hip against the seat frame, lifted yourself up bodily and stood fully on the pedal. Menaced by larger and faster cars, yet without the ability to cleave to the side of the road as you would on a bike, it was far more ter-rifying along a dual carriageway than cycling the same road. Gradually, we left the chaos behind and were soon km/h-ing up the river gorge road towards the tiny village of Saint Dalmas de Selvage, nestled under the Cime de la Bonette's peak.

Our plan, like our motivations, was not 100 per cent clear.

Suffice to say, however, that our first point of call was a bistro, where we would meet the bike riders and photographer for lunch.

Beyond that, I hadn't really thought. It seemed highly unlikely that the 2CV would make it up to the top, but I was looking forward to giving it a pop. And it was, I reflected, as we navigated the sliver of road squeezed between rock wall and mountain stream, the ideal moment to put a bit of Tour lore to a hands-on, *Blue Peter*-style test. For it was this diminutive French car that supposedly was used to test the difficulty of Tour climbs. Look on the route sheet for any given day, and unless the race has taken a trip to Holland there will be categorised climbs on the agenda, each one counting towards the King of the Mountains competition. Fourth category climbs are – the story goes – so called because they are scalable by a 2CV in fourth gear. If you've ever driven a 2CV in fourth gear you will understand perfectly that this means they are the easiest possible hills for Tour riders. Third category climbs could be climbed in third gear; second category in second gear and so on. And the biggest hills, the *hors catégorie* (beyond categorisation)? Tour de France founder Henri Desgrange had to drive up them in reverse. Could this underpowered icon actually have dictated the climb categories? We were going to find out . . .

∧

But first a historical diversion. Because, if this chapter is designed to clear up a few misconceptions about the mountains and the Tour, then the first thing we need to admit is that it actually wasn't the legendarily fearsome figure of Henri Desgrange we have to thank for the introduction of the high mountains to the race. Instead, it was a combination of Desgrange's anxiety, boredom and sadism and the promptings of a little man called Alphonse Steinès that was responsible. Steinès, one of the forgotten men of the early Tour de France, was born Johann Stenges in Luxembourg, but like Desgrange, who was slightly his elder, he was a central figure in Paris, the crucible of French cycling, in the 1890s and 1900s. Steinès had worked with Pierre Giffard, the founder of the Bordeaux–Paris and Paris–Brest–Paris races, and had played a part in organising the first Paris–Roubaix, before Desgrange asked him to help shape the Tour de France route after the 1904 race.

The Tour had had a tough year in 1904. Its second edition had been run over exactly the same course as the first, but it had been spoiled by several of the competitors, including the previous winner, Maurice Garin, cheating by taking the

train. The top four finishers were subsequently disqualified, and the scandal badly hit the race's reputation. One of the measures taken to restore trust was that stages would henceforth only take place in the daytime, to minimise the opportunities for cheating in the dark. But this change was also in part intended to improve the spectacle and make the race more exciting. This was where Steinès came in – because Henri Desgrange, for all his vision and drive, was conservative and cautious. The great man has a deserved reputation of being a despot, but at crucial moments his nerve failed him. He did not, for example, attend the *Grand Départ* of the first Tour de France out of fear, we can only assume, of it flopping.

It took someone like Steinès to push him – and the race – out of his comfort zone. Steinès was one of the most knowledgeable men in France about the state of its roads. He had long been in charge of the 'Sports Societies' column in *L'Auto*, which meant keeping in touch with cycling clubs across the country, and regularly criss-crossed France to meet the paper's regional correspondents. Not only that: in 1903 he had worked with a motorcar manufacturer called Martini, testing its new hydraulic brakes on every single passable road col in the Alps – 48 in all – and it was probably this that helped convince him that the high mountains were not only feasible by bicycle, but would also add a unique allure to the race.

The first part of the project was to convince Desgrange to change the route at all. Courageous in itself in that it must have involved significant dissent – in so many words suggesting, well, isn't doing the same route year in, year out, a little, erm, *boring*?

'With obstinate perseverance,' he said in an interview much, much later, 'I convinced the boss, Henri Desgrange, that a Tour de France should follow the coasts and climb mountains on the roads closest to the borders.'

A tour of France that actually went around France: revolutionary. Thus, where the 1903 and 1904 editions ate up France in six great long stages, the 1905 race skipped around in 11. It visited Caen on the Normandy coast for the first time, and took in Les Landes, the windswept sandy pine forests south of Bordeaux which, being totally flat, need not concern us here. It also paid its first visit to the Ballon d'Alsace, a 12-kilometre climb to 1,178 metres, which fulfilled all Steinès's requirements: it was right on the border with Germany (France's loss of the Alsace-Lorraine region in the Franco-Prussian War of 1870 was a sore point to say the least); and it was a real mountain that would inject the race with some pizzazz. To say that this was the first mountain pass the Tour ever climbed would be lying: the Col de la République, near Lyon, probably claims that honorific. At 1,161 metres, that col is barely lower than the Ballon, and was on the *parcours* from the very beginning. But although it is high it is not quite a proper climb, and the earlier point about branding still obtains: Desgrange probably saw he had missed a trick with the Col de la République – had not fully comprehended at the time what would constitute drama and hype in his new race – and now he was going to brand the hell out of the Ballon. His paper was going to make a right old fuss about this being the ultimate test of a cyclist's prowess.

The Ballon was, as we shall soon see, a success. A later stage took in the Col Bayard and the Côte de Laffrey (1,246 metres and 910 metres respectively), two climbs in the foothills of the Alps, which led to letters to the paper praising the strength of the men, who had ridden from Grenoble to Gap in four hours – a journey that would have taken a carriage with six horses (and four extra reinforcements on the hills) twelve. But, to cut a long story short, they were all relatively easily passed. So much for the ultimate test. More was needed.

The final impetus to push the race into the high mountains came, probably, from a certain François Faber. Nicknamed the 'Giant of Colombes', he was not so much tall as prodigiously strong, strong enough to nullify any excitement in the 1909 Tour. A strapping brute of a rider, he simply rode away from the peloton on several stages, and soloed for up to 200 kilometres at a time in race-winning breaks. This kind of blanket domination was not, from the newspaperman's point of view, edifying. Dull racing and zero competition did not sell papers. The Col Bayard and the Côte de Laffrey, obstacles once hyped as terrifying and fearsome, were not enough to slow Faber down, but for all his strength, he was heavy – posterity puts him at around 88 kilos. So, in the autumn of 1909, Desgrange let himself be convinced that the race should head into the high mountains of the Pyrenees. The itinerary was announced in January 1910 to little fanfare in *L'Auto*, with two stages, Perpignan–Luchon and Luchon–Bayonne, replacing the traditional Narbonne–Toulouse single stage. Then, towards the end of the month, a notice naming the principal towns each stage passed through. No commentary, no explanations, no details of the cols to be traversed. Even so, fans and locals joined the dots, and put two and two together to make oh-my-God-are-they-mad?! Outraged letters started flooding in.

'You're taking the racers where there are no roads,' said one correspondent. 'The routes you've chosen are cut off by snow, ravines and waterfalls,' said another.

Were they? Truth be told, nobody at *L'Auto* knew. Looking at all the evidence of how events unfolded, it seems that Steinès actually did not travel the Pyrenean course at all before the route was declared. He had taken it on faith that there was a decent road where there was a squiggly line drawn on his map. But in his zeal he had made a mistake, and consequently, it seemed, Desgrange had overcommitted.

Even in the early 1900s there were minimum standards for roads, and in France there was a nascent national road network. The trouble was, these *routes thermales* (so called because they linked the spa towns of Eaux Bonnes, Argelès Gazost, Luz Saint Sauveur and others) that crossed the now-famous cols of the Peyresourde, Aspin, Tourmalet, Aubisque and Osquich were not classified as part of it. The Tourmalet was, it was generally agreed, more or less OK in a car, but the Aubisque was nothing but a loggers' track (according to one of the letter writers), wide enough only to be used by oxen bringing timber down from the forests to the sawmills in the valleys. Their loads either took the form of large 'packets', or whole trunks dragged behind them, which scored deep, long grooves into the path's surface. 'There were holes there you could bury a man in,' Steinès later said.

And getting a car over the cols was one thing, but it was also beside the point. What about a bike? It wasn't completely unheard of. A publicity picture from 1899 for the Savoie region tourist board shows three riders – including one woman, which seems remarkably progressive for the time – merrily scaling the Col du Galibier, one of the Alps's biggest climbs. However, these *cyclotouristes* were taking advantage of an ingenious service: they were being towed, all three, by a mule. There had also been cycle races staged locally up the Tourmalet since at least 1902, when the Touring Club de France put on a 215-kilometre race that scaled the mountain twice. But was it was possible to ride the Tourmalet during the Tour de France, and to ride it with so many other terrible ascents all in a row? Desgrange was prone to hyperbole, and would never use one doom-laden adjective where three would do, but even he sounded sincere when he wondered if the high mountains were an obstacle too far: 'I lived through the most intense emotions of my sporting career in front of these men's effort on this abominable climb with its horrifying gradients . . . in front of their moans of anguish, in front of the collapse of certain men, at the end of their powers, at the side of the road,' he wrote. 'I felt, I must admit, that all these men had pushed far beyond their limits. I felt true remorse and was afraid, very afraid, of having gone too far.'

And that was only a smaller col, the Alpine Col de Porte, the year before. His worries over the Tourmalet – even now known as the Tour's jewel in the Pyrenees, and an absolute bastard to climb from either side due to the unrelenting gradient – were real.

After that January announcement and the resulting furore, whenever the Pyrenees stages were mentioned, the paper's tone was defensive. But they weren't mentioned all that much. The publicity machine was very different in those days, and Desgrange on the whole stuck to endless explanations of the rules and regulations – the editorial equivalent, perhaps, of closing his eyes and sticking his fingers in his ears and hoping the problem would resolve itself on its own.

It didn't, and the situation came to a head in late May. With the race only two months away, two of Desgrange's men, a journalist, Charles Ravaud, and another who is only ever referred to as 'the Inspector General Abran', drove down to give these two monster stages a go. They seemed to manage the entire route of the first stage, including the fearsome Portet d'Aspet, in their Imperia car with its Dunlop tyres (they made sure to advertise what they were driving), and Ravaud mentioned that on the Portet d'Aspet he wouldn't be surprised if, come July, many drivers had to reverse up its fearsome bends.

However, on the second stage their success was limited: their path up the Aspin, Tourmalet and Aubisque was blocked by snow.

The eagle eyed of you reading this may, by this point in the stacked switchbacks of this story, feel you have spotted some holes in the 2CV-categorisation theory. And there are fatal flaws – although maybe not the obvious ones. It is clear from the numerous references to cars reversing up the mountain tracks that drivers in the early days did find it difficult, and that car gears may really have been a useful metric of how fearsome a climb was. But the Inspector General Abran drove an Imperia, Desgrange preferred a Hotchkiss, and it was a Mercedes and a Dietrich that also got into trouble. In 1910 the 2CV was only a twinkle in its maker's eye. Yet that does not disqualify it: the *Grand Prix de la Montagne*, the official name for the Tour's climbing classification, only began in the 1930s, and it was only upon the race's resumption in

1947 that the mountains were divided into categories. However, this is still a year before the advent of the 2CV, and at first there were only two categories, which rather puts a dampener on *any* gear-related conjecture. More categories were added over the years, but they have never been totally consistent and there is no overriding objective logic to them: they have always been subjective and mutable. What may be a second-category climb in one Tour may end up a first category in another, for reasons of its placement in the stage or simply at the whims of the race director.

So, viewed one way, our experiment was a success: the 2CV theory was discredited even before we turned the key in the ignition; viewed in another light, one might say that our careful and highly rigorous investigation was based on a false premise and therefore useless. I hold my hands up and admit it: I'm no scientist. But I'll leave us trundling up the mountain for now and get back to 1910, where the Tour de France remained in a fix.

After the failure of Ravaud and the mysterious inspector general, Desgrange was furious: furious that the world's greatest race had been put in jeopardy and that, after going out on a limb against his better judgement, it was possible that he personally might become a laughing stock. Both parties report 'stormy conversations', with the result that Steinès was dispatched with his bicycle in early or mid-June – barely a month before the race – to recce the proposed route properly. 'I was determined to make it through, whatever the cost,' he wrote later. 'But I almost paid for this foolishness with my life.'

The story of Steinès's reconnaissance has been told and retold many times. Like most of the good stories about the Tour de France, its truth or otherwise is slightly beside the point, and it all happened more than a hundred years ago so it's not surprising there are many conflicting accounts of what went on. There has been a lot of exaggeration, guesswork and Chinese whispers – mainly about when it all actually happened (estimates in most histories range from late 1909 to May 1910) and what befell Steinès on the mountain that night. But, as it happens, we have two accounts of it directly from Steinès himself. One was published in *L'Auto* on 1 July, just before the race itself. The other was in a *L'Équipe* special edition almost 50 years later, in 1959, when Steinès was an old man of 86. In the accompanying photograph he has a long white beard, his trademark John Lennon spectacles and appears to be wearing a dressing gown and pyjamas. He is clutching something that looks suspiciously like a road map of *c.*1910 vintage, and resembles most closely Santa Claus on one of his evenings off. Both accounts, despite the years between them, concur on all the major details.

Steinès must have known as well as anyone how unpredictable the weather can be in the mountains, even relatively late in the year, but he was unprepared for the serious late-season snowfall in the Pyrenees in June 1910, which coated the tops of the highest peaks with deep fresh drifts. It didn't impede Steinès initially. He negotiated the Perpignan–Luchon stage and much of the second (including the Col d'Aspin where Ravaud and Abran had failed) successfully on his bicycle. After the Aspin, he stopped at Sainte Marie de Campan at the foot of the Tourmalet for some food, and received bad news: the Tourmalet was probably impassable. Definitely, probably, or maybe it wasn't. Nobody knew for certain, and nobody nursing their drink in the warmth of the local *auberge* seemed much inclined to find out. But Steinès could feel, you imagine, the malevolent heat of Desgrange's wrath on his back. He decided he must press on. A local man volunteered to drive him up (in a Dietrich, if we're still keeping an eye on the cars), and in the lengthening shadows of the evening they set off.

The going was good until, two kilometres from the top, they were halted by banks of snow covering the road. It was 7 p.m. and a heavy fog was competing with the approaching night to see which would fall first. The Dietrich was forced to turn around and Steinès, though hemmed in by snow, was at a metaphorical crossroads. To turn back would be to admit that he had let his mouth write a cheque his bike couldn't cash, and above all to fail his *patron*. 'It's great to play the big man, to show a courageous face, when you're chatting by the fire,' he wrote, somewhat self-congratulatingly in *L'Auto*. 'It's another thing to see that man in the face of adversity.'

What sort of man was he?

He resolved to make it, come what may, and found a shepherd who agreed to take him to the col. Together they began the climb. Steinès's inexperience made him a slow and perilous walker, and he fell into a crevasse more than once. An hour later they reached the trig point marking the top (given in those days as 2,133 metres, not the 2,115 metres the road is now) and the shepherd, refusing all pleas, imprecations and finally threats, refused to neglect his flock any longer and lead Steinès down the other side. Snow lay even more thickly on the downhill towards Barèges, and Steinès, alone and unsure of the way down, crawled on all fours for four kilometres over the snow, through the dark, slid, rolled and hit his head. Enveloped in clouds, unable to orient himself or even know how much time was passing, since his watch had stopped at ten past nine, he simply headed in what appeared to be the least dangerous way down. Eventually he reached a stream, which he followed to a waterfall, which soaked him, before carrying on downhill. Then he found some bicycle tracks to follow and, finally, a road; and when he found that, he fell to the floor with exhaustion and started crying. He'd crossed the Tourmalet by night and made it safely to Barèges. But only just. It was 3 a.m. and there were search parties out combing the mountainside for him.

'I escaped all by myself,' he wrote as an old man, 'but not without injury and not without terrible dangers. I lived through hours of mortal anguish, without help, in the sinister nocturnal silence of the high mountains.'

Nevertheless, Steinès communicated back to Paris that the Tourmalet was perfectly passable.[2] And it was by this confidence trick that he turned the Tourmalet from a 'wrong turn' (which is what the name means in the local dialect) to a 'must have' – from *un mauvais détour* to *l'incontournable*, as the French know it today.

---

2 Or so says the famous telegram he is meant to have sent to Desgrange – *'parfaitement praticable'*. Actually, Steinès says he telephoned, so perhaps the telegram is another invention by historians after the fact.

If only this had been the end of his problems.

There was still the matter of the Col d'Aubisque, which, though lower, was reckoned by many to be harder than the Tourmalet, and was definitely in a worse state of repair. The next day, Steinès battled over it through a storm, both riding and pushing his bike when the track got too bad. Arriving safely on the other side, he stopped for the night and learnt that only a few days previously a car had been attempting the crossing when it skidded on the loose stones of the track surface and rolled 400 metres into a gully. The car (a Mercedes) was completely destroyed, and all four passengers had died.

The following day he paid a visit to the *Génie des ponts et chaussées* in Pau, to talk to the chief engineer in charge of the local roads and bridges. At first, the man was horrified that anyone might consider sending a bicycle race up what was clearly an unsuitable track. The Mercedes catastrophe had shocked the valley and he would happily do something to make it safer, the chief engineer said, but he didn't have any money.

'You have to make the road good. The riders will cross it in a month – mark my words, they will cross it,' Steinès replied. 'If it's a question of money we will provide it. But they will pass!'

The mention of financial help got things moving. Steinès put in a long-distance call to Paris and finally got Desgrange on the other end of the line, to whom he explained they needed around 5,000 francs to make the road passable.

'Offer them 500,' Desgrange said, and the line cut out.

That evening, Steinès dined with the chief engineer and the subordinate whose job it was not to maintain the Aubisque road. By the end, they'd agreed that Steinès would return to Paris and try to increase this sum. After calling in all the favours he could, Steinès scraped together 1,500 francs. The chief engineer found the same amount, and with these 3,000 francs the work started to make the road over the Aubisque from Arrens to Gourette passable for a bike race.

I read Steinès's account of all this some months after my meeting with Jean-Marie-André Fabron who, though his official job title is *chef de la subdivision Tinée*, stands in a direct line of descent from that chief engineer in Pau; his conversations – or lack of them – with the Giro organisers about snow on the Bonette seem familiar. *Plus ça change*, I think. It seems correct to say that race organisers are always on the edge of a *folie de grandeur* – that their o'erleaping ambitions to bring us the highest peaks, the greatest excitements and spectacle always risk falling flat. The history of bike racing in the mountains has probably always been one of big gestures and big risks, for the organisers as well as the riders.

For all the uncertainties and difficulties in its preparation, once the riders are over the start line the 1910 stage is a huge success. The winner, Octave Lapize, duels with his teammate Gustave Garrigou up and down the monstrous cols. However, while Lapize is humbled and has to climb off his bike and walk some of the way up the Tourmalet, Garrigou, first man over, wrestles his machine up the whole way and doesn't put foot to ground. Desgrange's money man and deputy, Victor Breyer, is there on the top of the Tourmalet to see the first men over and receive Lapize's famous hurled abuse: 'You're all assassins!'

Either there was a lot of murdering going on or it's such a good line the reporters take it and run with it, as it's riffed on in the paper three times over the coming days. In the second instance, the organisers' car draws alongside a labouring Lapize on the Aubisque, and the rider is asked what's up.

'I'll tell you what's up, you're criminals, you hear?' he replies. 'Tell Desgrange that from me. You don't ask a man to make an effort like this, I've had enough.' In the third instance, Steinès conducts some interviews after the stage: 'Desgrange is an assassin,' is Lapize's verdict.

Emboldened by this reaction, perhaps – and by Faber's amazing third place overall – Desgrange thinks bigger and higher. The next year will include the Ballon d'Alsace, and in the Alps the Col du Télégraphe and the mighty Galibier. The mountains have given him suffering, spectacle and drama, and already forged some of the myths that will sustain the Tour for the next hundred years and more. Steinès makes even more grandiose claims, however, when he tells his version of the Tourmalet story in 1959. This modest sum of 3,000 francs and the publicity generated by the Tour, he says, led to the *routes thermales* being classified in the national road network for the first time: 'I say that without the Tour de France, the world's tourists might not even today know the splendid, admirable, unique *Route des Pyrénées*, this trophy of France in its incomparable natural setting.'

In other words, when Desgrange gave the mountains to cycling, he gave them to everyone else as well.

As for us, we got to the top, eventually. Just not in the 2CV. It motored happily up to Saint Dalmas, where we found the photographer and assorted bike riders already tucking into a lunch of cured meats and cheeses made of the milk from the flocks of sheep that grazed on the banks of the tiny river below. We joined them and mixed in a little red wine to give us courage for the ascent ahead. But even the wine could not convince me that the 2CV would successfully take us much further. Even though our late-model van was, comparatively speaking, supercharged – 602cc rather than the 398cc the smiling little rust buckets were born with in 1948, and therefore something like *trois* rather than the *deux chevaux* of its name – it didn't inspire confidence. To cap it all, it had been decided we would be taking the hidden back road to the top, past Saint Dalmas to the Col de la Moutière and then around. This had the benefit of being stunningly beautiful and deserted, and the disadvantage of being much steeper, with three kilometres of unpaved track at the end. I was uneasy and, surrounded by models, the old advice from *Walden* flashed through my mind: 'Beware of all enterprises that require new clothes.' And I remembered from Steinès the folly of unadvised motor trips in the mountains. In 1913 he had the privilege of reading his own obituaries after the car he was travelling in during a Tour de France recce (a Hispano-Souza, if you want to know) rolled over while trying to avoid an accident. It left him with multiple fractures, wounds bad enough that he was not expected to live. Upon awaking in the hospital, he read the words written over him on his deathbed and – ever the diligent journalist – offered to write his own instead, so that there were no mistakes.

Despite my pessimism, the Fourgonnette took the first steep slopes with aplomb. However, about halfway up it started to labour. Something began to smell and the clutch ceased to engage or disengage the gearbox, and I enviously thought back to the unasked-for luxury of both reading and writing one's own obituary. The burning smell got worse. Eventually the forward motion ceased – no explosion, no flames, broken bones or disfigurements, barely even a cough from the engine – and we had to park it on the verge and let it 'rest'. Then we carried on up to the top, the Col de la Moutière, a desolate place where I had my first real look at a wartime Alpine bunker. The compact, forbidding concrete outpost stared out over the desolate landscape, still standing guard in a way that captured my imagination.

The Fourgonnette revived on the way down, and we got it

back to town without accident or injury. But I took the experience as proof, if any was needed (it wasn't), that a 2CV did not dictate the Tour's climbing categories. Neither did our valiant 2CV, to my knowledge, appear in a single publicity picture taken from that shoot. Was it all in vain? Your guess is as good as mine. Much later, in a fit of vintage postcard buying – the results of which you will find scattered through this book – I came across something. A picture from the early days of the Col de la Bonette with, you've guessed it, a 2CV parked at the top. So it was not the road's fault. Perhaps it was simply a bad 2CV. Perhaps our failure was due to bike riders jumping in and out and a photographer hanging out of the back doors. Perhaps it was because we were going at barely a walking pace and stopping frequently to let the riders

catch up. I recalled that the *hors catégorie* – the slightly non-sensically named 'beyond categorisation' categorisation was born in 1979, around the same time as our Fourgonnette. Let's call it an *hors catégorie* photo shoot.

Chapter 3
CONTROL, AND LOSING IT

Or, pain and its consolations, racing with or without a
brain, and Freud and flying stones to finish off

It's summer somewhere in some nameless mountains in
France, and I'm riding with my rather fitter and speedier friend
James. But that's OK, because he's stopped for a pee behind
a road sign and I'm forging ahead up the slope at my own
pace, knowing that he will catch me soon enough and force
me to speed up to, and then past, the point of hot discomfort
once again. In the meantime, though, there's some pensioner
on a mountain bike a couple of hairpins up the road. A
damselfly snared in the surface tension, a trout circling below.
I glimpse him periodically through the cherry and the apricot
trees, and a little further up, strobing in between the neat
rows of the vineyards, frozen zoetropically each time as if in
a motion study of a cyclist. He's pedalling very smoothly, but
I figure I'll reach him easily, breeze past him with a cheery
'*Bonjour*', maybe slow down to exchange a few words – if he
can squeeze any out without keeling over – and then I'll pedal
off again, all *souplesse* and mountain-goat ease. Five minutes
later, I'm breathing loudly and mashing at the pedals, while
the old timer is still just spinning along. He's barely any closer
and I can feel my features are set into a familiar red scowl
of effort. James rejoins, smells the sweaty tang of competition
in the air, and also takes up the chase. An eternity passes
and I'm on the edge of breathless collapse but we're within
hailing distance of the guy, whose scrawny legs seem barely

to be pushing the cranks around. I struggle to compose myself and to project the nonchalance I had once imagined I'd have in this situation. We draw alongside, force out a '*Salut*', and the plastic bulge on the down tube of his bicycle frame makes everything clear: he has a battery, and, therefore, a motor. Mechanical doping. He was a lure, and we swallowed it, hook, line and sinker.

The point to be drawn from this is not that we should hate electric bikes. (I did at that moment, but, all in all, I was rather pleased he was even able to ride in the mountains, which I don't think would have been open to him otherwise.) Nor am I highlighting how much I cared that we'd bust our guts in a rigged and unfair contest. The point is more that anyone can ride up a mountain. OK, not everyone; but most people aged between seven and 77 with a good basic level of fitness can, even without motor assistance. If you don't think so, give it a go. You won't look elegant like Fausto Coppi or soar like Marco Pantani – it will more than likely be a bloody ugly, dishevelling and discomfiting slog – but as long as you're prepared to dig in and turn the pedals for far more time than is reasonable or dignified, you will probably get to the top.

However. Very few people ever actually *race* up a mountain. On group rides we may attack relentlessly and tear strips out of our mates, or when riding solo set our sights on beating some nameless other up ahead, but even if we participate in an Italian Gran Fondo event or an Étape du Tour (the annual amateur sportive run on closed roads over one of the Tour de France's stages, which are hotly contested by an elite few), for most of us these are just a long, lumpy day out on the bike. Yet racing in the mountains has, in the century since Desgrange's experiments in the Pyrenees, become central to our appreciation of our sport. Whether it's the Pyrenees, the Alps or the Dolomites, the mountains are where, as a rule, the Grand Tours are decided. And for armchair fans, a race inching up and snaking down passes is one of the most beautiful spectacles pro cycling offers. We can share in the satisfaction of beating gravity and arriving at the top, but very, very few of us get to ride at top speed up a mountain, taking on an opponent, taking on a race, sprinting uphill for fame, glory and a place in the history books.

What does racing in the mountains actually feel like and how do you do it well?

∧

When I first met Joe it was at a mutual friend's birthday barbecue, one attended by several pro cyclists who lived in and around Nice. He was a lanky 22-year-old American neo pro who had moved to France only a few months before, at the start of a two-year deal with Team Sky. Joe – Dombrowski – had excelled in his previous two years with the Livestrong development team, winning the Girobio, the 'Baby Giro', which vied until 2012 (Joe's year happened to be its last running) with the Tour de l'Avenir to be the most prestigious amateur stage race on the calendar. Previous editions had been won by riders such as Francesco Moser, Gilberto Simoni and Marco Pantani, and Joe joined these celebrated names thanks to a solo win on the Passo di Gavia. The Girobio used to be something of a crystal ball into which pro teams and agents would gaze, divining future promise in the swirling shapes of the peloton within, but the race was not closely followed by many fans, even the diehard ones. What really got Joe recognised was his performance in that year's Tour of California. Stage 7 had a summit finish, a 5.5-kilometre climb with an average gradient of almost 9 per cent that took the riders high into the San Gabriel mountains to the ski lifts on Mount Baldy. At Baldy's foot, the 21-year-old had found himself in a whittled-down peloton of elite climbers, and when Robert Gesink jumped on a stage-winning solo break Joe did his damnedest to go with him. Although he eventually came in fourth, just off the podium, his finishing position ahead of respected climbers such as Tejay van Garderen, Tom Danielson and Chris Horner caused a stir. He arrived in the top echelon of the pro ranks at Sky, the team of the moment (alongside his friend Ian Boswell, who had also transferred from Livestrong), marked out as a climber of great potential.

Life seemed good at that birthday party, an event notable in my memory for the sight of a lot of skinny guys with razor-sharp sock tans digging into a wide selection of French patisseries, and for a kind of sugar-fuelled hysteria that dissolved slowly into guitar playing and singing in the warm Riviera night. However, Joe's two years with Sky did not pass as anybody might have hoped. In the tumult of moving from the States to Europe, with all the attendant disruptions and new experiences, he didn't seem to get the right support settling in, and his neo-pro schedule, given the big jump in difficulty represented by the World Tour, was gruelling. After a fitful start to his second season, Joe didn't race after the Tour de Suisse in June, sidelined by injury and a mysterious loss of form. Finally, an endofibrosis of the iliac artery was diagnosed – a hardening and constriction of the artery to the leg which restricts the flow of blood. It's a problem that is increasingly common in pro cyclists, but one that's still quite difficult to detect, and it had left him with a significant lack of power in his left pedal stroke. He was faced with an operation and a long, enforced layoff. The problem was only successfully resolved towards the end of his contract, at which time he left Team Sky.

When Joe signed with the American World Tour team Cannondale-Garmin for the 2015/6 season it seemed almost like a new opportunity, maybe even a second bite of the apple. Later, he would tell me it 'felt like a fresh start'. 'Starting from zero, with a bit more perspective and more of a platform to launch from.' I'd followed Joe's interrupted progress from afar, and this fresh start coincided with the increasing urgency of my questions, scrawled in notebooks or pinballing around my head, that would eventually become this book. He would, I thought, be an interesting foil to my musings on mountains. One: because he was a pro. Many pros are, of course, just like us in that they love cycling purely for the simple act of cycling (they are *much* better at it though); but they are different in that they need to know more, to understand more about the craft of cycling well at the extremes – at extreme speeds and in extreme environments – and in their ability to negotiate the demands and pressures of competition. Two: he was pretty young (24), and still learning. One of the aims of this book is to understand and to convey – to whatever extent that is possible – what it feels like to be in the mountains in a race like the Giro or the Tour de France; and I figured someone thoughtful, and still fresh enough to be discovering and absorbing new ideas and new feelings, would help to do that. Plus, after his disappointment at Sky, this was the moment he'd really need to start showing what he was made of.

So I got in touch, and he agreed to help.

I don't like interviews. They're often a process that can be formal and uncomfortable, even oppositional, for both sides. So Joe and I just chatted. Over the course of about a year, at sea level and at altitude, on the transatlantic internet and in many different physical locations, we talked and talked and batted things back and forth. And though some of it fits neatly into different scenes and different physical places, I'm going, with his permission, to marshal his insights and arrange them so that they're sometimes found far from where they started, in a way that helps me tell this story.

⋀⋀

We're sitting in the January sun, on the terrace of a café on the seafront not far from Joe's place in Nice, and, fittingly, we're eating tuna Niçoise salads. Being next to the sea, talking about the upcoming Giro with somebody who really knows it – not only that, someone who is actually going to be racing it – definitely promotes a feeling of being on holiday. Even though he lives here, I think Joe sometimes feels the same, and it's exciting that the Giro is coming to his back yard. The backcountry around Nice, which more or less culminates in the Col de la Bonette, has some of the most spectacular and deserted mountain roads around. If you're a cyclist interested in climbing (like, for example, Joe . . . and Chris Froome, Peter Sagan, Geraint Thomas, Nairo Quintana, Tejay van Garderen, Richie Porte, Romain Bardet and numerous others who base themselves in the area) it's pretty much a playground, and the only criticism that could be levelled at it, training-wise, is that there's barely a flat road on which to do your TT efforts and motorpacing (i.e. the things lots of climbers think are the boring bits). The decision to locate here is easy to justify: 'It's like, why does a five-hour ride in the mountains pass so quickly, but a five-hour ride on the flat seems to drag on and on?' Joe muses. 'The climbs provide a bit of interest rather than the monotony of cruising along on the flat all day, and it's the exploration of the climb itself, too. You don't say – at least I wouldn't say – I'm going to explore these flat roads today, but I would go look on the map and look for new climbs I've never done, go and ride a new climb just because it's there.'

It turns out that Joe is just as keen on exploring for the fun of it as any amateur cyclist, simply riding to see what happens if you turn left instead of right. That crinkle of the map as you pore over it, the alluring invitations of squiggly roads crossing contour lines. But now, with the second-largest race in the world coming to town, his detailed knowledge of the region assumes another dimension. The Bonette he hasn't ridden all that much, but the Col de la Lombarde, the second-to-last climb, leads up to the ski resort of Isola 2000, which is where Joe and friends often go for altitude training. I've been up and down the road a few times, by bike and by car, so I figure that after so many visits, and long descents from altitude to cycle in the valley, Joe will know it by heart.

There's a definite feeling of a hometown challenge coming on. I tell him that, all things considered, he'd really better do something special on the Bonette stage – for the sake of giving my book a cracking ending, if nothing else. This is probably the first, but by no means the last, time that I make this comment. I would call it a joke but that would imply that, on some level, I'm not deadly serious.

Joe's was not a 'normal' entry into the pro ranks, if such a thing exists. He came to road cycling relatively late in life, around the age of 18, and did a couple of years at university before quitting to have a proper stab at being a pro bike racer. His official bio says he is 6' 2" and in the mid sixties, kilo-wise, though when you stand next to him in Lycra he appears taller and skinnier than that. In the seasons that have passed since that birthday party he has matured and got visibly stronger, but, with his tousled hair, cyclist's tan, youthful face and glasses, if you passed him in the street in Nice you might be forgiven for thinking that he was an exchange student. He made it as a bike racer despite the late start because he was naturally very talented. His VO_2 max (the measure of the body's maximum oxygen consumption, which is a major determinant of potential at endurance sports, and largely genetically determined) was very high. But the top level demands a lot more, and Joe's about to give me a taster of the psychology and the roadcraft of racing in the mountains.

'Before, I could just go uphill fast. So as long as I could get to the climb without crashing, or wasting too much energy, and being reasonably close to the front, then I would probably go all right. But when you go up to the World Tour, everyone is gifted with good genetics,' he says. 'There's still a difference there, but ... those margins are smaller. So suddenly just learning how to ride in a bunch, how to be efficient, all the details become more and more important.' Details, details, details. Like what? 'Like ride as much as possible, sleep as much as possible and eat ...' he stops to think. We have finished our salads and Joe has declined dessert. We both have an espresso, his without sugar. In my head I fill the gap with my own choice of words. 'Well,' he finishes.

He tells me of the people who have taught him the ropes. Not recognised climbers, actually, but seasoned old hands like Bernie Eisel and Mathew Hayman. In the early days at Sky, Joe was sometimes tasked simply with following Hayman as he performed his team duties on the narrow, twisty European roads – very different from the Stateside superhighways of Joe's youth. Race objective: learn to move around the bunch with Matty. Understand peloton dynamics, the fluid shapes of an ever-changing thing, a composite creature with a hundred brains. The wind and how to stay out of it, gaps that disappear before they even open up; elbows, swearing, aggression and intimidation for the sake of it, being hustled out when you're just trying to deliver bottles. All symptoms of the pressure and the heightened competition that comes at the top level. Positioning yourself so that, when the move is being made, knowing that this is the move to make, you can leap to freedom, escape to where you're able to act, where you're in control.

'Whenever I've won a bike race it's always been alone and it's always been on top of a mountain,' Joe says. 'Other than as a Junior, that's how I've always won. And whenever I've won like that, I've always felt very in control, like, I have this.' He pauses, reflects and then continues: 'I don't know if it's because, when someone else is dictating the pace, a lot of times you're not able to handle it. You just feel out of control. And really you are, because if you were in control then you would have stayed with whoever you were trying to stay with – and eventually won.'

This may seem self-evident, but I'm not sure I've ever heard it formulated as clearly. Climbing a mountain is an uncomfortable thing. Go fast enough and the discomfort turns to pain. Race, and it is one of the most prolonged and focused ways of inflicting a certain type of pain on yourself or your rivals there is. Each revolution of the pedals is measured out in screaming muscles, and air gasped into and ripped out of lungs. In the fight against gravity normal limits cease to apply. Eventually, it becomes unbearable. And what then? Are you still in control, managing your suffering? You have a choice: 'Ultimately, when you're climbing, at some point you give up, don't you? Unless you win,' Joe says. 'At some point you decide to give up. Anyone, even the toughest guy out there, could keep going at the point they get dropped. But at some point you decide to get dropped.' In other words, there is rarely anything completely inevitable in that gradual inching away, the slow-motion disaster of losing a wheel. The number of people who make it *literally* to their last pedal stroke is minuscule, vanishingly small. The mind goes before the body. For Joe, the antidote when climbing is to try not to think about it. Sounds simple, doesn't it? 'You just have to dissociate with what you're doing,' he says. 'You can't really think about how uncomfortable it is, because then you just create excuses for sitting up. You think, yeah, this sucks, maybe I'm just not on that good of a day, maybe I'll sit up now. So it's like, goodbye! and then you just ride easy. But when you get to the finish you think, why did I do that? It's like this endless cycle – you're not really happy at any point in time, because when you're on the rivet climbing you're thinking, why am I doing this?'

Why am I doing this? It's one of the fundamental mind-games of the fight that goes on in the mountains: the mental fight in which you wrestle to control the physical and mental, all too aware that the impossible situation you're in will 99.9 per cent of the time only resolve into another impossible situation. There's only one way out. 'The only point in time you're happy is if you actually rode all the way to the finish as hard as you could,' Joe continues. 'And even then you're just happy afterwards!'

That said, giving it all unto the death is not always the right thing to do. If you're a *domestique*, making a specific effort or doing a job for your team leader, the best thing to do is to acquit your duties and then sit up to conserve your strength for the next day. In that situation, nobody is going to applaud you for putting yourself through the wringer racing for 30th place. But if you don't have the perseverance to keep going to the bitter end on the climb, how will you ever have the commitment to prevail on the larger, more important level of the race?

Is this core psychological ability to commit beyond what is reasonable something you've just got to have, or can you learn it? You could make arguments for both sides, citing riders who had the physical talent but just never had it 'in the head' to be the best, and the counter-examples of riders who matured, changed team, or underwent some experience that transformed them from quitter to contender. We probably all have a favourite theory. But how you make your commitment count, rather than just wasting your energy, is definitely something that can be learnt.

It comes back to control, and to knowing when to think, and when not to. Joe told me a few stories that might make this clearer.

The Rettenbachferner climb is in Austria. It leads from the town of Sölden to the Rettenbach glacier, a year-round skiing area in the Ötztal Alps. If you're looking for a climb to help people understand what it's like to race up a mountain, then this is probably one to choose. It's a pig. A long, steep, high pig: 12 kilometres at 11 per cent, starting around 1,400 metres and finishing somewhere close to 2,700 metres above sea level. It features fairly regularly in bike races like the Deutschland Tour and the Tour de Suisse, and, since it was built for ski-station access, it's well surfaced, well maintained and has a regular gradient: steep and unrelenting right from the bottom. That makes it Joe's kind of pig. The pig was included in the 2015 Tour de Suisse, a race to which Joe had been sent with the plan of riding for the general classification (GC), the overall race lead. I wondered how anyone might prepare for something so brutal, so, in one of our first conversations, I asked. He told me about scouting it using old race footage on YouTube: checking the foot of the climb for sharp turns or pinch points; the short downhill section in the middle; how exposed it got at the top. The climb was to come at the end of a hot, 200-kilometre-plus stage; given the position and the gradient, the team mechanics fitted a cassette with a 32-tooth cog to give Joe and the other riders a chance of spinning up in relative comfort rather than grinding it out slowly in too large a gear for the circumstances. 'The team put me in a good position at the bottom, and I was pretty much right where I needed to be,' Joe said. 'I didn't need to hit the bottom of the climb right at the front because, basically, there was an hour to sort yourself out – and it's a big road, you can move around. I was actually feeling pretty good.'

When a peloton first hits a climb, the work rate often jumps because, as sure as eggs is eggs, certain guys will accelerate. Sometimes, it's the non-GC riders with fresh legs and limited objectives – they want to make a break, catch the break or have a crack at the stage. Sometimes, it's purely because in the heat of the moment some guys lose their heads and rocket off unsustainably.[1] Not this time: the bunch went gently, perhaps because of the starting altitude or the climb's reputation. 'Then, maybe six or seven kilometres in, the real attacks started to go, the race-winning moves: the guys who would go on to win the stage were kind of there, and that's where I started to drift back,' Joe explained.[2] 'There was no

---

1 On a side note, isn't it wonderful that everyone, from six-year-olds on their first bike to blokes on a sportive to veteran pros, gets overexcited and jumps around like jelly beans in such situations? It says something about the spirit of the sport.

2 On another side note, Joe shared with me an observation by his team boss, Jonathan Vaughters. The nub of it is that there is a physiological reason that riders tend to get dropped every four minutes. According to Vaughters (according to Joe), people start getting dropped after four minutes, and the big selection is usually after eight

sudden implosion or anything, but I was riding at my limit, they went and I just rode to the finish as fast as I could go. It was not a bad ride but not a super ride. I'd been hoping for a bit more.'

So a damp squib, race-wise. (In fact, a bad first couple of stages put him a handful of minutes down, and the whole Tour de Suisse wasn't a memorable one for Joe.) One of those moments when commitment – or its lack – might not have made much difference. A sputtering out.

But hang on, that's not quite the story here. The real point is what happened to Thibaut Pinot on that stage. Cut back to that select front group, and to people falling off the back. Pinot, the young star riding for La Française des Jeux, was there with Joe and then, quite early on (let's guess maybe eight minutes in) he was dropped. Joe takes up the story: 'I'd got tailed off, and I was doing what I could, riding my own pace to the finish, and I remember seeing him come back. You don't take in so much on your periphery because you're so focused on what you're doing, but I remember thinking, oh man, he came back! The nature of the climb is you can see a few switchbacks down. He was well behind, and then he came past me again.' Joe continued: 'For one, that's pretty strong, mentally, to stay inside yourself, because if you go way too hard at the bottom then you blow and you're not going to come back. But also to have the mental fortitude to say – I'm assuming – I'm going to power-meter this, you know, stay within what I can do. And I'm going to sit on that all the way to the finish . . .'

---

minutes. After that, the intensity goes down every four minutes and the pace steadies until a winner from the final group emerges. 'So basically, when you're at the bottom of that climb, absolutely nailed, you have to think, OK, if I can get past this four minutes, then the next four minutes I'm good,' Joe said. Whether this is bike-rider lore, like not eating the crust of your baguette, or actual real hard science, I do not know.

That takes foresight and not a little bit of control. Pinot won the stage and took the jersey that day.

Chris Froome, apparently, is good at doing the same thing – getting dropped, riding the hill his way, coming back relentlessly – when he's not just outright winning, of course. When it's done well it's about confidence in yourself but, more than that, a will to force reality to conform with your desires. I'm going to detour quickly into rowing here, and borrow shamelessly from one of the great sportswriters – Simon Barnes, of *The Times* – and tell you about Matthew Pinsent. Pinsent is, if you're not familiar, a celebrated British rower, and one of our most decorated Olympians. In his book *The Meaning of Sport*, Barnes tells the story of Pinsent at the Athens 2004 Olympic Games: how Pinsent's coxless four was neck and neck with Canada in the final race; how Canada edged ahead and it seemed inevitable they would win; and how Pinsent, singlehandedly, pulled the race back from an impossible position. 'Pinsent took the crew over the line by means of a massive outpouring of the self. He refused to accept the plain and obvious fact of defeat and remade reality in front of us,' Barnes writes.

In cycling, mountains are where this feat of imposing one's will onto reality tends to take place. All the greatest riders do it: Eddy Merckx attacking on the Col du Tourmalet in 1969, cresting and looking back and then, seeing nobody descending behind him, soloing 130 kilometres over the Col d'Aubisque and winning the stage – sealing his grip on all the Tour de France jerseys that year, as well as the team and combativity prizes. A young Marco Pantani on the Passo di Mortirolo, smashing the climb record (and Miguel Indurain in the process) . . . or in 1998, on the Col du Galibier, on a stage to Deux Alpes in cold, heavy rain. Stephen Roche on that stage to La Plagne in 1987. The most recent example that springs to mind is Cadel Evans in the 2011 Tour, proving that even minor figures – relative to Merckx and his ilk – can have superhuman moments. That day, the French expressionist Thomas Voeckler was in the yellow jersey and the Tour was in the balance when Andy Schleck, one of the real favourites, launched a surprise long-range attack on the Col d'Izoard. Nobody would help Evans, who was among Schleck's most dangerous rivals, shut the attack down, and so he single-handedly dragged a small bunch, including Voeckler and Alberto Contador, another of the GC favourites, 25 kilometres up the Galibier into a headwind. Such was the force of his desire that in the final couple of kilometres he dropped both Voeckler and Contador, and finished with a small time gap to Schleck that he would easily obliterate in the time trial two days later.

But back to Pinot, whose ride up the Rettenbachferner exemplified the current thinking about the most efficient way to ride up mountains: no explosive efforts, ride your own pace, let the attackers burn their matches to no avail. It was riding and using your brain.

There are other ways to be clever when climbing. For example: drafting on climbs (something that amateur cyclists surely never think about). Joe again: 'I make this mistake frequently,' he says. 'We'll be on, say, a 5 or 6 per cent climb and so we're climbing at 27 km/h, and me, I have a lot of drag because I'm so tall, so not being on the wheel at that speed, even though it's not super fast, makes a pretty big difference.' So you have to stay on the wheel. But what if it all kicks off? 'A lot of times when there's a lot of accelerations my tendency is to want to ride more steady. I could follow, but it's costly' – here he means that pushing into the red too much can leave you unable to dig deep to follow the big moves later – 'so there's that moment's hesitation where I say to myself, "I'm gonna ride my own pace." Then all of a sudden, that group of guys moves up the road together and you're the only one not in it and they're all benefiting from each other's draft and you're pushing watts in the wind by yourself.'

Maybe that's using your head too much.

He continues: 'Or you have these fast climbs with a little bit of headwind, and they wait and jump around the switchback where it turns to tailwind. You don't jump, and then you make the next switchback, turn and it's headwind, and there's five guys rotating up there and then you're just riding by yourself in the headwind, so then you're screwed.'

Does he mean that, using your head can – paradoxically – sometimes mean losing it?

'Yeah. In some instances you have to ride like Pinot and use your head, and stay within yourself and time trial it, and other times you have to kind of ride without a brain. Even for just a minute or two.'

And here we're back, full circle, to pain. When it gets too much, when you really have to climb well, you just have to grit your teeth and get on with it. 'You have to be training good and eating good, the power has to be there, your weight can't be too high, but then when it comes to actually performing on the day, for the most part climbing well is about just turning your brain off,' Joe says. 'Like, sometimes I think I could be a better bike racer if I was a bit dumber. A lot of great bike riders are kinda stupid. You know, have nothing going on up there, just primal instinct.'

Of his big results, Joe has had a couple of contrasting wins. The brainer, if we can call it that, was at the Tour of Utah in 2015. The race had started disastrously when Tom Danielson, their designated GC rider, disappeared from team dinner the night before the first stage to take a phone call and didn't come back to finish his burrito. It was the US Anti-Doping Agency informing him he'd tested positive for testosterone (he has denied taking it deliberately, blaming contaminated supplements), and so he was forced to withdraw.

The team was in disarray and morale was low. But in the first stage Cannondale's Alex Howes took second place in the sprint, the mood lightened and the team began to work towards placing Joe at the top of the GC.

Stage 6, the penultimate stage, finished on a 15-kilometre climb up Cottonwood Canyon to the Snowbird ski resort. They made a plan the night before: teammate Ben King would get in the break and Joe would attack and join him at around 5 kilometres to go. The next day King did in fact get in the break, and near the bottom of the climb Joe made his move to bridge over. 'I go across to him, he does a suicide pull[3] and we just smash everyone on the final climb,' Joe says. Plan: executed. Jersey: taken. The final stage included two categorised climbs. The first, Wolf Creek, was quiet; the second, the 2,726-metre Empire Pass, saw Joe stick to Michael Woods, his jersey challenger, and endure a fast descent to the line where the two men finished in the group just behind the break – with Woods unable to make up any of the 50 seconds Joe had gained the day before. 'I'd say I come into the races now with bit more depth, and I'm a bit more calm under pressure. You know guys are going to attack you, you know guys are going to try to take the jersey on the last day, whatever, but just being confident: I was good yesterday, so I'm sure I'll be good today. I don't need to panic over anything,' Joe told me.

The other win – let's call it the no-brainer – was in that Baby Giro stage on the legendary Gavia, the same side of the climb that made Andy Hampsten famous. It had been a crazy race, and not untypical of the chaos of Italian amateur racing – 'There's really no team in control the whole time, there's loads of crashes, everyone's yelling, but the Baby Giro is a cool race,' Joe says. Despite a runaway dog almost

---

3 A 'suicide pull' is where a rider sacrifices himself for a teammate, riding so hard he is effectively 'dead' when he pulls off.

unseating him in the early time trial, Joe took the leader's jersey. But he then punctured on the *strade bianche*, the white gravel roads of Tuscany, and lost a lot of time waiting for a team car to appear out of the dust.

You must have been frantic, I say.

'Yeah, I had no teammates there,' he replies. 'Like, shit, I'm losing this race now, just standing on the side of the road. I was two minutes down because of that, and [the Russian rider Ilnur] Zakarin took the jersey.'

The second-to-last stage was a killer: two first-category and three HC climbs, finishing on the Gavia. 'We did 5,200 metres of climbing in 160 kilometres, in just under six hours,' Joe says. 'It was literally just up, down, up, down, up, down, up, down . . .' He counts the ups and the downs in his head, and finishes: 'Up.' At the top of the penultimate climb, he reached into his pocket to find the energy gels he could have sworn he still had were no longer there (he'd later find them stuffed between his pinned-on race number and the pocket). He descended, but at the bottom of the Gavia, he had neither teammates nor a team car (the car had suffered a flat tyre). And no water. 'So I was like, I have no food, no bottles, and there's still a 20-kilometre finishing climb to go. I'm gonna bonk for sure. I'm rooting around, nothing.'

Nothing to do but turn off the brain, and hope.

Joe continues: 'I went from the bottom of the Gavia, just full bore, so I was all by myself for like probably 45 minutes. With about 5 kilometres to go, the team car came up. But it wasn't ours, it was the Dutch national team car, with Marcello Albasini, our director, in the back seat. He said, "Hey man, you're gonna win, keep going, you're going to win!" I was like, "Can I get a bottle?!" but it was too late, I had to keep going.

'I was super focused so I didn't think about it, but when I got to the finish I was completely fucked. Another few kilometres I would have run out of juice, I would have lost 10 minutes. I was literally cross-eyed when I got to the finish line.'

'Why am I doing this?'

When it gets tough the pros ask themselves that question too. Pain and pain management are in the job description, and that must be a difficult thing to reconcile yourself with. And aside from the suffering of making an effort or hanging on while a rival turns the screw, there is the psychological pain, the affront to the ego, of being dropped. The only resolution to the impossible situation is the impossible situation. If I took any one thing from that (tuna) Niçoise conversation with Joe, it was that mountains are an opportunity for a rider like him to control and manage suffering – to deal with his own and make life insufferable for those around him. This makes the mountains – in addition to being a beautiful backdrop for this battle for control – an external manifestation of this largely internalised struggle of muscles and wills. A darkness visible. (Whether or not the spectator's voyeurism is healthy is another question.) It's what causes Joe to say, as we sit in the sun and talk about glorious, sunny five-hour training rides on deserted switchback climbs, 'That's when I can't believe I get paid to do this!' And then, in the next breath: 'The thing is, there's other times when I'd say, I would pay anything not to do this.'

Without the incentives of racing, let alone professional sport, what do we amateurs get out of cycling up a mountain that mitigates this? Succeeding in a challenge; feeling the achievement of reaching the top; being relieved of our effort in a place in which we are allowed not to pedal any more . . . certainly all of that. But part of it, I'm sure, is in the complicated relationship between pleasure and pain itself.

Some 'normal' people (i.e. non-cyclists) can have a very limiting attitude towards pain. Regularly – not all that often, but regularly – I crash when I'm riding my bike. Thankfully I've never had a bad one, but maybe once a year it gives me something to think about. I remember an old friend wincing, once, when he saw my bloodied fingernails and palms, and gravel and twig scrapes all up my arm, that had been caused by a tangle of handlebars and a rather graceless high-speed belly-flop into a great big muddy puddle. He could not imagine willingly participating in an activity in which physical pain was at some point and on some fundamental level inevitable. Or not any more: I remember him, us, as seven-year-olds, covered in grazes from exploring, or football or whatever, when our bruises were the visible proof of the fun we'd had. Even now, I cannot see a world without those highs and lows. That physical pain (and I often think this even when I hear of greater hurt, of friends badly injured descending or in traffic accidents), weighed against the pleasure cycling provides, seems a small price to pay. That muddy-puddle day, my friends said that all they could see, as I flew headfirst off the bike, was me smiling.

In 1899, an American psychologist and philosopher of the emotions, William James, wrote: 'I cannot believe that our muscular vigour will ever be a superfluity. Even if the day ever dawns in which it will not be needed for fighting the old heavy battles against Nature, it will always be needed to furnish the background of sanity, serenity and cheerfulness to life, to give moral elasticity to our disposition, to round off the wiry edge of our fretfulness, and make us good-humoured and easy of approach.' It's pretty certain he wasn't talking about bike riding, but I think his point stretches: the peaks are good at keeping us on the level.

I'm not claiming that my thoughts on pleasure and pain are typical, and only the weirdest masochists must actually like crashing, but my position, refined through numerous scrapes, is probably somewhere on a spectrum which has, at its far end, incidents like Tyler Hamilton winning solo in the Pyrenees, after an 80-kilometre breakaway, with a broken collarbone (he rode more than 3,000 kilometres in the 2003 Tour de France with said injury, finishing fourth).[4] Somewhere also on the spectrum is the more usual 'no pain no gain' training mentality, and still elsewhere is the suffering of riding up a mountain. These are qualitatively different from the other real pains in life – the heartaches and deceptions, the illnesses and goodbyes – in that they are mainly a product of our own will and are therefore entirely optional. And given that climbing a mountain is optional, it's worth asking why we choose it. In other words, asking what this pain *means*. 'Pain is a march by protesters who've forgotten to paint their signs,' wrote Tim Krabbé in *The Rider* – a great way of expressing the idea that, when cycling, it is a signal whose meaning we determine, and that we can choose our attitude towards it. Jens Voigt, for a long time many cycling fans' favourite hard man, called pain 'my favourite enemy' and 'my old friend'. For him, it had a multiplicity of meanings. When he felt it in training, it meant he was training well; when he was racing, it was an indicator that he was doing his job (and even that it might be time to attack, because he knew that if he was hurting others would be too); when he was injured, it was proof that he was still alive and all the relevant bits were still attached.

For non-racers, there's probably something of the last one – that enlivening feeling – in the pain of climbing a mountain. Plus the aforementioned knowledge that we're pushing ourselves, achieving something . . . and in that there is, maybe,

---

4 Pain was his speciality. At the previous year's Giro d'Italia, Hamilton broke his shoulder and ground his teeth so hard that he had to have 11 of them capped or replaced after the race. That time, he finished second.

a promise of happiness to come. Because, much more than in the muddy-puddle scrapes, pain on a mountain is not simply the by-product of pleasure but in some way necessary for it. There's something to make you smile in it. Tim Hilton, a British club cyclist, writes in his memoir, *One More Kilometre and We're in the Showers*:

> Suddenly I was a bird: uncatchable, self-contained, soaring and zooming towards the horizon, free from human worry and therefore happy. Cycling is about physical pleasure and happiness . . . Pleasure is more or less our goal and daily bread; and at some point in a good ride pleasure and suffering are one and the same thing.

It is a complex alchemy that turns pain into pleasure. We come back, again and again, climb the same hill 10 times in a row to teach our bodies to endure the suffering. For all the pleasures training brings, it is also a way of discovering pain. By training we understand and extend how much pain we can inflict upon ourselves. Pain becomes our currency and our goal. It is something to rely on, to control and to harness. To relish. 'It never gets easier,' Greg LeMond, three-times winner of the Tour de France, is supposed to have said. 'You just get faster.'

Some of this became clearer to me one June day in 2009, somewhere near the top of the Col du Galibier; certain things came sharply into focus just as everything else disintegrated. The Galibier and its precursor, the much smaller Col de Télégraphe, are two of the most legendary Alpine climbs, first crossed by the Tour de France in 1911, and very often ridden in tandem. They rise a total of 1,900 vertical metres over 35 kilometres, from lowland to ski resort to a desolate, barren theatre of high peaks. That day, about halfway up the Galibier, after 120 mountainous kilometres in the saddle, I realised I was running on empty and that, with no possibility of going back, stopping or finding any food, the only option was to keep on going . . . and that consequently I was pretty much done for. I was at Plan Lachat, the point in the climb where the road reaches the head of a valley and crosses the beautiful chattering stream you've been riding next to, takes a zigzag up the steep valley side into a hostile, less earthly place. Increasingly lightheaded, I climbed higher and higher, and as the world grew bigger around me, my sense of self diminished. I toiled interminably, past the last ruined livestock shacks and growing pockets of snow and ice, as the wind chilled and a gathering storm blocked out the sun above the steep road ahead. And then to a soundtrack of Pharoah Sanders in my headphones, a spectacular implosion like a supernova becoming a black hole, and a deconstruction began. My vision darkened around the edges and the world collapsed in on itself, folding like an empty cardboard box into two dimensions and, trapped between a rock and the infinite sky and dwarfed by the vast indifference of the mountains, as hail fell from clouds dark as bruises all around me, something in my mind cracked and two beams of sunlight, God's fingers, reached diagonally down into the valley below. And what is it but fragments of your own self you would discard that you may become free?

It was my best day on a bike ever.

Sometimes, days when the thinking stops are the most pleasurable. Often I go out into the hills on my bike with the intention of puzzling through some problem, or a writer's block; and once the kit is on and the pedals turning, what happens is . . . nothing. Sweet respite from the everyday cares. Things that pass through instead:

- What's the difference between a seed and a nut?
- My stupid brother

- A ham-and-cheese sandwich
- That girl (the girls) I should have kissed at school but didn't
- What age that guy who just passed was when he bought that car he's driving
- Hub airports and the Airbus A380
- Bunkers
- 74 divided by 16
- Where do flies go when there's a storm?

Everything and nothing, in other words, interspersed with long periods of glorious blankness. And then, in the shower afterwards, the thoughts start flowing and the door unlocks and the breakthrough comes.

Sure, that's a bit different to the sort of nothing you get from climbing a mountain. That requires total concentration and commitment, of the sort you can lose yourself in: if you're doing it right, you can only think of one thing – up. And, in a fragmented world of WhatsApp and Facebook and cat GIFs, and jobs that steal our time but not our attention, to have a single, all-consuming purpose is a release. It is so satisfying and so outside normal experience that it might only be interpreted as happiness. Up, up, up. One thought . . . and simultaneously none. We are conscious animals – half ape, half angel, said Benjamin Disraeli – but every now and then, we want to forget, even for a brief moment. When I'm climbing well, through pure effort I ride away from thought and leave my conscious being struggling a hairpin or two behind. I drop myself. Zeno's paradox: what is in motion is neither in the space where it is nor in the space where it isn't. And then total exhaustion, alone in a hailstorm on the roof of the Alps is, perhaps, another step further down the road towards the old sublime notions of ecstasy and oblivion.

Freud famously speculated on why people often performed

actions that did not simply increase their pleasure or diminish their unpleasure – beyond the pleasure principle, he called it.

One motivation, he theorised, was that the repetition compulsion we feel is an impulse to re-enact unpleasant or painful experiences to master or prove ourselves superior to them (hill reps, anyone?). He also theorised there were 'death drives', a deep desire of conscious matter to return to a former, pre-conscious state of being. They are 'a manifestation of the inertia of organic life', he wrote, 'the drive to return to the inanimate'. Beneath it all, desire of oblivion runs. And, in Freud's opinion, we gain some deeper satisfaction from our unpleasant tasks because we have 'safeguarded our own particular path to death' – followed our will, in other words, past the point of perversity and even into nothingness. I can see that in riding up a mountain: in that pain-filled path into the sky there is a reaching for an inner stillness, an inertia through repetitive, mind-numbing upwards movement. And what have the immortal climbers (Vietto, Coppi, Gaul, Merckx, Pantani) done, but aggressively followed their own way – chased it with particular alacrity and to the detriment of all else – to its logical end?

I've been back to the Galibier several times, struggled up it again, more or less slowly, ridden away from thought, felt better than that first time. And I've come to the conclusion that maybe Freud only got it half right. All living matter wishes to return to the inanimate, yes, but all stones dream of flying.

Chapter 4

THE KINGS OF THE MOUNTAINS

Or, did one man's untimely demise doom all climbers to
unhappiness? Ice cream and wine, and lightness and sacrifice
in literal and metaphorical ways, and riding on the moon

Is there anywhere in the world where Sunday afternoon
doesn't feel like Sunday afternoon? Or any job that doesn't
leave you with the eternally nagging feeling, on those Sunday
afternoons, that you should really be sitting down and doing
your homework and getting ready for school the next day?
Bike racing, possibly. I am with Joe on such a Sunday, at the
French National Sport Museum, which is housed in the OGC
Nice football stadium, and I am trying to shake off that des-
ultory feeling. He, on the other hand, has done his scheduled
training for the day and, having achieved something – having
already done his metaphorical homework – is seemingly feeling far more satisfied with life. In the pantheon of entertaining
visitor attractions, this sport museum is not up there with
Disney World, but it contains some diverting things, not least
of which is a collection of historic bicycles. Aside from a
beautifully carved wooden hobby horse and a penny farthing
from the distant reaches of history, there's one of Richard
Virenque's old rides, a T-Mobile time trial bike and a slender
steel-framed machine in a familiar dark orange colour – a
bike that belonged to a late-period Eddy Merckx. We scrutinise

the decaying tubular tyres, thin alloy rims and elegant Campagnolo gears as if looking for the secret to greatness. 'Do you think it was really his?' Joe asks. Then an idea: he takes a picture with his phone that he sends to Axel Merckx, Eddy's son. This kind of historical verification is, of course, not available to mere mortals. However, when you have spent two years riding for a team run by Axel and count him among your good friends and confidants, I guess it's normal. The moment sticks with me, and I begin to ponder the ties that bind cyclists to the history of the sport. To state the obvious, professional riders' relationship to cycling history is far more direct than mine or yours. Pros are likely to have met some of the legendary riders who have come before them, to start with. They may well have received advice from or even been coached by them, and if they reach the highest levels they will be aiming for results that are comparable to those of the stars who've turned pedals before them. Win a Classic, or a Grand Tour stage on a famous climb like Alpe d'Huez or the Gavia, and

they can look the greats in the eye. For most fans the relationship to cycling history is more distant and mediated: perhaps a glimpse of a former champion from the crowd; reading about glorious exploits past in an autobiography; watching a TV programme or looking through the vast archive of books, old photos and magazines that create the legends of the sport, and sustain a history that is rich with myths and meaning.

More often than not, these myths are born and live in the mountains. To give an example: Mont Ventoux is a remarkable enough place in itself, but nobody rides up it without a certain sense of its history in cycling. Maybe that's Pantani and Armstrong's thrilling (and, unfortunately, drug-fuelled) duel in 2002, or the heavyweight Eros Poli's unlikely break for victory in 1994. It might be Eddy Merckx receiving oxygen at the top in 1970 or Charly Gaul, 'The Angel of the Mountains', who won the first summit finish on Ventoux in a remarkable time of one hour, two minutes in 1958. For many, the mountain's menacing reputation is indissolubly linked to Tom Simpson, the British cyclist who collapsed and died on its upper slopes in fierce heat in 1967, but for some – mainly very old Frenchmen – it conjures up the image of Jean Malléjac, who almost suffered the same amphetamine-fuelled fate 12 years earlier, in 1955. Many pros are no different. In that Tour in which he placed tenth on Ventoux, Bradley Wiggins seemed absolutely aware of what his climbing prowess meant, and where it fitted into the history of the sport.

Here's another: the Tourmalet is Octave Lapize shouting 'Assassins' at the Tour organisers; it's Eugène Christophe breaking his forks on the way down and stopping to mend them at a blacksmith's forge; it's Eddy Merckx on his solo break in 1969; it's Robert Millar or Richard Virenque, or Andy Schleck duelling with Contador in the mists. To each their own hero, depending on predilections and, well, age; but we nearly all build something of our relationship with the mountains out of these myths. At the heart of it all is the singular figure of the 'climber', a new kind of rider invented by Desgrange when the Tour introduced cycling to the mountains. The climber was a complicated man, who from that moment on complicated the idea of cycling. Something intruded that was not, as far as I can tell, there before, something of a different order – because what climbers do, at their best, transcends ideas of athleticism, physical endurance and winning or losing. I'll try to explain: we admire and respect fast riders, dominant riders, and those who win Grand Tour stages on the flat. We marvel at the sprinters' courage, their skill and vision, tally up their wins and are impressed, but somehow, I believe, they don't occupy the same place in our hearts. A sprint is quicksilver rough and tumble, often too quick to be seen properly, and a second-placed sprinter is a sorry figure. Whereas a climber on a lone breakaway into thin high air (or two riders battling in the mountains) produces a spectacle that seems beautiful regardless of whether he succeeds or fails, or really achieves anything other than climbing the hill gracefully at all. There is something alluring and self-justifying there, something that heightens the emotions and quickens the pulse. Just as the mountains introduced something intrinsically beautiful, climbers introduced a new layer of mystique. More than other riders, the stereotypical climber is someone uncompromising and somehow unknowable: solitary, difficult and often troubled. But are these things inextricably linked? Is this the only way for climbers to be, and how does this lineage bear on the climbers of today?

∧

René Pottier was a Frenchman with drooping moustaches and a demeanour, if we are to believe the photos of him that

survive, that naturally found rest somewhere between lugubri-
ous and haunted. He also did a nice line in racing
headwear – again, if the photos are believed, alternating
between a trademark linen cap (which resembled nothing so
much as a shepherdess's bonnet) and a stripy woolly bobble
hat. Born in 1879 near Paris, Pottier was small, light, intensely
focused and solitary. His talent shone from an early age, and
before turning professional in 1904 he had already broken
several track cycling records. The 1905 Tour de France was
his first. It was also, as we discovered in Chapter 2, the first
Tour to feature a 'real' mountain climb, the Ballon d'Alsace.
The Ballon came in the middle of the 299-kilometre Stage
2, a stage which started off slowly. Riders were saving their
energy for the 12-kilometre climb, with its 8–10 per cent
slopes. When it arrived, a lead group quickly broke free containing all the era's big names: Hippolyte Aucouturier, Émile
Georget, Louis Trousselier (the Tour's eventual winner) and
Henri Cornet (the previous year's champion). One by one,
Pottier dropped them all, climbing at an average of 20 km/h
on his single-speed bike. Only Pottier managed the climb
without putting foot to floor and taking a break, though Cornet
hung on the longest. At the top Pottier changed back to his
all-purpose machine (riders were allowed to swap between
bikes with a different gear ratio on them, suited either to
climbing or riding on the flats) and set off again for the finish
line at Besançon, but he was caught on the descent by
Aucouturier and came second. Wrote Desgrange: 'The climb
of the Ballon d'Alsace ... was one of the most emotional
spectacles I have ever seen, and it confirmed above all else,
that man's courage is limitless and that a well-trained athlete
can claim the unlikeliest victories.'

Pottier abandoned during the following stage because of
tendonitis, but in 1906 he repeated the feat on the Ballon.
This time he won the stage, one of five he took that year on

his way to winning the Tour overall. So dominant was he that, during one, he was so far ahead that he stopped at a roadside bar and drank a whole bottle of wine. An hour later, as the peloton came past, he remounted, gave chase, and caught and beat them. If he sounds carefree, he was not: 'He won without showing any joy or effusiveness. Silent, stubborn, severe,' wrote one newspaper. 'In every situation Pottier kept a cold, neutral expression, from which one could only divine one thing: willpower.' But his talents when the going got tough were undeniable, and he was loved for it: 'If Pottier had a chance to shake off an adversary on a climb, it was over, one would not see him again,' ran the same article. 'The harder the race, the more it seemed it was to his taste.' On the Ballon d'Alsace, it is said, he was cheered on his way by a thousand staff from Peugeot, the bicycle company that sponsored his team and had a factory nearby. In 1905 he had been the *'meilleur grimpeur'* – the best climber. It was after this repeat that Henri Desgrange coined the name *'Roi de la montagne'* – 'King of the Mountain'.

Less than six months later, he was dead. On 25 January 1907, Arthur Barthélemy, the racing equipment director at Peugeot, went to the building where many of the racing cyclists in the town of Levallois kept their bikes. The door was locked and the wine merchant adjacent said that Pottier had not returned the key to its habitual place. Barthélemy went to Pottier's house, but he was not there. His wife had supposed that he was with Barthélemy. Worried, they ran back to the store, broke the door down and found Pottier. He had entered, locked the door behind him, taken his bike down from its hook and then hanged himself from a rope affixed to that same hook. He was 27.

Despite desperate interrogations by his wife, his brother, all the press, there was no apparent motive for Pottier's act. Some suspected a mental breakdown, but he had seemed

cheerful at lunch and had talked about participating in the forthcoming Paris–Roubaix. It was whispered later that his wife had been having an affair, but nothing was ever proven and she was beside herself at the news. 'This is maybe the first time in this brave man's whole life that we must set down what moralists call a failure of courage,' wrote Desgrange in his tribute to this 'introspective, quiet, fierce, uncomplaining' man.

In these qualities, as in his enlarged capacity for suffering while riding uphill, Pottier set the mould for climbers to come. The best climber prize continued to be named every Tour, though until 1930 the honour was just a mention in the paper. Then, a chocolate manufacturer called Menier put up some 5,000 francs for the *Prix Chocolat Menier*, *Prix de la Montagne* (the next year it would rise to 35,000 francs). However this was still not a classification as we know it today – it was a nomination, not a proper competition like the points classification or the GC. According to some sources the Menier money was actually shared between the top five or six climbers, who were picked out subjectively by the organisers, and not just given to the first-named rider.

In 1933 the official mountains classification, the *Grand Prix de la Montagne* (GPM), was born.[1] The next year the competition would really take off, with the advent of *Le Roi René* – King René.

With a nod to Donald Rumsfeld, there are at least three categories of truth that pertain to the Tour de France:

1. True truths (things that are – Eddy Merckx won five Tours)
2. Untrue untruths (things that are false – Floyd Landis's 2006 performance was fuelled by beer and bourbon alone)
3. True untruths (myths that are probably untrue but carry the weight of truth – Jacques Anquetil used to put his bidon in his jersey pocket while climbing, to save carrying the weight on his bike)

For me, for a long time, the greatest true untruth of them all was a story about René Vietto and his toe. Vietto was France's first *grimpeur* superstar. A child of the sun, he was born to a dirt-poor family in the hills above Cannes on the Côte d'Azur,

---

1 The distinctive polka-dot jersey didn't arrive until 1975. Some people say that the design came from the then sponsor, Chocolat Poulain; others, that race director Félix Lévitan was paying homage to an old track star, Henri Lemoine, who was famous for riding in polka dots.

and worked from the age of seven with his mother collecting jasmine flowers for the local perfume industry. Through a friend he got a job as a bellboy at a hotel, then as an usher at the local casino. He saved his tips, bought a bike and began to ride, further and further until he was doing out-and-backs to Marseille 175 kilometres away; faster and faster until he was winning races (the local 'Boucle de Sospel' over several mountain passes was his first pro-level victory); and higher and higher, up over the Col d'Allos and the Col de Vars to the top of the Col d'Izoard – and then back down to the shining sea again, over 500 kilometres in a single go.

Col d'ALLOS 2250 m.) – Tour de France 1926

In 1934, at only 20 years old, he won the Tour de France's King of the Mountains classification in its second year. He had seemed also to have the yellow jersey within his reach until, descending in the Pyrenees, his team leader Antonin Magne broke a wheel, and René, the dutiful junior teammate, gave him his own so that Magne could continue on. A photograph of Vietto sitting on a wall sobbing, waiting for another wheel (and with every passing second watching any private ambitions of wearing the yellow jersey slip away), sold hundreds of thousands of copies of the next day's paper. The following day, Magne punctured on another descent, and Vietto rode back up the hill and surrendered his wheel again. These potent images of sacrifice (and not the aforementioned toe story) endeared him to the French and *Le Roi René* entered into the realm of myth.

Vietto rode the Tour again in 1935 after winning Paris–Nice that year. But in the years after that, his sporting career was hampered by knee injuries that required multiple operations, and fast cars and the good life took precedence over racing. In 1939 he was back, and placed second in the Tour, only for war to interrupt. He would never win the Tour de France but would, by the time he retired in 1953, be the rider who had spent the most days in yellow without winning in Paris (only overtaken in 2012 by Fabian Cancellara), and that mountains prize in his debut Tour might be considered the pinnacle of his achievements.

In spite (because?) of this failure to scale the highest peaks of his sport, he was, and remains, an icon in France. The most elegant climber of them all, still fondly remembered by those too young to have seen him race for his rolling, high-tempo cadence *en danseuse*, and his style: attack, always attack. Always ride your opponents off your wheel and solo into the distance. If we are to judge Vietto by results alone he was a beautiful firework that exploded brilliantly but was eclipsed by bigger bangs. It might be said that he was loved unreasonably – as much (more, even?) for his failures than his successes, which is something that happens to climbers. Some believe he didn't quite live up to the myths that were built around him, but maybe that's precisely why they grew. He was taciturn, irascible and intense, but this hid certain acts of kindness and courtesy towards others. 'His attitudes and whims . . . hid shyness and tenderness. He intended to keep a part of himself a mystery,' wrote Tour historian Jacques Augendre. Maybe it's easier to project our own hopes, fears and desires onto a blank surface, and maybe René knew that. He seemed naturally to lend himself to legend.

In the Esterel, the wild red hills to the west of Cannes, there was a goat who, when Vietto was out training as a young man, would greet him from the side of the road. For years it would bleat him a welcome as the Cannois passed through just after midnight on his regular 350-kilometre there-and-back to Marseille. When Vietto retired, the goat died.

In 1934, René won a Tour stage in his home town, Cannes, over much the same route as his Boucle de Sospel win, having led from the Col de Braus onwards. At the finish line there were riots. His supporters – the whole crowd – lifted him off his bike, pummelled him, manhandled him in joy. Some race official tried to intervene but one burly fan took exception to this nobody's interference, hit him and knocked him out, and René was safely carried to his hotel. The KO'd man was Jacques Goddet, the Tour director.

In 1981, just before that year's Tour started in Nice, the 68-year-old René was knocked over by a car. During the subsequent physiotherapy he was put on a mechanical contraption to strengthen his legs. He immediately started pedalling furiously. 'Calm down, M. Vietto!' said the nurse. 'What do you think you are, a Tour rider . . . ?'

In the 1947 Tour a plane crashed into the mountainside as he climbed past; earlier in that race, incandescent at being reeled in after a 120-kilometre lone breakaway, he had kicked a kerb in Brussels. One of his toes went badly septic, threatening to curtail his Tour (and now we reach the toe). Since the Tour stopped for a rest day in Nice, close to his home, he arranged for his doctor to come and cut it off. Then he got on his bike and resumed with the other riders the next day. In other words, instead of abandoning the race he abandoned the toe. He'd lugged it through the Alps but jettisoned the excess ballast ahead of the Pyrenees.

'I always liked being operated on,' Vietto said in a TV interview towards the end of his life. 'When the surgeon took something off, I used to tell myself: "You'll be lighter on the bike. You'll climb better."'

The legend continues that the toe was preserved in a jar of formaldehyde and kept on a shelf behind a bar in Marseille.

Is it weird that I became fascinated by this story?

Aside from being a useful bit of weight saving for a climber, the severed toe began to represent for me a tangible link to the heroic age of riding, to those dusty, sweat-encrusted men of old with their woollens and their goggles and caps, and their spare tubular tyres wrapped around their shoulders like boa constrictors, who were 10 times the rider you or I could ever be. The toe story was only a footnote to the Vietto legend, but there were enough reports of its fate to make me believe that at its core there was a grain of truth. If it existed, it might be the key to all these mythologies, a way of sorting fact from fiction even as the sands of time threaten to bury the distinction between the two. If, like its original owner, it no longer was – an imaginary relic of unimaginable hardship – that fact would in itself say something about how we worship our idols, and about the sacrifice industry that connects cycling present to cycling past. What is it we take with us and what do we leave behind?

A final possibility was that it was simply a piece of dead flesh in a jar. The truth status of Schrödinger's digit bothered me for quite a while. Until eventually I thought, fuck it, and I decided to go to Marseille to find out. Before I did I contacted Vietto's son, Jean Vietto. Jean Vietto lived in Nice, just along the coast from Cannes, but he was a long-distance truck driver and never home so our conversations only ever happened in writing. And I also found someone called René Bertrand, who was possibly René's greatest fan and I arranged an appointment to see him. But, upon arriving in Marseille, it seemed propitious to have a drink first.

And that is how I find myself sitting in the covered terrace of a bar on the old port. The locals are wrapped in dark coats, long scarves and gloves, but there are tourists walking around in shirt sleeves. The winter sun angles fierce and low through the cross streets, streams through the masts moving gently on the water and filters through my carafe of rosé, casting an appealing colour on the Formica table.

It is not the right bar. That much was obvious before I went in. There is no toe-in-a-jar next to the Pernod. But it's a start. If nothing else, I am getting into the swing of things. I have joined the old men, in their caps, jackets and wire-rimmed dark glasses, in drinking wine in the morning. I'm not sure Vietto would have approved. He came from a life of privation, and when he was at his best he was an ascetic, and something of an extremist. For Vietto training meant riding a gearless fixed-wheel bike at least 100 kilometres further than the race he was preparing for. At the height of his career, he would organise Côte d'Azur training camps for his teammates, during which he would ride them into the ground without mercy: puncture and you'll be dropped; stop to pee and you'll be dropped; eat and you'll be dropped. He would deliberately go out in terrible conditions and every man was expected to finish the ride, even if that meant hundreds of kilometres solo after bonking (one of the many colourful expressions cyclists have for completely running out of energy during a ride).

'René practised a very hard training regime,' said Apô Lazaridès, his protégé and *domestique*, in a TV interview as an old man, with Vietto by his side. 'I mean, he did a lot of kilometres, and he didn't allow eating. His discipline was something else. I remember putting in the kilometres with him once and I said, "René, I'm hungry, I can't go on." "Eat grass," he told me. And I ate grass that whole day.' Jean Vietto, René's son, confirmed this. 'There was one time with Apô when he just threw away their bag of food and their bidons, and both of them suffered,' Jean wrote. 'Apô once said to me that my father had been hard on him, but it was a necessary suffering to surpass yourself.' Jean continued: 'Once, [Vietto] punished himself by putting the bike on his bed and sleeping on the floor himself.'

'For me,' René said, in that TV interview with Apô in the 1970s, 'sleeping is dying and eating is poisoning yourself. *Voilà.* Go to bed at 2 a.m., get up at 4. Get up at 4 a.m. and leave at 5, whatever the weather.' Apô laughs at this, but nervously, and has the look of a man who is glad he now runs a mini-golf resort next to the sparkling Med and always sleeps soundly until at least sunrise.[2]

---

2 The coda to the toe amputation story is that after his own toe was amputated, René Vietto coerced Lazaridès into cutting off his own toe, the better to understand the suffering a rider must endure to win the Tour de France. However, since René never won the Tour this flies in the face of logic (not that logic is always a climber's close companion) and I never found any evidence. As a further aside, René really

My game plan here in Marseille is devastatingly simple. Go to a bar. Check the shelves for jars. Cross it off the list. Go to another one. Somewhere in the middle I will visit René Bertrand. Then perhaps another bar. Check the shelves for jars. Tick another one off the list. It is not without purpose: it will be in the service of finding one of cycling's lost relics (and daytime drinking is always purposeful, however gratuitous), but I confess that at a certain point, even pre-rosé, I am losing focus on the toe. The sun. The boats. The Ferris wheel rising above the quay. Enough dilly-dallying. Time to go to see Bertrand.

René Bertrand was born on the same day as René Vietto, but 14 years later, which means that he is a sprightly 87 or so when he buzzes me into his building and meets me on the landing beneath his two apartments – the one he lives in and the other that houses all his cycling memorabilia. For years Bertrand owned a bike shop in Marseille, and, with Antonin Magne, was a *directeur sportif* for the Mercier team in the 1960s. Whenever the big cycling stars came to Marseille, they usually passed by his shop.

'I was a fanatic,' he says. 'In 1934 I was six and my father took me to see the Tour in Marseille. I lived in the Rue d'Aubagne, a hundred metres from the start. Magne was in yellow, but I wanted to see Vietto. It all started there.'

Later, the men became friends. Bertrand became a dealer for Vietto's bikes. When Vietto came to Bertrand's daughter's wedding in Marseille, Bertrand drove him home, all the way to Cannes. Now he is the guardian of many of the artefacts of Vietto's life: the race number from his first win in the Boucle de Sospel, his contracts, the last bike he ever raced

---

didn't seem to like sleeping or eating. After he retired, he planned to undertake a week-long, 3,500-kilometre solo tour of France powered only by a single *musette* full of vitamin biscuits, to prove that food wasn't necessary for nutrition. The attempt never took place.

on. Snapshots line the walls of Vietto at all stages of his career, as well as other greats including Gino Bartali, Jacques Anquetil and Raymond Poulidor as well as Marcel Cerdan, France's greatest ever boxer and lover to Edith Piaf, who was another friend. We talk about Vietto's successes: Paris–Nice in 1935, his most prestigious overall win (he always liked to perform on his home roads) and his year as national champion, of the Free French at least, in 1941. But big victories were hard to come by: 'Vietto and Poulidor were the two least lucky guys in the Tour,' Bertrand says.

Like many of his generation, Vietto had the best years of his career taken away from him. In 1947 he was the only pre-war star to line up and, as such, he was favourite to win. In the pan-flat second stage he soloed away from the break to win in Brussels, proving his form was good and that he'd worked on his flatland riding. Later, he won in Digne, and defended his yellow jersey through the mountains, only to lose it after 15 days to Pierre Brambilla, in a disastrous

139-kilometre-long time trial. 'He did 180 kilometres on his own, on the *pavés*,' Bertrand tells me. 'That was hard work. He shouldn't have made that break to Brussels, he paid for it later.' The Tour was won by Jean Robic, a relative unknown, after the Breton attacked and dropped Brambilla on the penultimate stage.

Did he regret never winning the Tour?

'Oh yes, he never admitted it, but it was something he missed,' Bertrand says. 'But he didn't make excuses, he didn't say, "Oh, this or that happened."' Jean Vietto added: 'People often asked him the question. The war really destroyed everything for him. He'd thought he'd have time to try and win other, later Tours.'

But what about the toe?

Jean Vietto again takes up the story: 'In those days, toe clips were made of iron, and in Paris–Roubaix, passing over a pavement, one of his clips cut through his shoe and his little toe was [eventually] amputated,' he wrote. 'Years later, he gave it to M. Pierre Gueydon (a friend of the Bertrand brothers).' If Vietto had been suffering with his toe since Roubaix, some months before, perhaps the injury was inflamed by his second passage on the northern cobbles in the Tour. What's sure is that it wasn't amputated in Nice; instead, on the rest day, his doctor pumped him full of penicillin and sent him off again to win. The toe was taken off after the Tour, after Vietto lost. We can only guess how a septic toe, septic to the bone, might have affected his performance. And it was indeed preserved. For a while at least, a friend of Vietto from his military service kept it at his bar, in Marseille, which was called Chez Siciliano.

What about the toe, though, I ask Bertrand.

'Oh *putain*, the toe,' says Bertrand. He goes into the kitchen, opens a cupboard. Closes it again. Opens another, gets on

his knees, roots around as if looking for bin bags or sink unblocker. And then he takes something out.

It's a glass jar with a toe in it. A shrivelled, brown, desiccated toe. Surprisingly large and with a nail and present up to the knuckle – in other words, with at least half an inch of unexpected exposed bone, an extra joint that makes it look almost like a finger. It's the pale bone on which the rest of the beckoning digit rests I notice, more than anything, in that first moment. Around the top of the jar is written: 'Vietto' and '*Doigt de pied*' ('toe') as if one might otherwise mistake it for a cocktail snack, or another ex-rider's ex-toe one had lying around. I have the feeling that a curtain has been pulled back and I am looking at some rarely glimpsed medieval relics of the saints which have been taken from their resting place and exposed, if only briefly, to the light of day, and that they will soon be returned to the dark in order that they continue to burn brightly in the imagination, to exist solely as an image guiding the faith of millions back to a truer time, one of hardships, struggle and sacrifice. It is one thing seeing photos of racing from the so-called 'Golden Age' of cycling, but to know that this exists, that this and things like this actually happened, is something else.

Another bar on the port. I have nothing left to find, but a celebration seemed appropriate. The sun is slipping through the masts of the sailboats, between the motor yachts and down, behind the buildings lining the quay. I have a finger of Pastis left in my glass. *Doigt de pied* is literally 'foot finger'. I'm still thinking about this encounter with the raw stuff of legend.

'Papa didn't regret it, and often said it was with this "sacrifice", and the photo that immortalised his choice, that he made his name,' Jean Vietto wrote to me, describing his father's feelings about the wheel-giving. 'Pride and sadness all at once.' A career-defining, maybe even a sport-defining, incident – because isn't this salt-sweet, storybook combination of selflessness and suffering more or less unique to cycling, and one reason we feel justified in believing it is better, or at least deeper, than other sports? 'Don't write that I lost my chance by saving Tonin [Magne],' said Vietto about that same incident, in an interview towards the end of his life. 'We've no right to diminish his performance. And anyway, it would be false. In reality I lost that Tour in one of the northern stages, following four punctures, one after the other. [Raffaele] Di Paco helped me out by giving me a tubular tyre . . . without him, I'd still be on the side of the road.'

Which maybe shows that when it comes to legends we remember the mountains and not the flats (no pun intended), and that reality is inevitably more prosaic than myth. Unless you happen to be looking for an amputated toe in a jar.

Jump to an interview with another octogenarian, but in Toledo, far away from Marseille, in central Spain. It is only as we are finishing up when it occurs to me that not only would my interviewee have an affinity with Vietto, but it is a fairly sure thing they would have met. We are in a former garage on the outskirts of town that is now in part a warehouse for the barriers and other things involved in running the Vuelta a Toledo annual stage race, and in part an office, HQ and self-administered fan club for the Eagle of Toledo, Federico Bahamontes. Did you know Vietto, I ask through my translator. 'Oh yes,' he said, and his eyes fill with admiration.

Federico Bahamontes does not admire many climbers. He rates himself, but that's natural when you have a good claim to being the best cyclist ever to ride up a mountain. 'The mountains [are] the basic truth of cycling for Spaniards . . . and the cyclist [is] the only being capable of using the strength of his legs to challenge the force of gravity and fly,' wrote veteran Spanish cycling journalist Carlos Arribas in the *El Pais* newspaper.[3] The first winner of the Tour's mountains classification – the year before Vietto – was a Spaniard: Vicente Trueba, the diminutive Spanish climber known as the 'Flea of Torrelavega'. However, the Eagle of Toledo soared higher. In the 1950s and '60s he won the King of the Mountains six times, and the equivalent at the Vuelta twice and the Giro once. Only Richard Virenque has since equalled that Tour tally. Virenque, in fact, won seven, but his performances were tainted by the Festina affair (the major doping scandal in which a car from that team was stopped at the Belgian border just before the 1998 Tour and industrial quantities of performance-enhancing drugs were found, pointing to a large-scale team-administered doping programme). From 1993 to 1998 Virenque rode for Festina, and four of his polka-dot jerseys were won in that period. He finally admitted to doping in court in 2000.

Bahamontes, however, claims, and with some force, never to have doped – in an era when doping products were less effective than in the 1990s but their use equally rife. He is 88, but he has the demeanour and vigour of someone 20 years younger. His handshake firm, his step sure. 'All the people who raced with me are now dead because of what they were taking,' he tells me. He is still pin sharp, still totally in control of his faculties (and, moreover, also has all 10 toes), and though he sounds fierce his forthright opinions are delivered with the twinkling humour of your favourite granddad. Nobody in his era measured up, according to Bahamontes, and nobody since has either, and if that's what he believes, then he will damn well say it. Only Charly Gaul almost made

---

3 This was quoted by Alasdair Fotheringham in his English-language biography of Bahamontes, which is an excellent account of his life, including the grim details of his childhood. Details in the Further Reading section at the back.

the grade, and Bahamontes calls him 'my number one enemy'.[4] Are the riders of today comparable to those of old? It has been one of the themes of our discussion. Their bikes are lighter and their times are faster, but can you swap brute force and feeling for power meters and heart-rate monitors? If mountains are about myths, can this rationed and rationalised experience hit the same peaks?

Bahamontes may still be pin sharp but, that said, he doesn't immediately remember the Col de la Bonette. Bahamontes was the first man over it in the 1962 Tour de France, its first

---

4 Charly Gaul is another singular figure in the history of the climber. Gaul was a former butcher's boy from Luxembourg who lived up to his nickname, the 'Angel of the Mountains', climbing like a dream and looking absolutely angelic on the bike. But his baby face hid a sadistic, killer competitive streak. Well versed in the suffering required to be a great climber (and reputedly a big consumer of amphetamines), Gaul got better as the weather got worse. He won the 1958 Tour with a day-long break into an infernal storm in the Alps, and also won the overall and the mountains prizes in the 1956 and 1959 Giros d'Italia. However, he was as unpopular with other riders – he barely communicated, even with his team, or did routine things such as share his winnings out – as he was idolised by the public.

'Charly Gaul, he was the only one that could keep up. He was the strongest rival I had,' Bahamontes told me. 'On cold days he was super dangerous but on hot days I always beat him.' In 2000, in L'Équipe, the venerable cycling journalist Philippe Brunel wrote: 'In the furnace of the 1950s, Gaul seemed to ride not against Bahamontes, Anquetil, Adriessens, but against oppressive phantoms, to escape his modest origins, riding the ridges to new horizons, far from the life without surprises which would have been his had he stayed in Luxembourg.'

After he retired Gaul disappeared from public life and only resurfaced, fat and old and barely recognisable, in the 1980s. He had spent the intervening time living as a hermit in a hut in the Ardennes forests.

As he explained in an interview upon his re-emergence, which was then summarised in that L'Équipe in 2000: 'I bought myself a little portable television and I connected it to the battery of my car to watch the Tour de France. When the battery ran down, I called the man at the garage. I had travelled plenty enough. I told myself, "You're happy here, at peace." There was nothing but the trees and the water. I passed my days planting vegetables. Deer used to come and eat at the end of my garden.

'How do I explain what I did? Well, it's difficult to go back into normal society. Today, of course, I laugh about it, but that period was essential: without it, I wouldn't have been able to tackle the final slope, that of old age.'

Later still, he befriended the brilliant, troubled climber Marco Pantani, who was seeking help through a psychological crisis after he hit a car during a race and had to learn to walk again.

ever inclusion in a bike race. He was also first in 1964, its second outing. (Both times the race went to the full height of the Cime loop, the first time from south to north and vice versa the second.) Between 1964 and 2015, only two other men have had the honour of leading a race over the Bonette. The second was Robert Millar, in the 1993 Tour de France. The Scottish climber won the polka-dot jersey in 1984 and was for many years Britain's greatest Tour de France rider; leading over the Bonette came late in his career, and he did not win the stage. The third man was the South African John-Lee Augustyn who, as I already mentioned, overshot a turn in 2008 and hurtled off the road just over the top. The mountain made such an impression on him that he later started a clothing company named after it. However, for Bahamontes, who did not crash, it is initially unmemorable. I am not completely surprised. There were many mountains in his career, it was all such a long time ago and I'm not sure Bahamontes ever willingly let anyone ride over a major col before him.

Alejandro Martín Bahamontes (according to the church register) was born in a small village near Toledo in 1928. The family was poor but the Spanish Civil War and the Franco regime lowered them, like many, into abject poverty. For a while his father broke rocks as a road-mender's mate; for two years, the 11-year-old Federico had to help him. As a teenager, Bahamontes stole stale bread and rotten fruit, and even killed cats to stave off his family's hunger (cats that, Alasdair Fotheringham writes, his mother gutted and stuffed and which the family called 'baby goats').

Riding a bike was part of this struggle to survive. By 18, Bahamontes was working as a market trader, unloading lorries and then picking out and selling on the rotten fruit the stall-holders didn't want, and he saved the money he made to buy a bike. The plan was he would ride from village to village, illegally picking up bread and beans and flour which he would then sell on the black market in Toledo. Anyone caught doing this by the *Guardia Civil*, who patrolled the roads, faced a prison sentence. Often he would ride in the middle of the day, when it was hottest and the police would be on their siesta; needless to say, speed and cunning were an asset: 'All my strength came from the market,' he tells me. It is difficult to imagine this poverty as he sits here now in his office, behind a huge desk, in front of a picture of himself as a handsome young man and next to a stern statue of an eagle. Bahamontes entered his first race almost by accident, when he met some friends on the road who were going and he tagged along. He came second. His first proper win was the mountains classification in the Tour of Avila, which he rode as an amateur, and he worked his way around Spain's regional Tours – usually riding to and from the start, however far that might be. From his earliest races he always excelled in the mountains. 'Whenever I arrived in the mountains I was happy,' he says.

Truly, for the first few years of his career, he thought of little else. He won the King of the Mountains in his first Tour, and absolutely dominated from then on. Unlike Vietto or Charly Gaul, who would emerge to be his main rival, his style wasn't pretty. He would stand on the pedals, curiously upright, with his shorts hitched high and his hands shifting forward and back over the bars. It was, however, devastatingly effective. A favourite trick would be to attack, slow down so that he would get caught by the bunch and then go imme-diately again, crippling his rivals. Either that or recover and eat a little, and then launch off for the next lot of KoM points. 'My tactic from the beginning was attack, attack and attack again,' he says. The French press called it racing 'à la Baha-montes', a backhanded compliment that implied he didn't take it seriously enough. Remember that idea that there is

something gratuitous in the climber's art? Bahamontes is in part responsible for that. There is a story that one year he stopped at the top of a col during the Tour de France, and, having claimed the KoM points, got off his bike and ate an ice cream and waited for the peloton to come. Like the toe story this one is more or less true: it was the Col de Romeyère in the Vercors region, the year was 1954, and it was a very hot day. The main reason he stopped was that he was riding on a wheel with broken spokes and needed a replacement, but the ice cream was a pretty classy touch, and one which did not dispel accusations that he favoured spectacular over effective racing: that he was erratic, quixotic even, and excessively individualistic. At times it was more than that: he was self-isolating and troublesome. He took his wilfulness to extremes, seeming always to contrive to be discontented wherever he was, and he changed teams at least once a year for most of his career. Was it a fair criticism that he cared about the King of the Mountains competition to the detriment of everything else? 'Always, always,' he says, smiling. 'I never thought about the general classification. I was always trying to get the mountains classification. In 11 Tours I made the podium 10 times in Paris.'

His one Tour overall win came in 1959, and it was inspired by the great Fausto Coppi, whose team he had signed for that year. Coppi, as they say, made him an offer he couldn't refuse: 'Coppi said to me, "Why do you always ride for the mountains? You should do the GC!" I said, "GC? I'm not made for the flats, but I climb well in the mountains and that's what I'll do." Always I targeted the GPM. All the cols in Spain, Italy, France, I won. Every day I rode for the GPM, it was mine.' The conversation with Coppi happened in the winter off season: 'We were eating before going hunting and

he said to me, "If you want to come to my team, you must go for the GC." I said, "With Coppi, yes!" If somebody says to you, "Come play football for Real Madrid," you sign immediately. Coppi was my Madrid.'

Bahamontes explains, in his characteristic mix of French and Spanish that pays little respect to the half of it I can understand without translation, that he arrived at the 1959 Tour in good shape: 'First stage, I went on the attack on the flat. I rode *à bloc* and I seem to remember I arrived two or three minutes ahead of the peloton. That was the moment I thought, I'll do the general and not the mountain.' He pauses for a second then adds, 'Then in the mountains I always went to the front, and I won the mountains and the Tour as well.' And he smiles.

Some say he got away with it because the other riders thought it was business as usual and he would do his usual trick of flopping on the GC. But I get the feeling that when he put his mind to something he was unstoppable.

I ask Bahamontes if a climber has to love solitude, as the stereotype suggests. The question is a royal road leading to several of his favourite subjects: suffering, sacrifice and how much better (that is to say, tougher) it was in the good old days. '[Climbers] have to have the capacity to suffer, so when they come to difficult moments they can deal with it,' he says, and as his thoughts turn to modern riders he segues into they-are-not-worthy-of-the-name territory: 'In the Vuelta España, for example, there are only four or five [modern] riders that compete for the classification. The others just sweat and get fat. They eat like kings and get massages and showers after every stage. They're like girls. They don't know how to suffer, the bike is hard.'

That's them put in their place, then.

His eyes are sparkling, he is enjoying himself. There is an element of him playing up to the audience. But there is no

doubt he is obsessively serious about the basics of his craft. First, there is that pure, iron will, which is probably innate. Or, as he says: 'You don't learn to be a climber, you're born one.' Next, there is work, sacrifice, suffering. And them alone. That's it. They become a mantra. For example, Bahamontes on racing with power meters and heart-rate monitors: 'It's ridiculous. I tell them the only thing they need is sacrifice and training,' he says. 'Fewer numbers, more reality.' Then the qualities needed to be a great climber: 'Great sacrifice. The key is in the sacrifice that you have to have if you want to be an athlete.' He continues: 'You have to *faire le métier*[5] strictly. If not, it won't happen. You can't climb cols without sacrifices.' He says he was always telling his teammates not

---

5 One of those expressions that really has to stay in French. It means learning the trade of a professional bike rider – see the Glossary for more.

to go out in the evenings, not to drink that Coca-Cola, not to have sex ('You have to save yourself. If you have relations before a race, you'll only be a *gregario*' [the Italian for *domestique*]), to go out training for another hour instead. Again: 'You have to sacrifice yourself. I used to have a director that used to make me go to sleep whenever he did, to make sure I didn't go out partying at night.'

It sounds pretty grim and pretty self-abnegating, but then, if you look at where he came from, and the national hero he became, the 50-plus years of comfort and relative wealth he's had since, I guess it makes sense. Bahamontes also said one particular thing that has stayed with me. Before my visit to Toledo I'd stayed with friends in Girona, and there had asked Nathan Haas, (the Australian pro rider for Dimension Data, who, it turned out, was a huge fan of the Eagle of Toledo) what he would ask Bahamontes, given the chance. At that point on a climb when the effort becomes unbearable, Nathan wondered, how did he carry on, and go even deeper? What was his key in that moment of suffering? 'I thought about everything I had done to arrive at this point,' Bahamontes replied, via me. The dedication, the sacrifice, the efforts he'd made and the life he'd escaped. 'There isn't the suffering now like there was before. The bad moments make you stronger. To get to the top, you must climb the stairs.' As was the way in this Spanish-French-English conversation, we circled around and came at the question again. 'We were poor, we had nothing,' he said later: 'There is no way back, the only way is forward. If you don't fight, you don't win.'

We kept on bumping into the differences between the modern and the old that day, and I felt for a while that I should put up a defence of the new, or give the modern pros some kind of right of reply. After all, Bahamontes had said to me that today's cycling was 'artificial' and 'cold' and that the riders lacked passion or temperament. The legends of old bestride the narrow world like Colossuses and we petty men walk under their huge legs and peep about to find ourselves dishonourable graves. But then I thought about how much Bahamontes and many of the previous generations are respected – by people like Nathan as well as by normal fans – and I thought it was probably unnecessary. There was self-aware humour in his words, and I think he acknowledged his status both as a legend with total freedom to speak his mind, and as a living link to a bygone age who could easily shock and thrill us modern softies. Beneath the jovial provocations, what he was saying – technology doesn't necessarily improve racing, money sometimes spoils things, hard work pays off – is totally uncontroversial. And I don't think he actually wanted people to go back to a time of 12-kilo bikes, misery and desperation in which you were only a few bad results away from eating cats. There is no way back, the only way is forward.

Bahamontes's hard line on training and dedication also reminded me of a conversation I'd had with Joe Dombrowski, when I asked him what he noticed when he saw someone climbing well: 'I guess you see guys who come into phases within a season when they're climbing really well, and mostly because they're super skinny, but they haven't gone so skinny that they're just useless either,' he said. 'They're toeing that line, which is a pretty fine one. Especially at the high, high end of the sport, because it's a power-to-weight game, and getting that weight as low as possible without having your power tank is a dangerous game.'

To me that sounds a lot like recognising the work and the sacrifice of the best riders – valuing exactly what Bahamontes did too.

I have brought along two illustrated magazines from the 1962 and 1964 Tours and finally the translator and I coax Bahamontes into remembering the Bonette. As he flicks through them it all comes flooding back. First: 'I should have won this stage in the Pyrenees!' Then, 'These are great photos!' And then: 'This is the Col de la Bonette. Wow, it was tough!' He looks at another photo of the climb winding its way up towards the sky. 'This I remember, because just a bit further ahead there was my name written in big letters in the snow. I don't know how they did it, but my name was written in black in the snow. It made me feel really emotional.'

But most of all, as he looks through my old magazines he says, several times, 'Another world.' He shakes his head, 'It was another world.'

~ ~ ~ ~

'Are you going to say in your book that bicyclists are all bloody mad?' my girlfriend asked as I told her I was heading back to France. This time it was for a special challenge. Nice–Bonette–Nice. From the Bay of Angels to the top of the highest paved road in Europe, and back again. Two hundred and thirty-five kilometres. Yeah, right, I thought, mad, and I mentally called upon a speech by JFK in mock justification of this epically need-less expense of energy: "But why, some say, the moon? Why choose this as our goal? And they may well ask why climb the highest mountain? We choose to go to the moon! We choose to go to the moon in this decade and do the other things not because they are easy but because they are hard. Because that goal will serve to organise and measure the best of our energies and skills, because that challenge is one that we are willing to accept, one we are unwilling to postpone, and one we intend to win."

I'd been thinking about it for a while. Ever since, in fact, my first ride up the Bonette one October. Like Everesting, this ride, climbing from the Mediterranean to the top of the highest road and freewheeling back down, promised to fulfil my desire for something geometric and conceptual. Something as pure and as flawless in theory as a mathematical formula, but beautifully futile, and in practice as hard and hot and dirty as hell. I had been working too hard and too much, struggling ignobly in the city, and despite a huge lack of recent bike time or fitness I was overjoyed at the prospect of a good honest fight in the mountains.

We left our apartment at dawn and cycled slowly through dark streets towards the expanse of lighter and lightening sky between the tall buildings that showed us where the sea was. There, my two companions for the day took their bikes to the water's edge to dip the back wheel in, while I selected a pebble from the millions around the high water mark to accompany me on the journey, and put it in my jersey pocket.

We rode with the sea to our left until we reached Nice airport, then looped under the promenade road to turn right into the Var valley, the wide, rocky expanse so poorly filled by the Var river in normal weather but terrifyingly quick to rise when spring thunderstorms added to snowmelt in the mountains. North we pedalled through the detritus of civilisation – shoe warehouses and discount stores and DIY yards and motels and tyre shops – that has collected in this wide valley crowded all around by hills, where once there were fields and greenhouses growing fruit and vegetables. At the top, at the confluence of the Esteron, Vésubie, Tinée and Var rivers, the land split into four and tunnelled into the foothills along four smaller gorges. We followed the Tinée, on a road overlooked by a 19th-century fort cut into the rocks, a reminder that Italy was close over the ridge of peaks to our right and that these neighbours had not always been friendly. Though the sun had risen on the coast it was still almost night in this narrow cleft, but it soon opened out and we rode past riverside meadows and through small villages, still morning fresh and cool. The road rose at a gradient of two or three per cent, one of those false flats that are deceptively hard to ride up fast and which would be equally deceptively hard to ride down fast. Meadows of cow parsley, cherry trees and

plums. The occasional cow or horse, and in one field an old and very patched-up helicopter, its rotors spinning lazily, next to a plastic water tank and other sundry supplies it would soon transport, in a net hanging from a rope underneath, to shepherds in the summer pastures up above.

Roughly speaking, the gradient of ecological change is a thousand times quicker vertically up or down than horizontally north or south, so by journeying up to 2,800 metres we would be taking ourselves to the equivalent of somewhere inside the Arctic Circle. It was also true that we were turning back the clock as we went. Not that they didn't have iPhones and broadband and the other accoutrements of modern life up here, but the décor and the signage were slipping in time. The hotels in villages, dormitories for the local ski stations, had last been renovated in the 1960s or '70s, and were full of fading plastic furniture and Formica or, even better, elegant wood, tiles and zinc in a state of genteel dilapidation. At the bar, a farmer or hunter or two with a little coffee, and the local taxi man walking the precarious high wire between his two main occupations, drinking and driving.

Gradually civilisation fell away.

At Saint Étienne we were three hours and 45 minutes into our day. We ate pastries and drank two coffees in the warm sun, refilled our bidons at the tap and then remounted our bikes. This was where the real climb started, and even with 90 kilometres of slight uphill behind us we still had 1,600 metres to climb – a vertical mile – ahead.

'I like climbing. But 24 kilometres uphill and 2,860 metres [sic] of altitude is daunting even when you are motivated and have a plan (first to the top),' wrote Robert Millar in Michael Blann's book, *Mountains: Epic Cycling Climbs*, about his ascent of the (other side of the) Bonette in the 1993 Tour de France. His rival in the race to the top that day was Pedro Delgado, and he was determined to break the Spaniard. He continued: 'I'll ride 10 kilometres hard and see what happens. On a normal col that would put me close to the top, but here it won't even be halfway. Strangely it seems a reasonable thing to do.'

We would not be riding hard. Our whole strategy for surviving the day relied on taking it moderately. After all, at the top, we would still only be halfway to our journey's end. We had been riding through soft sedimentary limestone and bright red mudstone, but at Saint Étienne a wall of granite reared up, the first outlier of the Argentera massif that separates Italy from France and which includes Monte Argentera, the tallest peak in the region. Past the village we plunged into forests of scrub oak, spruce and beech, and chestnuts that once were cultivated and had now again run wild, on overgrown terraces shored up by drystone walls stacked steep on the river banks. We cycled past Le Pra, officially abandoned for fear of landslides, but where a few people remain in summer, and crossed the bridge over the Salso Moreno river, which was so named – 'brown sauce' – by Spanish soldiers in the 18th century because it runs dark after heavy rain.

The landscape told a story of occupation, use and desertion. It had meaning, and this road was our narrative through it. Some people ride bikes on these roads to escape. Some because it's a socially acceptable way of being on your own. That's a good reason. Racing is a good one too. To think or to staunch thought; to help you sleep at night or get up in the morning. All good. So is going fast. I ride, I realised once, partly to make stories in the world. To make sure that there is a beginning, a middle and an end. A narrative of effort across the landscape in a world where our attention is otherwise pulled constantly in many directions. Fitness alone is the worst reason to ride a road bike. Robert Johnson, the bluesman, spent his life playing the blues to seduce women and to escape the hounds of hell. Not to perfect his command of the pentatonic scale. When Johnson performed at a jook joint he would single out one woman in the audience and fix her with his gaze, sing only to her, without regard for the rest of the audience – try to sleep with her, and never mind her boyfriend or whoever else she was with. I think that's what bike racers call focus. A jealous boyfriend was what killed him.

Not that one can totally scorn fitness. It is a means to an end. I was finding the Bonette was increasingly difficult. What had looked to me geometric was actually hot, sweaty chaos. Wherever there is interaction between place and time and an expenditure of energy there is rhythm, yet my rhythm was increasingly ragged. Sometimes before the beat, sometimes after. A jazz drummer would be ashamed.

As Duke Ellington said, 'It don't mean a thing if it ain't got that swing.'

My companions were slowly pulling away. In this situation, there is no way to bluff yourself faster. Even going slower is a kind of bluffing. When you're not fit the only speed you can ride up a mountain is the speed you can go. I was alone. I settled in and was at peace. The year that Robert Millar and Pedro Delgado were sprinting for the top the great French rider Laurent Fignon was also climbing alone. He describes it in his autobiography, *We Were Young and Carefree*:

> The next morning, on the road to Isola 2000 we climbed up the Col d'Izoard and then the Col de la Bonette, the highest pass in the Tour. I can remember it very clearly. I rode up the whole climb in last place. Because I wanted to. I put my hands on the top of the bars and savoured it all to the full. I was breathing deeply as I lived through my last seconds in bike racing, which I had thought would never end for me. This col was all mine and I didn't want anyone to intrude. Climbing up over 2,700m above sea level like this gave me a host of good reasons to appreciate everything I had lived through on the bike. I had plenty of time to let my mind wander. It was a poetic distillation of the last twelve years. A little fragment of my being, breathed in and lived to the full, at my own speed.'

Once he'd descended, he climbed off the bike and retired.

Up above Bousiéyas, I was climbing through the high sheep pastures. Around the Camp des Fourches lay meadows full of tiny beautiful wildflowers. Purple and white saxifrage, yellow primroses, moss campion, peacock-eye pinks and orchids, and giant thistles that the sheep shun. On the slopes underneath a Second World War bunker, a sprinkling of white daisies looking from afar like the last remnants of snow. Higher up there is glacier crowfoot, glacier buttercup, alpine bellflowers and barberry, a peculiar and tenacious rosette-like plant with furry leaves and a delicate white flower. High-altitude flora these, because now we were very high and each breath was hard won. The trees had gone, the grass, disappeared – I must have been near where Bahamontes saw his name in the snow – and I was surrounded by grey flysch, a crumbling, dark, slipping, sliding rock. The Tinée river was now a tiny ribbon, or several tiny ribbons joining to make one. Here in the cirque beneath the Cime was its source, where it bubbled up, and I pondered the minor miracle of water, which can only descend and is nowhere seen to go up, appearing at the top of a mountain. So easily, it seemed, while I was labouring and so short of breath.

Periodically good feelings returned, but mainly it was the beauty of it, the opening out to a world of light and sky and an uninterrupted view across a sea of peaks, that carried me through, the infinitely unfolding world shifting infinitesimally with every pedal stroke. The pain that comes and goes is part of this lesson in relativity. I am small, this mountain is big. The storm is terrible when I'm in it, but while the sun is shining and on me and those clouds are distant they are but a picturesque ornament to the mountainside. I am here. Soon I will be there. Even the mountain is not permanent, but compared to the barracks below . . . the road, the paint on the walls, this sunshine, my discomfort. This too shall pass.

'They rode on the moon,' *L'Équipe* wrote in 1993, about the Bonette Tour stage. My riding companions were waiting for me at the top in the lunar barrens, stamping their feet, jackets on, to keep warm. A passing cyclist offered to take our photo together, but we did not hang around for that ritual.

I thought of John-Lee Augustyn as we descended through the corner where he took his fall. 'I was scared that I was going to fall to Hell but luckily it was just a slide. You don't know what's waiting on the other side,' he told the *Daily Mail*, describing his relief at finding himself on a slope and not in a crevasse. 'Yes, people will remember me being first over the Bonette but I think they will remember me falling off it more.'

A quick hamburger pit stop at the *gîte* in Bousiéyas and we dove back down, snaking through the turns, overtaking camper vans, hunched tightly down onto the handlebars, knees knocked in, for all the pleasure of gravity's free speed. And then we were in the valley again, howling into the headwind on the false flat. Riding in a tight group of three, taking turns to push it on the front and peeling off to recover in the windbreak at the back. Push, breathe, rest, breathe, repeat. Soon we were back on the bike path down the Var, and then we hit the coast. Finally, just before six, we were back at the beach where we started, busy now with summer crowds, and

we jumped in the sea in our bib shorts, to replace salt sweat with salt sea and wash off the dust of the highest road in Europe.

Oh yeah, and I left the pebble at the top, next to the memorial inscription at the highest point. Because all stones dream of flying, right?

Chapter 5

HOW KoMs CONQUERED THE WORLD

Or, the mountains of King George and pushing the envelope in search of up

It is a few days before one of the major World Tour races, and Joe Dombrowski and his flatmate Larry Warbasse (who is also an American pro cyclist) have convened a barbecue for their friends, some of whom will be racing too. There aren't too many carbs on view, but we eat delicious chicken and sausages and salad on the terrace, and at some point the conversation shifts round to the Col de la Madone.

You might have heard of the Madone. It was made famous by Lance Armstrong in his book *It's Not About the Bike* (now found filed under 'fiction' not 'autobiography') and he recounts how it was where he went to test his form, his watts-per-kilo and all that kind of thing, sometimes with the notorious and disgraced Dr Michele Ferrari. Armstrong frequented the Madone when he lived in Nice. It starts very close to the promenade in the seaside town of Menton, around 35 kilometres away, and then winds up into the mountains, reaching a height of precisely 927 metres in *around* 13 kilometres. That 'around' is important, as you'll see. It's a small road with very little traffic, and therefore a good spot to do a 30-minute all-out training effort. Before the 1999 Tour Armstrong vowed to take his time below 31 minutes. 'If I went to the Madone two weeks before the Tour and went as hard as I could, I knew if I was going to win the Tour or not,' *Cycling Weekly* has quoted him as saying. He did get under that magic 31-minute goal just before the 1999 race and duly went on to win ... and the rest, all the rest, is, as they say, history. The Madone has, thanks to Lance, become something of a celebrity climb. The Trek Madone bike range was named after it, and when roadies come to the area to cycle it's one of the first to tick off the list.

However, the Madone had pedigree before Armstrong. It was Tony Rominger, a Swiss pro who won the Giro and three Vueltas in the 1990s, who first used it as a training ramp when he moved to Monaco. It has pedigree after Armstrong too, because there is still intense interest in the Madone from local pros. Just a week or two before the barbecue it was reported in the cycling press that Richie Porte had beaten Chris Froome's Madone time, and Porte was now the acknowledged King of the Madone among pros. Both of their times were significantly quicker than Lance's, but I confess to the assembled barbecue-munchers that I'm unsure how comparable any of the times are because there is – in the non pro-cycling fraternity, at least – some confusion about where all these guys were starting their stopwatches. Confusion, in part, because a sub-50-minute time is hugely respectable for an amateur, and that gap of 20 minutes – 20 *minutes* – makes you feel they might as well be riding another hill altogether. Around the table it is quickly agreed that the Team Sky start is at a certain bus stop, while most people think that Lance began at the Menton-with-a-slash-through-it city limits sign a little further down. There's even a moment where it looks like someone might text Lance to find out.

But I don't really mind if we get to the bottom of it or not. I like the legend, and I like it that it's still a real live thing that inspires passion. That even when they're off duty the pros' competitive instincts still stand all aquiver about a certain climb that has never featured in a real race, and that there is a circle of friends and rivals where it carries significant meaning.

Tony Rominger	31'30"
Lance Armstrong	30'47"
Tom Danielson	30'24"
Chris Froome	30'09"
Richie Porte	29'40"

That said, the Madone is not one of Joe's favourites. The ride along the coast to the start is a bit hectic, and the Madone's surface is too patchy and its gradient too irregular to make it a must-ride destination for training intervals. He confesses he's never done a proper effort up it: 'I mean, it's a good ride, especially in the wintertime because it's south facing and it's close to the coast,' he says, 'But, I think, part of what I like about riding in the mountains is being "out", and on the Madone I don't really feel like I'm out, you know.' He continues: 'There are lot of pros who are kind of too cool for Strava but are into the Madone. I mean, I don't care if I have Strava KoMs or not – Strava's fun and I like to show people what I'm doing. But there are certainly a lot of pros who are not into [Strava], and it's interesting that the Madone is more or less the same thing – except it's done by word of mouth, and I would say it carries a lot more weight. It really is a thing. Like, to the point that Chris and Richie will go up there with full race kit and race wheels and see how fast they can go.'

You'll notice that Joe used the 'S' word there, a word without which no discussion of the modern art and science of riding up mountains would be complete. Strava: a website and smartphone app for recording your rides – distances, routes, speeds – and sharing your achievements with an online community, which has over the past few years become something of a phenomenon, with millions of enthusiastic users around the world. Perhaps its most addictive feature is the King of the Mountain and Queen of the Mountain (KoM and QoM) leaderboards. Search for the Madone on Strava and there will be at least one user-defined 'segment' marking the start and the end of the climb, probably plus a few segments for key bits – the first half, say, or the last kilometre.[1] And each segment will have a leaderboard showing the fastest times recorded on it. Strava allows cyclists to record, compare, congratulate and boast, providing inspiration, motivation and validation in different quantities depending on the individual user, but for Michael Horvath, one of the founders, the most important thing is the 'friendly competition', and the connection to people who are passionate about the same activity.

Strava – the name means 'strive' in Swedish – was created by Michael (who is of Swedish extraction) and his friend Mark Gainey. They had been on the Harvard rowing crew together, but after graduating found themselves no longer at the heart of a group of buddies who pushed each other to train harder and get better at their sport, and so they began to train less. 'What was missing in our lives was that sense of team that we had at Harvard,' Michael says. 'And we thought, what if we build a virtual locker room?' However, this was in the mid-1990s, and the internet was not ready for it: people did not put personal data online, websites were nowhere near dynamic or sophisticated enough to handle it, and GPS tracking was only accurate to around 50 metres. They shelved it and did other things, including launching an unrelated tech start-up. When they thought about it again, in the mid-2000s, technology was catching up with their ideas. They began to

---

1 There are rather too many segments on the Madone and other famous climbs, actually. The genius of the segment, as well as its Achilles heel, is that it is user defined, and so it is difficult to stop the proliferation.

create the virtual locker room – the social aspect that would later chime with millions of users. But the KoMs and QoMs that are the hyper-addictive hook came from the work of a software engineer called Davis Kitchel.

Kitchel was the third original member of the Strava team. He had also been an elite rower and he was working on rowing technology ideas for Dartmouth College, but in his spare time he was tinkering with algorithms that would let him take two different GPS tracks of him cycling up a hill (one that happened to be near Mont Ventoux in France) and compare them. The emerging program would, he realised, also have to consistently recognise the starts and finishes of uphill stretches of road – i.e. know what a 'climb' actually was – and then categorise them in Tour de France-style numbers, so that cyclists would know how hard it would be.

The ur-segment was being born.

'To me it intuitively made sense to create this thing that is now "segments",' Davis says. 'It was born out of the idea that there are these really important stretches of road which are a big part of the reason people are on their bike in the first place. It's a piece of geography that's always there. There are sprints and other things that are important and also exciting, but they can happen anywhere. The climbs, they're there forever, and their story is constantly being written by people riding them.' He continues: 'There's a clarity, a purity of what climbs mean to cyclists. Everything else falls away when you're on a climb.'

Gainey was on the west coast of the States; Michael was with Davis out east. Davis says the first segment ridden by anyone other than him alone was likely on the east coast, where he and his friends had a Wednesday group ride. Then Gainey recruited five people in the San Francisco Bay Area, and Davis and Michael five people near them, and it grew from there. The first version of Strava was green, not its now-ubiquitous orange, and it consisted of just a leaderboard, where the small group of friends who'd been invited to join were ranked.

People liked it. They went riding more often. Soon, some began calling in sick to work so they could ride their bike and take back a lost position on the leaderboard. The team had hit upon something. Michael takes up the story: 'At the end of summer we took stock and realised that people were really motivated about this idea of comparing themselves against others going uphill. We said, "This is it, the killer proposition." It resonated with the audience we had and it was all built around the uphill experience.'

When the site launched publicly in 2009, the leaderboard and the KoM were there (the QoM would follow in 2010). But – of course – Strava did not invent competition, friendly or otherwise. It had simply tapped into cyclists' pre-existing thoughts and desires. Hotels in Alpine resorts, for example, used to keep books to record times on the local climbs, but the urge to compete – and to climb – goes back much further than that. 'I don't think it would have worked otherwise,' Davis says. 'It's difficult to put things in people's heads that aren't already there.' Adds Michael (I talked to them separately, but their stories nicely interweave): 'It ties into the tradition that the hills are the biggest challenges you can do on the bike, they're naturally places where you want to keep a record. Some people think it's really important to be competitive, others think it's just fun; some people just want to measure their own slow decline, like I'm doing right now!'

With Strava the difference is that these measurements are not just written in a book, and it's not just the inner circle who know that Richie Porte is fastest on the Madone.[2] The

---

2 OK, that's a bad example, as his ride was reported in *Cycling Weekly* and the mountain is famous enough that we can all know. Plus neither Porte nor Froome

whole world can now see that Kenny Elissonde (a Frenchman formerly of La Française des Jeux now riding for Team Sky) has the Strava Madone KoM, and that Ian Boswell of Team Sky has the KoM for the first half. At least, those stats were correct around the time of that barbecue – Boswell had just swiped his one, to his delight, so some poor rider out there was getting the dreaded Strava email: 'Uh-oh, someone has just taken your KoM on . . .' However, with a peloton of pros on their heels, I would bet that those Madone KoMs have swapped hands more than a few times since then.

OK, so you're an average guy with a full-time job and you like beer and pizza a little too much to count yourself as a dedicated athlete. On your favourite Strava segment you're probably up against whippet-thin 19-year-old headbangers at the very least, not to mention the possibility of elite racers and professional cyclists and triathletes. You're never going to be in the top 100, let alone the top 10, on Box Hill or Mount Baldy or the Madone. But what if you segment the results by weight? And by age? (What one Strava employee has called 'dad filters'.) Or look at your own performance over time and train to beat your personal record? It's enough to make any and all of us reach for the skinsuit and the race wheels on every little training spin.

This phenomenon is known as social facilitation.[3] It was observed and named in the 19th century by a psychologist at Indiana University called Norman Triplett. He dug through the records of the Racing Board of the League of American Wheelmen and realised that cyclists who raced against competitors were faster than cyclists who raced alone. It may

---

use Strava – at least in their own names – but I hope you get the point.
3 I have to thank Tom Vanderbilt, who wrote an insightful interview with Michael Horvath for *Outside* magazine, for this term and the link to Triplett.

seem self-evident to us now, but other people – 'friendly competition' – help us push ourselves and get better.

And we all want to be better, right?

A

It was thanks to Strava that Everesting became a thing. To recap: in the early 1990s a certain George Mallory, South African-born but resident in Melbourne, Australia, had been offered a place on an expedition following in his grandfather's footsteps climbing Mount Everest via the North Ridge. And while the 30-something Mallory was an experienced climber (given his grandfather's renown, George Mallory II is reluctant to talk up his own climbing skills), he had a full-time job, and the idea of training for Everest was daunting. 'I was really invited on that trip because of my grandfather's good name, not mine!' he tells me. The first time he went to the Himalaya he had, 'through misadventure', spent a night outside at 6,000 metres up: 'No sleeping bags, no down jackets, very little. To substantially understate the story, we got very cold but managed to survive. No frostbite or anything, but desperately cold,' he says. 'As you can imagine, I didn't ever want to do that again. And so when I got invited to climb Mount Everest I was resolute there was no bloody way in the wide world I was going to run out of energy on the mountain and not get back to a tent . . . Which is why I started hitting Donna Buang as hard as I did. And it worked.'

Mount Donna Buang is in the Victorian Alps about an hour away from Melbourne. It is quiet and pretty, surrounded by forests and wildlife, and the road up it rises 1,100 metres in total. Figuring that no preparation could be too gruelling for an Everest ascent, George devised what he then thought of as the ultimate bike challenge. He took his inspiration from a rock-climbing exploit he'd read about called the 'El Cap day'. In wintertime, the legendary El Capitan rock face in the

Yosemite National Park is out of bounds to climbers because of the weather. So in the 1970s a group of climbers known as the Stonemasters, which included the legendary free-solo (that is, on your own, without ropes) climber John Bachar, used to scale multiple separate routes around Joshua Tree until they had totalled the same height – 3,000 feet – in a day. It was a technical challenge, a training exercise, even a bit of a game. In a similar vein, Mallory and a friend climbed five separate routes on the south wall of Blouberg (a famous South African climbing spot) in 24 hours, including two by torchlight, which sounds to this non-climber like no mean feat. And then, having emigrated to a new country, and with Mount Everest looming on his metaphorical horizon, George decided to cycle eight times up Donna Buang, 8,800 metres of up: it would be the El Cap day on a bike.

'In all earnest, in the Himalaya even too much stamina is not enough, if you want to be safe,' he says.

On his first attempt at what he came to call 'Mount Everest in a Day', he had barely started his second rep before his quads shouted at him to dismount. On the second attempt (on New Year's Day), he got to the top of the second rep before quitting. Undeterred, he went and bought a better bike and continued training. The next session saw him get to four, almost the equivalent of the height of Mont Blanc. By autumn of that year he had achieved six. Feeling winter's cold breath chilling the back of his neck, he planned an attempt for the big one, more aware than ever about how far away he was from achieving it. He wrote, rather gracefully, in an account at the time:

> Two laps more than the six I had managed previously does not sound like an outrageous increase, but I was destined to learn the hard way, that the human body is not a machine. Marathon runners know that half of 42 is not

21, but 35.[4] Although there is no limit to our endurance, we force back the boundaries in ever smaller increments and the effort required for a single forward step becomes ever greater. Mathematicians would say our limit is like an asymptote which we can approach but never reach.

On that day, the last Sunday in March 1993, he was forced to stop, because of exhaustion and a sore knee. He had failed, and his plans were put on ice until spring came and the weather improved. 'During the winter months which followed, I dissected every detail of the past attempt. I assessed each of the principal variables and devised a strategy for another attempt,' he wrote. In the meantime, he kept up his expedition training mainly by walking up and down his closest hill wearing a heavy backpack.

Life and the weather forecast conspired against him early in the Antipodean summer, and it wasn't until 31 October that he finally had a chance to get back to what he called his 'treadmill'. Treating this sortie to Donna Buang as a training session, he neglected to bring his final cassette tape. Even the soundtrack to his previous attempts had been well planned: Dvorak or Beethoven for a mellow start, followed by rock music from Bryan Adams, The Cure or Midnight Oil, then Jimi Hendrix or John Mellencamp to raise the energy and, finally, Dire Straits's *Alchemy* to reinvigorate the legs on the final lap.

George forced himself to think of the first four laps simply as 'a chore'. On lap five, although he no longer felt strong, a sense of relentlessness took hold; six went OK; after seven he felt 'wasted, but not quite exhausted'. And though he did

---

4 42, of course, being the length of a marathon in kilometres, and the implication that the last push to the line takes 50% of your available determination to complete.

not have his Dire Straits, after almost a year of trying, having been awake since 2 a.m. and by the light of the rising moon, he completed the eighth ascent. 'I should have been awed by the occasion but instead could only feel my sore backside and painful feet,' he wrote. Then he climbed the observation tower at the top, for the first time ever, to take in the view over the blackness, carefully freewheeled back down and went to bed. He'd cycled 272 kilometres and climbed 8,800 metres. Everesters these days will know you have to pedal every single one of those 8,848 metres, and he had wondered briefly if he ought to ride another kilometre to make up the symbolic last 48 metres that would take him all the way to the metaphorical peak, but he decided against it.

For him, at that time, the challenge was complete: 'It had taken me one step closer to the asymptote. How would I take the next step?'

George II made it to Everest – the real Everest, that is – and was gratified to find that apart from the Sherpas he was the fittest person in the expedition party. He summited one fine morning at 5.30 a.m., just after sunrise, and was down at high camp again by 9.20 a.m.

When he returned from Everest he pushed the Mount Donna Buang challenge further, until he had achieved an incredible 10 ascents – 11,000 metres – in a 24-hour period. Then he tried 11 (and aborted due to stomach problems) but after that, he wrote, he did not plan ever to go back to Donna Buang. He felt that, after all that riding and his time in the Himalaya, he was at a peak of fitness he would never reach again. His Donna Buang achievements were unimprovable. This particular chapter of his search for up had finished.

That was in 1996, and we may never have heard about any of this if it hadn't been for a friend of his who passed Mallory's 'Mount Everest in a Day' piece to the Australian website called CyclingTips. CyclingTips published it in 2012,

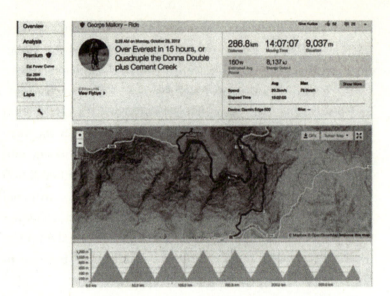

and the very well written account received a lot of online comments. Among them, some snark said: 'If it's not on Strava, it never happened!' And so George reasoned he'd better go out and do it again. Two tries later (one was ended by a broken spoke), and he had 8,848 metres to post on Strava.

That inspired a group of Australian riders who called themselves the Hells500 ('In Search of Up' is their motto) to exhort their members to go and have a pop at 'Everesting' too. And with Strava as a global platform – somewhere to record, validate and build a community around Everesting attempts – the idea spread to cyclists everywhere. Since then, there have been more than a thousand successful attempts, and some of the most famous mountains in the world have been Everested, as well as some of the world's most forgettable suburban streets and obscure dirt trails.

⋀⋀

And so we meet again on Firle Beacon. That's the potted history of how Jimmy and I ended up on top of the South Downs at 4.30 a.m. in the morning. Impressionable victims of cycling extremists dedicated to ensnaring not-so-young men and recruiting them via the internet to do inhuman things in the name of an unhealthy cult.

Basically, it had only been a matter of time.

When I first heard the word 'Everesting' and understood what it meant, something lodged at the back of my brain. Then sat there like a crystal under a microscope. I had harboured it secretly for a while, not wanting to let on for fear, perhaps, of talking too much and not acting. But it was a dark and heavy itch that needed scratching. Then I met Jimmy and we began to scheme. Our preparation was nowhere near as rigorous as George's had been, but the most well-thought-out part of it had been our choice of hill. Jimmy lived in Sussex, south of London, and was a specialist at a climb called Ditchling Beacon. He had, in fact, ridden up it for a Strava competition some 130 times in 30 days. (British cyclists, and especially those familiar with the traditional London to Brighton route, might recognise just how unhinged this is.) I liked the cut of his jib instantly. When I lived in Brighton, close to Ditchling, I had ridden up it a fair few times myself, and it turned out Jimmy and I had been independently mulling over an Everesting attempt on it. Only those pioneers who manage a 'first ascent' get their name and achievement recorded on the Hells500 Everesting map, so we decided to join forces and ride it together.

Ditchling Beacon is all of 1.5 kilometres long and according to Strava has an average gradient of 9.1 per cent. However, it is quite a busy road, and the descent is winding, with poor visibility and high trees, so we shifted our focus around 20 kilometres to the east along the same chalk ridge of the South Downs. Firle Beacon is less famous than Ditchling and it is also steeper. This was a good thing, because steeper meant less long: Firle was 1.3 kilometres at 10 per cent, so for every metre climbed we would have to ride ever so slightly less far horizontally. Over the course of an Everesting that meant something like 215 kilometres v. 195 kilometres, which to me was pretty clear cut. In addition, Firle is not a through road. At the top there is only a car park, for walkers, and it is also very pretty. In our choice of hills, we had a winner. Other than that, my preparation consisted of borrowing a friend's wheel with a 28-tooth cog on the cassette, to give me an easier bottom gear than I usually had. Oh, and I made a large stack of peanut butter sandwiches and bought a couple of 10-litre bottles of water. The forecast was promising a very hot day.

All too suddenly there we were. Bikes assembled, the sun coming up. And the scale of the task was sinking in. The top of Firle is 155 metres above sea level. That's 2,647 less than Bonette and 7,893 less than Everest. Each ascent would be only 128 metres. We had 68 to do. There wasn't much else for it but to start.

There was no first flush of enthusiasm, no losing one's head and pushing into the red – we would have carried that pain all day. Almost before dawn Jimmy's friends were with us for a couple of reps' companionship. The sun rose, the morning passed. Gently does it. Neil, a friend from Brighton, rode up and stayed for a long time, talking us up and down. Each time I reached the top I pulled a sweaty pencil from my jersey pocket and added to the tally on a length of masking tape I had stuck on my top tube for that purpose. Each one a bar on a five-bar gate, and the five-bar gates marching down the tube towards the saddle. At a certain point they ceased to matter. We knew we had to climb all day, and then some. What mattered was keeping moving and the fact that time passed. As long as we kept on going up and down and up and down and time kept passing, I was sure we would get to the top. Or the end, or whatever it was.

Same view from the bottom, same from the top, connected

by the same middle. But the details became endlessly fascinating: a scrap of sheep's wool caught in barbed wire; the deep furrows of a ploughed field seen through a stile; and around us moved the sun, pushing shade across the road. Cows on their way to pasture watched from the amphitheatre of the hill. Each ascent was different, because time was a river and you can never swim in the same river twice. 'Mountain climbing isn't all that important to me any more,' Rheinhold Messner once said. 'Not the climbing part. What counts is just to keep on going and going and going.'

It became very hot and my masking tape became soaked in sweat, blurring the pile of gates I was raggedly constructing upon it. My bib shorts started squeaking and squelching on the saddle. Another friend, Oli, rode over, and then two friends from Strava arrived, and suddenly we had a little happening. I reflected upon how little one had to do to convince men of a certain age and cast of mind to bunk off work and come and hang out on a hillside.

At around 2 p.m. we repaired to the pub at the bottom of the hill to eat chips and drink Coke. Neil left us there, a

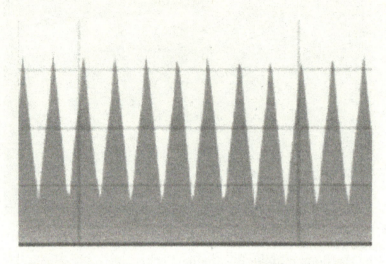

160.0 km   180.0 km

broken man, and we were, for the first time for hours, alone. The scale of the task bore down upon us. Thirty climbs to go, which at a sustainable pace – eight minutes up, three minutes down – would take us well into the night. What else could we do but continue?

The reps from 40 to 50 and the centimetres climbing to 5,000 and then 6,000 metres were hard won. Together alone in the heat on the unchanging hill, sweating, eating, drinking and dealing with the mental pressure of 12 hours in the saddle. To paraphrase another great Alpinist (and writer), Walter Bonatti, we were between discomfort and hope, going on, though slowly, one rep at a time towards the heights. However, in the furnace of the afternoon the difficulties and the unknowns seemed to multiply rather than diminish.

Within the infinite loop we had created other elements

began to repeat. The sun regained the horizon, the cows wandered back from pasture, Jimmy's friends from earlier returned, to ride a while or cheer us on at the top, having all managed to fit in a full day's work while we were there stuck on repeat. As the evening settled, in coolness, quiet and pastel-hued mists, with 10 reps to go I knew we would finish. The last few were accomplished in total blackness, and for the final one our companions left Jimmy and me to spin up on our own, chatting easily in the night. Sixty-eight reps, 13 hours, 56 minutes ride time, 8,894 metres, a ride profile like the teeth of a saw.

We parted then at the top of the hill without much fanfare, bikes slung into cars, kit placed into plastic bags to be incinerated later. On the way home I stopped at a 24-hour services on the motorway and ate all the Big Macs. Then a deep and dreamless, a calm sea of oblivion on the other side of the imaginary peak we'd just scaled.

It took me a few days, weeks even, for the events of that day to settle. We had succeeded but, bizarrely, it was an anticlimax. In all honesty I hadn't countenanced the possibility

of failure; correspondingly, there didn't seem to be all that much to celebrate. We had passed the time and the itch had been scratched but I was not elated. Physically I was tired, but not severely so, and that passed too. In that sense it didn't feel like I'd really pushed any limits, because climbing itself had never been a problem. The main difficulties had been the heat, eating properly and keeping focused – exactly the issues one might experience in any long ride. Almost immediately it seemed like a good idea to do another Everesting, to pass another day on another hill, to push a little further and see what would happen.

This deflation and the psychological effects took longer to process. We had surrendered all speed, all form, all vanity, simply to go up, and the world seemed a little smaller as a result. Or do I mean bigger? A normal bike ride, even taking in a mountain or two, now seemed much more manageable. There had been a flattening, an opening out. We had somehow changed what was possible. Yet there was no thunderbolt moment. Haruki Murakami's book *What I Talk About When I Talk About Running* explores his deep personal connection to that sport, and how it shapes the rest of his life. An accomplished marathon runner, he recounts at one point the story of his first 100-kilometre (62-mile) ultramarathon, and the feelings it left him with afterwards. It's worth quoting:

> I don't know what sort of general significance running sixty-two miles by yourself has, but as an action that deviates from the ordinary yet doesn't violate basic values, you'd expect it to afford you a special sort of self-awareness. It should add a few new elements to your inventory in understanding who you are. And as a result, your view of your life, its colours and shape, should be transformed. More or less, for better or for worse, this happened to me, and I was transformed.

With the Everesting all the right ingredients were there, but my cake didn't rise like Murakami's. This self-knowledge (and is it self-transformation too?) is perhaps one of the major things we seek in climbing mountains – real ones or imagined or even metaphorical ones, on bicycles or with ropes and pitons and ice axes. I had hoped that this Everesting would help me to understand something *in extremis* about the 'why' of it all, which would illuminate all those other, smaller challenges in the mountains. But no eureka moment yet. What counts is just to keep on going and going and going.

I meet George II in a steep small town in the Dolomites. He is in Europe on a tour of the great cycling climbs but it has been an unpromising day. Today he wanted to ride Monte Crostis (a really tricky climb last programmed by the Giro d'Italia in 2012, but not actually ridden because the descent is so hairy) and the weather had been so poor he hadn't been able to give it a crack. It is not late but the light is flat and fading and the clouds, as they do in the Dolomites, are threatening to slide in level with us at any moment, and cut us off from the sheer rock faces and luscious dark forests on the other side of the valley.

There is only one thing for it: pizza.

George is a compact, trim man, and very understated. If you didn't know about his dedication to climbing, you would not suspect from his outward appearance there was anything out of the ordinary going on. However, there is something hard as granite in his eyes and he is clearly in very good shape. Though he had promised himself never to go back to Mount Donna Buang, it had not lasted. He had regained his love for that mountain, and in fact in the years since he wrote his piece had shaved around 10 minutes off what he had supposed, back in 1996, was his best time for one ascent.

The personal best is now under an hour and he had, of course, Everested it when piqued by the CyclingTips comment. (By my count he has completed seven Everests, with the quickest in 10 hours, 12 minutes on what sounds like a miserably steep slope.)

And now he was in Europe. I couldn't help thinking of that line from his article: 'It had taken me one step closer to the asymptote. How would I take the next step?'

We order two pizzas from the counter of a takeaway-cum-sit-down joint in the deserted town centre and take a seat in the window, and George tells me that – at the age of 56 – he has just retired from his job as an engineer. His erstwhile profession suited his mathematical mind and his taste for numbers, data, precision. He is, it turns out, very keen on 'benchmarking' his cycling; that is, measuring his performance to some kind of yardstick or external standard. And cycling on the flat, because of the speeds involved and the sheer number of variables on performance, is not a good laboratory, he explains. It is the implacable force of gravity that creates good test conditions. 'I very quickly took the view that I was interested in hill climbing because I would be able to bench-mark. I would be able to obsess over my own results. You can with hill climbing,' he tells me. Obsessing over results meant spreadsheets: 'I [used to have] this giant spreadsheet of all the climbs I'd ever done,' he says. 'The spreadsheet had the distance and the elevation gain and therefore the average gradient, and then my best time on it. Then it worked out the rate of ascent.'

It sounds like it was almost a Strava-before-Strava, I suggest.

'Well it was . . . The thing is it only had my own data,' he replies. 'In those days all you could do was benchmark against yourself. I do honestly believe that for most weekend-warrior cyclists, most of the time, the best benchmark is your prior self.' (Thinking about the chasm between Richie Porte's time on the Madone and mine, I'm inclined to agree.) But as George II got more data, his knowledge of his own capabilities improved, the measurements he sought became more sophisticated and targets more exacting. 'When you spreadsheet it all out and you plot it out on a graph, you can see how your rate of ascent tends to taper off as the hills get bigger and bigger and bigger,' he explains. 'What you really want is to expand that envelope of rate of ascent plotted on hill height. So that led to the concept of the VAM envelope.'

To explain: VAM stands for the Mean Ascent Vertical (but backwards, as it was originally coined in Italian by that man again, Dr Ferrari). It is the number of vertical metres climbed in an hour, and it is a measure that most Strava users are familiar with. Let's say a nominal 'average' road cyclist may be able to ride a 500-metre-long hill at a VAM of 1,400. That means that if that effort were theoretically extended to last an hour, that rider would ascend 1,400 vertical metres. However, a 500-metre-long hill will only take a minute or two to ride; make that hill 10 kilometres in length and the VAM will go down to 1,000, or even less. For short bursts of high-intensity exercise the body can work anaerobically – without oxygen – but this causes lactic acid to form, which accumulates in the blood and soon causes muscle fatigue. Once lactate levels become intolerable, you have to slack off. Longer hills require aerobic work – efforts the body can sustain by delivering oxygen to the muscles – so they will be climbed slower and, as George II puts it, the rate of ascent will taper off. The interesting thing about VAM, from his point of view at least, is that on some climbs, generally the steeper ones, the rate of ascent will be better than on others (although there is always a point at which the gradient gets too much and your muscles give up). Find the hills that suit your abilities, and then train harder and better and more specifically, and you will start climbing longer slopes at a higher VAM. I think that's what they call pushing the envelope.

VAM was one of the reasons George started coming to Europe. 'By then my whole cycling psyche was dominated by rate of ascent. Everything was rate of ascent,' he says. He settled on a goal of climbing a hill ascending 400 vertical metres in 20 minutes – that's a VAM of 1,200 – and there were hills in the local Dandenongs range that were tall enough, but they were not steep enough to make it possible. 'I knew that in favourable conditions, for a hill that was fairly steep and had no dead wood in it – no flat bits or downhill – I was in with a prayer,' he says.

He worked out that the Portet d'Aspet, a 9 per cent climb in the Pyrenees, would be ideal, and headed off on tour.

That first time riding the Portet d'Aspet, he missed his target by a tiny margin, but the hunt for the perfect hill was on: 'Quite a big chunk of my motivation – not quite 100 per cent, but a big chunk – is to find hills that are closer to perfection,' he says. 'By which I mean, a nice hill with a nice surface, that's fairly straight so you can get a fast descent if you want one, and that is steep: ten-eleven-twelve, thirteen-fourteen-fifteen per cent, even. And the right size. Bigger is better.' Although he says he likes riding unknown stretches of road, it is undeniable that benchmarking on cycling's mythical climbs is more fun. Before setting out for his European missions, George scours Strava for climbs that will suit him. Then he checks the leaderboards to see if the age-group KoM is attainable (he has recently moved into the 55–64 category). If all signs point to Go, he then rides out and smashes himself to bits and, quite often, takes the crown with a good margin.

Monte Zoncolan is one of the Giro's most fearsome climbs, and it's slap bang in George's sights for this trip. It's phenomenally steep: 12 per cent for 10 kilometres, although, he says, 'It's steeper than the numbers suggest. I think the middle six kilometres average 16 per cent or something like that. It's absurd, it's ridiculously steep.' The Mortirolo, too, is a favourite: 'indescribably brutal' and the hardest HC segment he has ever ridden. 'If I'd had any strength I would have cried,' he tells me the next day, when the conversation swings back round to how awful it is to ride.

In my modest experience, I say, as someone with a climber's build if not a climber's talent, I agree with all his reasoning: the place I notice my advantage is on the steeper hills, where sometimes I feel good and more powerfully built riders start to go backwards. He fixes me with a stare and laughs – low-key high intensity is his thing – and says: 'Just in case there's any confusion about this, I don't feel great! I feel like I'm going to die.'

Later, I find out that George took the Zoncolan KoM for the 55–64 age group by a whopping seven minutes. He holds the age-group KoM for that particular awful Mortirolo route and, when his travels finally took him to Alpe d'Huez during the trip on which we met, for his chosen segment (there are hundreds) he bagged the age-group KoM there too, winning by a clear minute. The one he went for was the 'Official Chrono' segment, which finishes where the Tour de France does, about a kilometre higher than the standard 'tourist' finish. On the more popular 'tourist' segment, he is only fourth, which is impressive in itself. Alpe d'Huez is probably the most hotly contested climb in Europe, and I'm sure he was measuring out his effort for the longer course. But even so I can't help feeling he would have done even better if it had been a bit steeper. I suspect George would have liked it to be even harder.[5]

---

5 I have no love for riding Alpe d'Huez. It is almost always busy – with cars and coaches and other cyclists – and not at all interesting or scenic. But then I don't

Given the climbs he selects for his benchmarking – some of cycling's most famous, that sing siren songs to riders around the world – he must be, in his chosen (admittedly specialist) discipline, right up there with the best.

We're done with our pizzas and are on to our second beer when I ask George how his rock climbing has influenced his cycling. It's a theme he jumps on with enthusiasm. 'My approach to my cycling is heavily influenced by my rock-climbing youth,' he says. 'I can't believe that so few cyclists I know – and maybe I don't know many cyclists! – approach cycling like a rock climber approaches rock climbing.' To his way of thinking, any particular route up a mountain or a rock face is, in effect, roughly equivalent to a Strava segment, in that it's a certain agreed-upon mini course or challenge on which people test themselves and show what they can do. George II's particular proclivity – finding and picking off Strava segments that suit his abilities – shares similarities with how many rock climbers choose the routes they climb: they work out what is possible, what is stretching them, what will look good on their resumés, and then go climb. Though I'm taking his lead on the rock-climbing angle (I'm definitely no expert when it comes to mountaineering), from the cycling side of things it's a convincing argument, and rings true to me for a certain kind of rider and way of riding – although there are obviously many other ways of, and motivations for, riding your bike up a hill.

More significant is what rock climbing taught him about training to cycle in the mountains. Rock climbers worked out long before cyclists, he says, that short, high-intensity efforts would help their endurance efforts. He quotes a rock-climbing

---

have the desire or capacity that George and many others do to focus so purely on performance. Or, seemingly, the ability to bury myself in suffering to the exclusion of everything else. For me, the drama of Alpe d'Huez lives only in the race.

legend called Jerry Moffat: 'What Jerry Moffat said was an increase in power leads to an increase in stamina. But it doesn't work the other way around.' George II has devoted himself to proving this right: 'What I try to do in my training, which I've learnt from rock climbing is, if you want to get better on Donna Buang, you actually have to get better on the 50-metres-vertical sprint. Out of the saddle, fucking balls to the wall, fresh as a daisy having hyperventilated before, giving it the full fucking noise the whole fucking way, and getting to the top ready to die. A 500-metre-long uphill sprint. Really, if you practise those – and it's hard, it's really hard – you will get better at Donna Buang.'

When he says it's hard, I don't doubt him, and his delivery is convincing, to say the least, as are his Strava results. But everyone knows hill reps are good training. What I'm less prepared for, at least initially, is the technique he calls his secret weapon.

'One of the training techniques I've found effective – I mean ridiculously effective, more effective than anything else I can think of, even high-intensity hill reps – is stairwell run-ups holding your breath,' George II begins, looking at me in a way that suggests he feels he is letting a rather large and beautiful panther out of a sack. When he worked in an office block, every other day he used to run up and down the stairwells holding his breath during his lunch breaks, just in his normal clothes. He explains more: 'What you can do in a stairwell that you can't easily do anywhere else is you can measure very precisely what the elevation gain is, by measuring the steps and counting them. And when you train for it, when you hyperventilate and run up stairwells, you can get good at it.'

I'll confess at this point that I am slightly clutching at straws. Not at the concept itself – I've heard of tower runs, organised competitions where people run up the steps in skyscrapers, and 'vertical kilometre' trail runs – but at the basic, masochistic toughness of it, and the quality of the lateral thinking involved. If you can't train at altitude, hold your breath and run upstairs as fast as you can and get hypoxic (oxygen deprived): it's the next best thing.

George II continues: 'Anyway, if you run up a stairwell holding your breath, you get very seriously hypoxic very quickly. Because it happens rapidly you can get deeper into the red zone than any other way. I've twice fainted at the end, and on one occasion kind of rolled halfway down. Fortunately I wasn't damaged. You learn the signs, you learn to sit down before you pass out, so when you do pass out it's not consequential. But for the record, I've run up 24.8 metres of vertical in one breath. That's six-and-a-half storeys.'

'Bloody hell,' I manage.

It is fair to say I am sceptical that this is a reasonable thing to ask oneself to do. (However, I will have reason to change my mind – a reason other than George's achievements and his many, many KoMs – as we'll see in a later chapter.) 'Try it,' says George II. 'If you've got access to a stairwell, practise that. Try that every second or third day for a few weeks, I think you'll notice your climbing ability goes out of sight.' He muses with regret that now he has retired he no longer has a stairwell at his disposal to train on.

One other significant motivation for coming to Europe is for the physical experience of riding the famous climbs. It's a virtuous circle: seeing pros racing up a legendary climb on TV makes you want to ride it, and riding it gives you greater enjoyment of the race – an understanding of what's at stake and a connection to the pro riders and their physical feats. He mentions climbing the Col du Galibier, and then watching Cadel Evans struggle so valiantly and without help on the same slopes when he was chasing Andy Schleck in the race for the 2011 yellow jersey. It was, he says, 'just pure brute suffering and

prowess, [coming] from years and years of hard work and diet-
ing and obsession', and his voice is tinged with admiration. The
same rationale about the physical experience holds for mountaineering: 'If you haven't ever climbed up a snow slope with
an ice axe and crampons, it's really hard to know what it's like,'
he says. 'It was only really after I'd been Alpine climbing and
to the Himalaya that I could start to appreciate what my
grandfather had done, a little bit. The additional insight I got
from climbing Mount Everest myself is massive.'

George was aware of his grandfather's fame from a young
age, maybe from when a family member by marriage published
a book on Mallory and Irvine, and a copy got placed in his
school library – difficult, he says, for a kid who didn't want
to attract attention to himself. He confesses that in his younger
years it was even a bit of a burden. As he grew up he became
a student of his grandfather's achievements, his character and
his principles, reading all the books he could find. He tells
me about his grandfather's brief involvement with the Suffra-
gette movement, his association with the progressive Fabian
Society at Cambridge, and the ethical code by which he
conducted his expeditions.

'I'm a shadow of my grandfather,' he tells me. 'He was
hardcore.'

But I can't help feeling this might be an impossible bench-
mark to measure oneself against. And I don't think it's that
stark, or that simple. Later, I am reminded of a few lines
from a Louis MacNeice poem:

Pride in your history is pride
In living what your fathers died,
Is pride in taking your own pulse
And counting in you someone else.

We rode together the following day up the Passo Giau, one of the Dolomites' most famous and beautiful climbs, meeting in a car park at the bottom and heading off into uncertain weather. George was formidably in form, having worked hard on his fitness, as he always did before these trips, so that he could pack in as many consecutive days' riding as possible, to make the best use of limited time and still be competitive on the climbs. This ride up the Passo Giau was just a recce for him, and I was really grateful he was taking it easy on me. 'I'm comparative, not competitive,' he said at one point as we spun up through the trees, and I think that just about sums up his attitude.

Talking and riding with him gave me a lot to think about. George II's approach to his cycling was so different to mine, and yet we both used the mountains as the canvases on which

we drew our obsessions. 'It's like cycling in heaven here,' he said on that ride, and I thought, yes, heaven, but each man takes his own path to get there. And I could barely begin to imagine the internal vistas he had explored, the dark landscapes and sensations of pain on all those repeated ascents that had brought him here, to this mountain now, a few wheel lengths in front of me.

Still, so many things resonated. For one, he had talked of the emptiness of achievement, something that haunts many people who spend their time chasing goals, reminding me that desire is in the chase and not in the consummation. There's always another hill, another record. 'It is so vastly much better for your demeanour and your mental health and your enjoyment of life,' he said, 'to have ... to have meaning. If you've got something worthwhile to strive towards. I guess I learnt that especially on Everest: that almost within the same instant that you achieve something, suddenly it becomes worthless.'

But the thing that has stuck with me the most is the idea of pushing the envelope. Walter Bonatti, an Italian who was one of the greats of Alpine climbing, had a good phrase for it: 'What had enabled me to find the strength to resume climbing was the awareness that I had been struggling at the limits of the possible for days in order to solve my personal problems,' he wrote. The personal problems he was referring to were his part in a fraught Italian national expedition to K2, in the Himalaya, in 1954. While the expedition was ultimately successful, becoming the first to summit the second-highest peak in the world, Bonatti was accused by the summiting pair of using oxygen he was meant to be taking to them. Bonatti's rebuttal – that he couldn't have used it even if he had wanted to, and that actually they hadn't placed their high camp in the agreed place, forcing him and another climber to endure a night in the open at 8,100 metres (causing his companion to lose his toes) – was disputed and disbelieved for over 40 years. Vilified, slandered and disillusioned, he went solo, driving himself beyond what many believed one man could achieve alone.

'The limits of the possible': the phrase recurs in his writing, and is echoed in those of Frenchman Lionel Terray, another founding father of climbing in the Alps. 'Bit by bit I worked out for myself an ethic and a philosophy of mountaineering,' Terray wrote. 'In practice, the risk and suffering involved in picking the roses that grow on the borders of the impossible call for exceptional moral strength.'

I'm not trying to draw an equivalence here between the exploits of pioneering mountaineers and what normal amateur cyclists get up to in the mountains. But maybe their *in extremis* 'why' can illuminate something about us. Some of us, too, have that same affinity for these glorious worlds of light and beauty of the high mountains, the same thrill at the confrontation between nature and human endurance. We may, in our own way, share that same feeling, when everything is going well at least, of cloud-stepping, of dancing on space. And even if our achievements are nowhere near the same league, that Everesting pushed back the limits of my possible. Likewise, Murakami's ultramarathon. Or finishing an Étape, climbing Alpe d'Huez, riding the Madone in 29 minutes, 40 seconds, getting a PB on your local hill – each of these push back the limits, even if that's just in a very tiny, very personal way.

'Look, when you get to my age, any PB is a bonus. As far as I'm concerned, the sun has set. I'm into the twilight . . . I mean, PBs at 56, that's not normal,' George II said to me over that pizza.

Terray also makes explicit something else: that for many, mountain climbing has a moral code. Terray and Bonatti (and

Rheinhold Messner and many others afterwards) shunned certain comforts and certain pieces of equipment as being, in their own personal engagement with nature, somehow unfair. Bonatti, for instance, would only use traditional pitons (pegs to drive into cracks, in his day still sometimes made out of wood) and not the new 'spits' that started being used in the 1950s (pitons that were drilled into the rock face, creating new holds that previously had simply not been there). 'Using this type of piton,' he wrote, ' . . . cancels the impossible. And it therefore also cancels adventure. One might say it is tantamount to cheating in a game one has chosen to play voluntarily.' He continued: 'I think everyone should confront a mountain in a particular and precise way, obeying natural impulses, and be driven by precise, personal motives. Right from the start my motivation has been mostly of a thoughtful, introspective nature, ending in an assertion to myself about myself.'

I think George II would probably recognise this asserting-of-self-in-action in his grandfather. Do something long enough and hard enough and passionately enough and an ethos develops – or, more than that: it becomes an expression of the ethos that shapes the life. Recently there have been debates among the old guard of cycling's Everesting over whether a (very) few of the numerous attempts that now take place around the world every weekend are really in the original spirit of the endeavour. Should an Everesting course with a little downhill in the middle, where you can acquire a bit of momentum and gain a tiny bit of 'free' elevation on the downhill leg, count? This matters to George II. Because an Everesting, in his conception at least, is something hard and pure and uncompromising. It is about hoisting your ass up 8,848 metres, come what may, and to finesse that, one might say, is tantamount to cheating in a game one has chosen to play voluntarily.

These things are only an accomplishment if they are gone about in the right way. Mountains give us a place to show what we're made of. Picking the roses that grow on the borders of the impossible calls for exceptional moral strength. You cannot lie to a mountain.

Chapter 6

THE CLIMB IS NOT THE THING

Or, the world's greatest stadia, butterflies at the hardest
Grand Tour stage ever and the arms race of the 'extreme'

I am sitting with Joe Dombrowski again, at the seafront café
eating fish and salad. Or maybe it was the same time as
before; we went there quite a lot, it was always sunny and
we always ate fish and salad. The Giro is approaching and
we are talking World Tour, the select races that make up the
top level of competition in the professional road calendar.
Specifically, I'm asking him what was the toughest moment
he's faced so far. He thinks for a moment and then says it
was the team time trial in his first World Tour race, Tirreno–
Adriatico, a week-long race across Italy from coast to coast:
'It was really windy, to the point where I thought maybe they
were going to cancel it. We had a hit squad of a team – [Chris]
Froome, [Rigoberto] Urán and [Sergio] Henao – and I remember being nervous because there were a lot of roundabouts
and slick corners. I didn't want to cause a crash!' I remembered
that day; I'd been looking out for him and Ian Boswell, who
was also making his World Tour debut that season, excited
that they were getting their start. Joe continues: 'Coming off
the ramp, I think I was the last guy, and just . . . the jump!
I almost never got on the wheel. I think I did one pull before
I was dropped. Literally the first time through and I didn't

get back in.' He laughs. 'And I remember hearing the director on the radio literally a minute into this team time trial: "Guys, we've dropped Joe, just keep going now . . ." You hear that on the radio and it's just like, shit, I guess this is the World Tour.'

Actually, what I'd meant with my question was, could he remember a certain moment of racing in the mountains or on a climb that he'd found totally unbearable? Because even great climbers must find it tough. It never gets easier, you just get faster, right? Instead he'd answered with every skinny lightweight's *bête noire*: keeping up with the big boys in crosswinds on the flat. I guess it figured.

Then he tells me about the Vuelta al Pais Vasco, which is notorious in the peloton as one of the hardest races in the whole calendar. The climbs in the Basque Country aren't all that long, which means sprinters and the bigger guys can just punch their way over using reserves of power the *grimpeurs* don't have – i.e. the climbs are just at that sweet spot in a Venn diagram where one circle is pain and the other demoralisation. 'I remember going over some climbs in the middle of the race, and just thinking, I'm getting dropped and there's still well over 100 guys in the peloton and I'm meant to be a climber. Like, what am I doing here?' Joe says glumly.

In your first season, I suggest, you've got to let those moments go, and chalk it up to experience.

'Yeah, and realise just how big a step up the World Tour is,' he says. 'Like, you're not going to rock up and win the Tour de France, just chill out. Which I think the team tried to impress on me, but I didn't really fully grasp it until I'd gotten more experience.'

I can see what he means: you can know conceptually that climbing Mont Ventoux, for example, is tough, but that doesn't prepare you for actually doing it. And of course people will tell you a Grand Tour is fiendishly, awesomely tiring and difficult, but you can't really feel the truth of that road until you've ridden it. It sends me back to a memory of our time – well, let's be honest, his time – at the hardest Grand Tour stage ever.

A

There is not a single centimetre of flat road in Andorra, in the Pyrenees between Spain and France. I know because I checked. I went looking in 2015, on assignment for Strava to recce the course of that year's Vuelta a España Stage 11, and I didn't find one bit. The mountain principality is tiny, and is caught in a long steep valley between high rocks which, if you follow it from the capital, Andorra La Vella, at the Spanish end, takes you up over the highest road in the Pyrenees, the 2,408-metre Port d'Envalira, and down to another valley and the ski resort of Pas de la Casa. Pass through that and then you're out. France and the Col de Puymorens (1,920 metres). That's it. Andorra is an awful lot of uphill even if you stick to the valleys; if you branch out, you pass green terraces of land, beautiful, well-kept houses and gardens, sunflowers lashed upside down to barns to dry out, and deep dark forests on beautiful, tortuous roads that rise and fall at sometimes eye-watering gradients. Branching out is all that Stage 11 of the Vuelta does. It was designed by Andorra resident Joaquim 'Purito' Rodriguez of Team Katusha. In so doing he revealed himself to be both a sadist (he was tasking the pro peloton and also the forthcoming amateur 'Purito Cyclosportive' with some truly horrendous climbs) and a masochist (he would be riding it himself, and no doubt giving his all to win it). His route butterflied deviously in loops on both sides of the valley, passing multiple ski resorts on the way.

There have been stages of the Giro d'Italia that stand out for their combination of tough climbing and terrible weather, and there was a Tour de France stage in 1983 that featured

6,685 metres vertical gain in 247 kilometres, but this, the Vuelta's Queen stage, with 5,000 metres' climbing in 138 kilometres, taking riders up to a summit finish at 2,095 metres, will lay claim to packing in the most vertical metres per horizontal kilometre. Thanks to this it will be, according to some, the hardest Grand Tour stage ever.

Andorra is the mountain Monaco or the mini-Switzerland: its banks are notoriously discreet and until recently it had no income tax. The shops lining Andorra La Vella's streets alternate between those selling cut-price alcohol, cigarettes and electronics, and high-class boutiques selling Italian shoes or cigars, these latter mainly to walnut-skinned septuagenarians in smoked-glass shades and fawn mohair jumpers. There is also a surfeit of marble-bedecked spa hotels, which at this season of the year are almost empty, and so the photographer and I have snagged a rather good lodging for cheap. It happens to be where Team Astana and La Française des Jeux are staying for two nights – Andorra is also where the Vuelta takes its first rest day. The night we arrived we watched them – from the plush sofas of the lobby as we used the hotel Wi-Fi – troop in dispiritedly in a midnight thunderstorm after a five-hour bus transfer, and we watch them again on the rest day from the same sofas as they do the things bike racers do on rest days: use the Wi-Fi, talk to journalists, go on an easy spin, travel up and down in the palm-filled lobby's glass elevator. The muzak is unremittingly soft and relaxing, but the mood among the riders seems to be, let us say, tired and edgy.

Joe is staying in Soldeu, a ski resort at 1,825 metres, 800 metres above Andorra La Vella. His team's hotel is a rambling modern building, all glass and double-height spaces, which contrasts with the claustrophobic marble caverns of the luxury hotels downtown. Correspondingly, he seems more relaxed, ambling up to where I'm sitting in jeans shorts and a hoodie.

This Vuelta is his longest race yet and first Grand Tour, and it's also the first time he has pinned on a number since his Tour of Utah win. There were nerves, he admits, jumping into the unknown of a Grand Tour, and in his telling the first week contained more flats and side winds than he was truly comfortable with (or the average punter gives the race credit for: the public is by and large convinced that the Vuelta is a hilly race without much else to balance that out). But now, 10 days in, it seems he is coming into his element and any butterflies are gone. Well, all the butterflies except tomorrow's.

The team plan was that Joe ride for Dan Martin, their designated GC contender, and Martin started the Vuelta strongly. But a big pile-up in Stage 8 left him with a shoulder injury that forced him to abandon his third place in the overall rankings, and that has given Joe latitude to ride a bit more for himself when he thinks he might have a chance. He admits, cautiously, that before the race he picked out tomorrow's stage as one that might suit him, which leads to an interesting conversation conducted in semi-specifics and with a definite lack of overstatement. Clearly, he does not want to talk himself up too much – I'm sure he's worried about being over-presumptuous – and if it were me, the day before a big challenge, I'd keep myself to myself, for fear of jinxing it. Nevertheless, if you don't take the initiative . . . 'You pick your days and you pick your battles,' he says, and smiles. 'If you're coming into it with the mindset that this is an opportunity for me, then you have to stay focused on that and devise a plan.'

But how do you prepare for such a difficult stage, I ask.

'I think going into it knowing it's going to be hard is obviously part of the preparation,' he says, and doesn't elucidate more. I think, actually, that a good part of his preparation involves trying to stay as relaxed as possible, and not agonising and losing sleep over the big stages. Taking it easy when it isn't essential to be working hard. His growing stage-race experience – from the Baby Giro through to that moment being dropped at Tirreno-Adriatico and on to California, Suisse, Utah and others – has given him the nous to race a little more cleverly. For one thing, by cutting out wasted effort trying to gain seconds that will, paradoxically, hold him back from achieving something big. He explains: 'My thinking was that on a number of days here I've conserved energy. I've gone into it with the mindset of really targeting the second and third week, because there's some really good stages for me,' he says. 'I could have tried to ride for the GC, but it's my first Grand Tour, and do you try and do that, and fight tooth and nail to finish 16th . . .'

His point being that this won't receive much recognition or reward.

'Right,' he continues. 'Would I rather try and do that or try and win a stage? The danger is, if you sit in that 8- to 10-minutes-down territory, fighting tooth and nail to finish 16th on GC, it really limits your ability to win a stage, because then you don't have that leash you would otherwise.'

If you're too close to the top positions then, should you get in a break, teams will ride against you and the break will be doomed to failure. And the big stage tomorrow, for those wishing to contest the stage win, is all about making the right break.

'In the breakaway it's easier than being in the peloton, because you don't have to fight for position,' he says. 'There's not the surges, and up front you get as many bottles as you want, as much clothing, food, all that. Your car's right there.'

Joe had a long, fairly hard rest day ride, to keep the pipes open and recce a couple of the climbs; I went out for a twisty,

turny and up-and-downy drive, so we swap notes on the
course. Climb one is called the Collada de Beixalis and it's
a real stinker. Although the road book says it averages 8.7 per
cent over six kilometres, that average hides some terrible
switchbacks where the road is barely a car's width and the
gradient is easily at 15 per cent. And those bits come right
at the bottom. 'The road's so narrow and so steep at the bottom that it's about positioning,' is Joe's verdict. 'If you're out
of position you're not going to be able to do it.' The second
climb is not so bad, but the third and fourth are both over
10 kilometres long, and that fourth one, the Collada de la
Gallina, steep too: an HC after three category 1s. Climb five
is short and steep, and then the finishing climb to Cortals
d'Encamp is not so short and still steep: 9 kilometres at 9.5
per cent. Phew.

Tom Dumoulin of Giant-Alpecin is leading the general
classification, while Purito, the stage designer himself, is only
57 seconds behind in second place. It being only Stage 11,

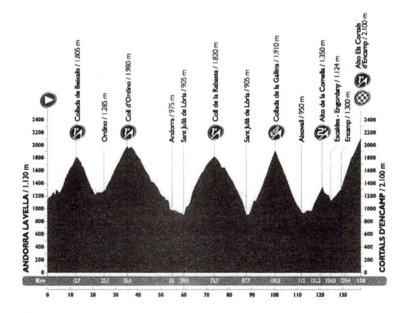

and only the first real mountain day, Joe is pretty sure that the GC battle will not ignite. Who might take the stage, I ask. Says Joe: 'My prediction for tomorrow is there's a breakaway of really strong climbers who are out of GC, and it goes to the line and one of those guys wins. And shortly behind that is the GC group. I kinda think Froome might . . . I mean . . . Purito is obviously always good, and it is his stage!'

Which, it seems to me, is saying that it's anybody's guess and that it's going to be chaos.

It is a measure of the respect in which the veteran Spanish rider Rodriguez is held that he has been allowed to programme a stage of his home Grand Tour. As climbers go, he is at the other end of the spectrum from Joe. Short and steep are his thing, and he has won the hilly Il Lombardia and the Flèche-Wallonne one-day races, the Tours of Catalunya and the Basque Country, as well as individual stages at all three Grand Tours, GC podium places and the Vuelta's mountains jersey. His nickname, Purito, refers to a type of small cigar that looks like a little stick of dynamite, and by extension to his explosive style.

If every rider got to design a stage, what would they do? And, broadening that thought out, I begin to wonder about the art of designing stages in general.

How the peloton plays a Grand Tour stage is a product of many things: GC positions, the composition of the break, individual rivalries, who feels good on that particular day, the weather and many more factors less tangible than that. But beneath it all is the basic composition of the stage, and that is decided by the race's directors and technical officials. Stage starts and finishes are often fixed long in advance and for commercial reasons, with towns paying large amounts of money for the prestige (and the boost to the local economy) that they bring. How the start and finish are connected is an art, one that relies on deep knowledge of bike racing, geography and local cycling contacts all around the country. These race directors are the spiritual heirs to Henri Desgrange and Alphonse Steinès, and their work is particularly in evidence during the mountain stages. Anyone who has ever ridden an Étape will understand that, at their best, mountain stages are not just a misshapen succession of random climbs: they are a carefully thought out sequence of challenges with an inbuilt rhythm and logic. If the race directors programme the stages well, there will be ebbs and flows, interweaving melodies and harmonies and moments of drama, from the Grand Tour's overture to the coda of the final ceremonial stage. Get it wrong and the symphony will sound flat, and the orchestra's soloists won't be able to show their virtuosity.

The mountains make a difference. That is to say, in cycling the characteristics of the venue itself substantially affect the contest, but in this the sport is not unique. Trail running, rally driving and other races that take place in the real world rather than a stadium also 'feature' the course, and even in a marathon the course can have a big bearing on finishing. But in road cycling, with its huge range of terrains and the collective nature of the race – the fact that, unlike in trail running, say, all the competitors stick together most of the time – the mountains assume the stature of an additional opponent. It is not simply one cyclist or one team against another, jumping when he knows the terrain suits him best, or testing his opponent when he seems at his weakest. It is both cyclists against the mountains. Every man for himself, and the mountains against them all.

'There is no cycling without mountains, in my opinion,' Michele Acquarone told me. I had decided, since my mind was focused more on the Giro d'Italia than the Vuelta a

España, to contact the Giro organisers, and eventually I found myself with Signor Acquarone at the end of a Skype line. Acquarone was the overall boss of the Giro for the organiser, RCS Sport, from 2011 to 2013, and he worked closely with Mauro Vegni, the technical director in charge of the race route in those years, to give the race shape and balance. And on shaping the race Mauro said this: 'There are three considerations to be taken care of. The first is that you need to consider the mountain not in a standalone stage but how it is placed in the general project of the whole race. You cannot think one stage at a time, you always have to think it through. The second consideration is the position of the climbs compared to the finish line. I'll give you an example. You can put the Stelvio in a stage, but if the finish line is well after Prato di Stelvio [the town at the bottom of the descent], riders will have all that time to recover from the climb itself, and so the technical factor of the climb will be diluted. This is absolutely a consideration that needs to be taken care of. And then of course the final consideration is how hard it is, the difficulty that the climb presents.'[1]

I asked Mauro if he had developed a particular approach to creating mountain stages. Dare I call it a philosophy? Yes I could: this was a conversation with a continental European, after all. 'There is absolutely a philosophy,' he exclaimed. 'It's made of two parts. The first part is tradition: it's incredibly important to consider the tradition of the climbs because the history of this sport was built on the most traditional climbs – like the Stelvio, for instance. On the other side is innovation. I'll give you a very precise example: think about Zoncolan. You can consider it as a traditional climb now, but you need

---

1 In 2013 Michele Acquarone was fired by RCS amid fraud allegations, which he denies completely, pointing to what he says are obvious forgeries of his signature on key documents. (The case is, as they say, ongoing.) Mauro Vegni took over as cycling manager at RCS Sport and I spoke to them separately.

to remember that it was introduced at the beginning of the 2000s. So at the time it was innovating. The Zoncolan immediately became an instant tradition. Another one to consider is Colle delle Finestre. It's considered already a traditional climb, but last year was only the second time they were racing it, so it was innovative. We're always mixing tradition and innovation.'

If you're not totally up to speed with the history of the Giro then I'll explain. The Passo dello Stelvio is the most famous climb in Italy. At 2,757 metres, it is regularly the highest point the Giro crosses and it is famous for the profusion of switchbacks stretching up and down two tight valleys near the Swiss border. The Zoncolan, meanwhile, which was where George II was heading when I met him, was actually first used in the Giro Donne, the women's edition of the race, in 1997, but it rose to fame in the men's 2003 Giro and quickly became a favourite with the fans. The west side is 10.1 kilometres at a horrific average gradient of 11.9 per cent. The Finestre is another brutally steep road, but this time with the added attraction of eight kilometres of gravel at the top. Since 2005 it has appeared three times; it has had the likes of Alberto Contador, Danilo di Luca and Mikel Landa slipping around on its rocky surface, just like their illustrious predecessors a century before, and it will surely feature again. Acquarone considers crossing the Zoncolan one of the highlights of the modern Giro. He liked the Finestre too, but not as much.

The other innovation Mauro and Michele both push – and here might be one of the Giro's competitive advantages over the Tour de France – is that over the last 20 years or so the Giro has looked to include mountains right from the start of the race. The Tour de France cannot quite do the same, or at least in the past it has mostly chosen not to. Much of this stems from the Tour de France being more wedded to its *grands sites* than either the Spanish or Italian races. A Tour without any one of the Tourmalet, Galibier, Alpe d'Huez or Ventoux is very unusual, and if there were two consecutive years they didn't appear traditionalists would be in uproar. These enforced stops oblige it to cleave to a route with substantial time in the Pyrenees and the Alps every year, with a couple of transition stages along the Mediterranean usually between them. It also regularly visits its heartlands, Normandy and Brittany, the Centre region (where, take it from me, some towns have nothing else to live for outside a Tour visit every few years) and Paris, none of which are very mountainous. This all contributes to the Tour's traditional three-week, three-act drama. Italy, on the other hand, is more flexible: with fewer must-visit places and more mountain ranges to play in right across the country, the organisers can be faster and looser with the action.[2]

Another driver of innovation might be that the Giro and the Vuelta organisers are aware of their races' inferiority to the Tour in the public imagination – which might logically lead them, in a bid for notoriety, to inject thrills and spills and to add difficulties for difficulty's sake. It could be argued that as in other areas of life (as, for example, violence in movies) in cycling there is a relentless logic of escalation: that once we have seen the steep slopes of the Zoncolan a few times, it will no longer sate our desire for tough racing and we need ever more extreme challenges to get the same fix. However, both men reject the idea that there is this kind of 'arms race'. 'Is there a need to be more extreme?' echoed Mauro. 'It's actually not there. The reality is that over 21 days you already have a

---

2 The same two factors are true of the Vuelta, which also in recent times has gone for a scattershot and hardcore approach to its mountain challenges – so much so that not one of the top sprinters contested the 2016 Vuelta. The race was simply not designed with them in mind so they avoided it, and the points jersey went to Trek-Segafredo's Fabio Felline.

hard race, so you don't need to be extreme. What you need to be is well balanced, and to give the fans and the riders a chance to challenge themselves every day in the stage.'

I'm not sure I totally buy this. I don't mean to imply that any race organisers make irresponsible decisions and purposefully create dangerous conditions, but, just as different riders have different tolerances for careering down hills or charging up them, so each race has a character and an appetite of its own, shaped by factors like topography, the national audience, the riders and, of course, the organisers themselves. Some races do push further than others when it comes to lining up extreme climbs and tests of physical and mental endurance. It's simply a fact.

It seemed inevitable in these discussions that the ideas of extreme terrain or extreme racing got mixed up with questions of risk and safety. The things were difficult to unpick. I asked Michele, too, about the risks of racing in the mountains and about pushing the envelope, and he, like Mauro, demurred: 'Sometimes the problem when we speak about innovation is that climbs are too steep or too narrow, and you cannot do them because it's too much. Even if fans want to see something crazy, if it's too much, it's too much.' He continued: 'We the organisers never need to create a dangerous race – we are the first who need to protect our stars. But we need to create a race full of opportunities for riders,' he said. 'I prefer to speak about opportunity in the race.'[3]

This seems more insightful to me. As Michele implied, a risk is a danger but also an opportunity – an opportunity

---

3 It was just before Michele's tenure that the Monte Crostis climb George Mallory II was interested in got removed from the Giro *percorso*, after the sad death of a rider, Wouter Weylandt, on a mountain descent in a previous stage. I never specifically intended to talk about extreme dangers and risks to life, but the subtext was there with both Michele and Mauro.

to apply judgement, talent and experience to influence a situation. We all take risks, in the sense of making calculated and informed decisions about the possible bad outcomes of an action, all the time, and bike racers take more risks than most. It's part of the job. Sometimes that's just a risk in a racing sense: make a move and if it fails you've lost the race. Other times, there are undoubtedly more serious consequences. But would anyone want it any other way? The general standard of fitness among riders, from *maglia rosa* to the humblest *gregario*, is probably higher than ever; frames are stiffer, wheels are quicker, brakes are better. To keep doing the same things would make races sterile – stale for spectators and riders alike. The course must provoke good racing and give enough opportunities for the best riders to differentiate themselves and make their talent and initiative count. New challenges must always be found. The question is, will the chosen challenges tempt sprinters, *rouleurs*, or climbers, like Joe? And where will the line between desirable opportunity and unacceptable danger be drawn?

In truth, these lines are moving all the time. Racing is always changing. To take one example from the past few years, here's a pet theory concerning 'marginal gains'. When Team Sky arrived in the peloton in 2009 they shook things up with their unwavering focus on optimising every area of a rider's life to make them quicker. Sky delved into nutrition and the cutting edge of sports science (not to mention mattresses, motorhomes and so on) more deeply than anyone before. But, subsequently, many other teams applied themselves in these areas and the gaps Sky opened up narrowed again. The general standard of training and scientific application has arguably never been higher, and the athletes are closer to maximising their physical and genetic talents than ever. Because everyone is closer to their limits it is increasingly rare that any Grand Tour contender has the sheer superiority to ride away from the others with, say, 40 kilometres to go on a high mountain stage. Gaps are smaller, attacks happen later. I'm not wearing rose-tinted spectacles and pretending that daring, long-range, Tour-winning heroics used to happen often, but they seem increasingly unthinkable. (An alternative version of this narrative holds that this is because the huge differences in performance occasioned in the past by doping are also being slowly erased, and let's hope this is also true.)

Either way, the unintended consequence seems to be that in the past few years we're seeing more and more racing downhill. Descending is not so much a matter of fitness. There is a larger psychological component and it cannot be trained in the same way, and so those who are real masters are increasingly exploiting this competitive advantage to win time. Vincenzo Nibali, a super descender, springs to mind, as does Romain Bardet, who twice in recent years has descended to a stunning stage victory. One was on the deviously tricky Col d'Allos in the 2015 Critérium du Dauphiné on the way to a solo win at Pra Loup. The second and most apposite was in the Alps during the 2016 Tour de France, when he attacked over the top of the Montée de Bisane climb and hared down a greasy descent to the finish. It was Stage 19, not all that far from Paris; Bardet was fifth on GC, less than five minutes behind the yellow jersey, and so he could not be allowed to gain too much time. Witness Chris Froome and Nibali chasing, and both at one point slipping and sliding on a corner. If the playing field of the climbs continues to be levelled, this will only start happening more. When the limits of the possible are reached in one sphere, it is natural that we start exploring them in another.

I also talked to Michele about sadism. Or, at least, I tried. Whether or not there was an element of sadism in sending riders up terrible mountain challenges – and in spectators delighting in watching them suffer – seemed to me a valid line of questioning. Surely there was something just a little bit cruel in the way fans sometimes glory in the hardships? Not for Michele. He refused to be drawn. For him, the delight was in watching them overcome these near-impossible obstacles: 'His challenge is your challenge and you just want to support him. Fans push riders because they want to help him,' he said. 'It's sharing the passion, sharing the fatigue, you know. It's everything but sadistic.'

He went on to describe the unique atmosphere in the high mountains on the day of the race: the eating, the drinking, the party. Those colourful, screaming, passionate masses that have become indelibly associated with the spectacle of racing up high; thousands of people lining the road all day in anticipation of an event that, even in the mountains – where speeds are low and the race strung out, and where a good vantage point affords a view of kilometres of road – will last a few minutes at most. The Zoncolan was the best venue for this in his opinion, but the Finestre was also good for fans. 'What do you call it when there are cowboys in Far West movies, there are even Indians, how do you say?' Michele asks.

Cowboys, Indians and the Wild West, I confirm, wondering where this is going.

'When you arrive at the Colle delle Finestre, in the last few kilometres there is great scenery, there are these big mountains around you and all the people that are watching down. It's great for fans because you can watch the road all down the mountain. And so there is everybody looking down, like Indians when they are looking for cowboys and then attacking. You have that feeling!'

Hmmm. So not sadism, but predation instead? But I get what he means. The atmosphere, the wait, the adrenalin and then the chase. It's a piece of theatre, a show, heightened by the most stunning setting possible. 'They're like our stadiums. We don't have the San Siro, we have the big mountains,'

Michele says. 'I believe the *tifosi* [the passionate Italian fans] are an important part of the cycling show. They create the mountain. What creates the mountain is the champion and the fans around him.'

That's the magic that racing in the highest peaks brings. A spectacular theatre and a community coming together in an audience, in the expectation of a breathtaking show.

In 1977 Nan Shepherd, a writer, naturalist and walker, wrote what is considered one of the masterpieces of mountain literature, *The Living Mountain*, about her beloved Cairngorms in Scotland. She was contemplative and lyrical, and did not always strive for the peaks, and there is one line from that book that here seems apt: 'To pit oneself against the mountain is necessary for every climber: to pit oneself merely against other players, and make a race of it, is to reduce to the level of a game what is essentially an experience. Yet what a race-course for these boys to choose!'

The whole of Andorra is a stadium on 3 September 2015, but the day starts quietly. The mountains around the city are wreathed in cloud and even the orchestral version of the lambada piped into the breakfast room, where team staff are breakfasting, has a melancholy air. The riders are still in bed. It is muggy, oppressive and close.

The morning progresses and my photographer goes off by bicycle to the spots he has picked out for the day's pictures. I sit in the lobby and plan my movements – the course is so compact that, like a cyclocross race, it will be possible to see the riders several times, either by walking a few minutes or simply waiting in the same place. I wander down to the start village just before the traffic in Andorra La Vella stops and the team buses begin to arrive. Compared with the Tour de France and even the Giro, the Vuelta is very relaxed, one reason why pros like it despite the frequent tough stages and climbs. The buses are not cordoned off and riders are walking through the crowd to sign on. The clouds are burning off and Team Colombia are outside their bus early, under a sun awning, on their turbo trainers warming up – a fair indicator that they expect the day to be lively. So are Katusha, Purito's team. Other teams are not warming up, which perhaps shows the limit of their ambitions.

Under the heavy sun the mood is one of trepidation mixed with nervous excitement. 'Purito is crazy,' says Esteban Chaves, team Orica-GreenEdge's Colombian climber, or so CyclingNews reports. 'The stage should have been held over two days. Seriously I think it suits riders like me, Purito or Nairo [Quintana]. We're all looking forward to this stage.'

I bump into Larry Warbasse, Joe's flatmate who is riding for IAM Cycling. 'I want to get in the break!' he says, 'But a lot of people do . . .' It's a sentiment I hear repeated by riders to journalists several times. Then I bump into Ian Boswell. 'My legs feel like shit after the rest day,' he says.

How hard is it going to be, I ask.

'I guess that depends how hard we ride it,' he says, grinning wryly as he turns and walks towards the stage where they're about to announce his name. Joe is by the Cannondale-Garmin bus, about to get on his turbo and preoccupied about whether to wear a base layer or not. It's the closest I've seen him come to being nervous. I leave them all to it and take my place on the street for the ceremonial roll-out through town before the gun.

The first 3.8 kilometres of the neutral zone are gently uphill. After that, another three kilometres of gentle uphill, then a left turn at a roundabout and straight into a narrow wall of road that signals the start of the first proper climb. The roll-out is not relaxed. Riders are bunched behind the race director's car, jockeying for position for when the gun

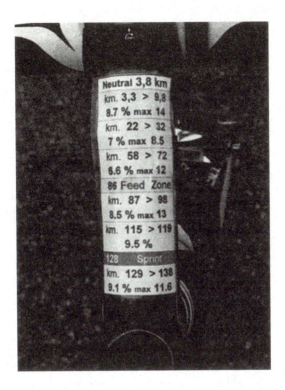

finally goes. It looks like there are a lot of elbows. The peloton disappears and the town is eerily quiet. I remember the drawback of watching a race by the side of the road: you have no idea what's actually happening. I stand by – not in, you understand – a McDonald's (whose reliable free Wi-Fi is the secret weapon of Grand Tour journalists Europe-wide) then rush to my next rendezvous with the riders. It is on a downhill, and as I wait I hear from another spectator that something has happened to Chris Froome. A crash somewhere near the start, and now he is behind, with his teammates, and Astana are putting the hammer down to inflict as much damage as they can. There was a break that got away on the first climb, but the guy next to me does not, of course, have detailed information about Joe.

I watch the break come past, a broken line of riders that

will try to coalesce again at the bottom of the downhill. An Astana rider is near the front, and that's significant: if Astana are motoring on behind the break – essentially chasing their own man – the Froome situation must be serious. Ian Boswell also comes swooping past. He is hunched over the handlebars, one of the front four or five. They are en route to the final couple of climbs. In the time it has taken me to check the internet and make my way across town (OK, maybe drink a coffee too), they have raced almost both of the butterfly's wings. It is a short stage and, despite the difficulty, it is passing quickly. There is no Joe, but no time to worry about that now. After a long gap the peloton comes through, another stream of riders all trying to hang together for dear life.

When the race has finally passed it becomes clear that I will not get up to the finish: the cable car to the top is too far away, and very crowded, and if I try I will likely miss them. This is always the way when chasing racing with no accreditation. The reliable option is a bar. So I find myself sitting at the back of a hole-in-the-wall bar squashed in with 30 or so Andorrans, watching Ian, a guy, like Joe, I know a little,

battling for a podium place with Mikel Landa and Fabio Aru of Astana, with a big lump in my throat. Ian stayed at Team Sky when Joe left, and became one of the team's trusted mountain *domestiques*. This is also his first Grand Tour, and watching him contest a podium spot on a stage is emotional. So much for the shit legs, I think. Landa takes the win and Aru comes in second, but Ian holds on for third.

I watch the riders streaming in behind Landa, Aru and Boswell, ashen-faced and spent, and reflect on the sadism thing. We want our champions to be worthy of our adoration and so we give them mountain-sized obstacles to climb. The high mountains, with their snow and their remoteness and their inherent danger, are literally and symbolically the biggest challenges we can ask of them. And, while it may not be sadism, precisely, it would be impossible to deny the thrill when the mountains exercise their caprice or take their toll.

Froome comes in eight minutes down, his hopes of winning the Vuelta gone. He cracked, everyone says, but the full story emerges overnight: he was knocked hard sideways into a barrier and a stone wall at the start of the first climb, and he has fractured his foot. His Vuelta is over. I speak to Ian the day after the stage, and he explains how he fought to hit the first climb at the front, made the break that went near the top and then rode all day expecting to be called back to help out. 'Once we got to the last two climbs, I hadn't heard whether Froome was in the group or not,' he told me the day after. 'I heard a lot of Spanish on the radio talking to [Mikel] Nieve, so I put it together that Froome wasn't there any more.

'Even going into the final climb I didn't expect us to stay away. We got to the bottom and Dario [Cioni, the Sky sports director] said, "You're racing for the stage win now." Half my mind was like, oh sweet, I could do well on a stage! The other half was, oh shit, I kind of wanted to be called back so I can do an effort and call it a day, because I'm pretty tired!

'I still have a lot to learn about racing in the breakaway,' he continued. 'When Landa jumped at the bottom, ideally I would have gone with him. Maybe that's a bit of a lack of confidence or experience not following that move right away. I eventually jumped and was able to ride my own pace. I had a bit of a side cramp from taking too many gels. There were a couple of kilometres there where I was actually kind of creeping.'

As for Joe, the evening after the stage he tweeted: 'Cycling is cruel. Objective: breakaway and go for stage. Reality: Crash at km 0, bash knee, go full up climb 1 and catch broom wagon on top.'

We don't catch up in person for a month or two after the race, by which time it's all in the past, another lesson learnt. 'I know I'm biased, but I don't think there's a harder sport in the world,' Joe says. 'And it's so humbling. You go from being in training where everything is under your control, and you think you're going good, because you're doing all the right things. Then you go to a high-level race and it's like nothing's in your control any more! And that can be quite uhhh . . . you know, shit happens.'

The best laid plans of mice and men go awry.

'Yeah. I mean, it sounds clichéd because people say it so much, but that's bike racing, I guess.'

Curiously enough, I reflect, for all our prognosticating that the GC battle would not ignite on that first mountain stage at the start of the second week, that's exactly what happened. Froome departed and Fabio Aru (though he would lose the red leader's jersey for a few stages) gained a chunk of seconds that were his springboard to winning overall. That's bike racing.

It might sound clichéd, but you have to recognise the truth

that gives rise to clichés – and you have to accept that bike racing is bike racing, or else you'll drive yourself mad. Some days you don't have the legs. Some days your head's not in the right place and you miss your chance. Sometimes you have bad luck. Shit happens.

Chapter 7
HOW THE ALPS WERE WON

Or, *routes stratégiques* to *routes touristiques*,
warrior scientists, and what did two Napoleons and
the Blue Devils ever do for us?

The twenty-fourth of July 1950. The Tour is in one of its favourite places, Pau, a rather beautiful hilltop town with grand promenades and gardens looking out towards the distant Pyrenees. It is a rest day and it is hot. Very hot. Each year, this part of south-west France becomes a cauldron as the summer heat, trapped by the mountains, rises and rises until it becomes uncontainable and explodes into violent storms. It is the day before this edition's first mountain stage, and Tour director Jacques Goddet has been playing with the race format to try to reduce the overall importance of the mountains. Time bonuses awarded to the first rider to pass over the big cols have been reduced from a minute for each one to only 40 seconds (which is still enormous by modern standards – no seconds have been awarded for classified cols for years). In a bigger break with tradition, the Tour is only spending one day in the Pyrenees – a single étape from Pau to Saint Gaudens over the classic cols of Aubisque, Tourmalet and Aspin – before it heads east across the Mediterranean towards the Alps.

Events will conspire against Goddet, however, and the mountains will reassert their importance.

Jean Robic was a curious and rather unloved French rider. He had won the 1947 Tour, the first Tour after the Second

World War, yet unspectacularly, never once wearing the yellow jersey on the way to Paris. Physically, he was unprepossessing: he was 5' 3" and 60 kilos, was going prematurely bald and had sticky-out ears. He was a rather obstreperous character and would, it was said, wait in the doorway when he went to restaurants until the whole room was looking at him; and then say, 'Yes, yes, it's Robic,' before parading through to take his seat. 'He had a face that was speckled like a bitter apple,' Tour historian Pierre Chany wrote. In 1944 Robic had fallen badly in Paris–Roubaix, after which he habitually wore a helmet, which in those days was virtually unknown among pros. Thanks to this, one of his nicknames was 'Leather Head', since contemporary helmets were made out of leather and resembled a bunch of bananas, or several saveloys, draped across the cranium; another, less unkindly one, was *Biquet* (which means kid, as in kid goat), because he was so good in the mountains. Not only could he climb well, he was famous for taking on heavy, lead-filled bottles before descending, to give him more speed on the downhills.

In 1950 the Tour was contested by riders in national colours, but despite his previous Tour win Robic was not given a spot on the main French team, where the ascendant Louison Bobet, with his matinée idol looks, was the preferred rider. Instead, Robic had to make do with the West regional squad. Grand Tours were much more national in flavour in those days, and there were five French regional teams bulking out the start list, not to mention the first ever official African presence at the Tour, in the shape of Nord-Afrique, which was composed of riders from the French colonies in the Maghreb. It was expected far more than today that the hosts would dominate their national race, but the French were up against it. Both Tours since Robic's win had been taken by the Italians: first by the pugnacious Gino Bartali in 1948; then in 1949 the peerless Fausto Coppi had overcome intra-team politics to beat Bartali – and everyone else – in the Alps. Both years the best the French could manage was third.

In 1950 Coppi wasn't riding, but the Italians were again dominating. There were two Italian teams: one comprised of younger or up-and-coming riders, and one of the stars and their water carriers. The latter included Giovanni Corrieri, who had won Stage 5, taking his total Tour de France stage tally to three; Serafino Biagioni, who would win stages and wear yellow the following year; and Fiorenzo Magni, who was in the prime period of a career that would include winning the Giro d'Italia, the Italian National Championships and the Tour of Flanders three times each. And there was Bartali himself. Like Robic, Bartali was never going to win a beauty contest, but physically he was more prepossessing. The son of poor, hardworking Tuscan peasants, he was stocky, with thinning hair and a pugilist's nose – God's boxer – and in the Italian public's mind he was the opposite of the debonair, adulterous Fausto Coppi. In 1950 Bartali was 36 and his best days were behind him (he had won the Tour twice, the Giro overall three times and its mountains jersey seven) but under his captaincy the Italians were imperious. So much so, they had been criticised by other teams and the press for riding unsportingly in a kind of rolling road block – similar, I imagine, to the kind of disciplined high-tempo collective efforts that Team Sky is sometimes criticised for today. Between the two Italian teams they had won five of the 10 stages before the rest day.

Much has been written about that Pyrenean stage from Pau and, like all the best Tour stories, there have doubtless been a few juicy details added and lost along the way. We know that Bartali was riding with Robic and Bobet, and the trio were chasing Kléber Piot, a Frenchman from the Île-de-France– Nord-Est team. Robic had led over the Aubisque but had crashed on the descent, scraping his side and damaging his derailleur, leaving Piot first over the top of the Tourmalet. They were all on the Col d'Aspin, which was mellower than the two preceding climbs and was the final obstacle of the day. Perhaps if there hadn't been a storm Robic might not have fallen – more than 50 riders did on the slick surfaces – and he wouldn't have been in a group with Bartali. Perhaps if there had been more than one Pyrenees stage the crowd wouldn't have been so large. Somewhere on the Aspin the crowd encroaches too far and impedes the riders. Bartali and Robic go down. The atmosphere is highly charged. The spectators believe it is Bartali's fault that Robic hits the deck. There is a mêlée, in which Bartali is insulted and hit. A knife is flashed. Both riders are quickly up and on their way again, but Robic's derailleur is now useless. He rides on single speed, losing time, until he finds a teammate to swap bikes with. Bartali is enraged and speeds on to the finish, overhauling Kléber Piot and winning the stage. Firenzo Magni, his young compatriot, takes the yellow jersey. The Italians have won, resoundingly. And Bartali tells his team manager, the old champion Alfredo Binda, that he is not sure he will start in the morning. He is leaving the race in protest.

It's possible that, in the hysteria, the threat of the knife was overstated. The famous Tour journalist and historian Pierre Chany has been quoted as saying: 'I saw this spectator, he had a knife in his right hand ... and a *saucisson* in his left.' But Chany has been known to favour a good story over the truth, and *L'Auto*, the organising newspaper, which had the best coverage of the race (and, admittedly, a reason to play the incident down), reported in the immediate aftermath that the supposed knife-wielding maniac was a woman. Whatever the truth, it is undeniable the prevailing sentiments were hostile and probably xenophobic. Magni, too, received blows, and that evening displayed a bruised shoulder where he had been hit with a stick. And Bartali had even more serious accusations. Not only did 'fanatics', as he called them, threaten to take his bike, 'on the descent, a non-official car pulled out in front of me and waved me past, the better to, 100 metres further down, squeeze me against a low wall, behind which was a large drop,' he said. 'I am a professional racer, a racer who wants to earn his living with his bike, not lose his life because some people think they don't like our way of racing.

'I don't want to continue.'

Binda, too, is eloquent: 'A man's life clings to so little when it is threatened. But I will exhort them this evening to start tomorrow. If Gino accepts my prayer, we might dare to hope.'

Overnight, a diplomatic mission from Jacques Goddet does everything it can to convince the Italians to continue. He even offers them a set of grey jerseys to race in, so they are not as conspicuous to angry fans. Magni is understandably reluctant to quit, as that would mean relinquishing his lead of the race, and there are noises among the *Cadetti*, the junior team, to support him and keep riding, but Binda cannot sanction a split. They will stand and fall together. The Italians withdraw at Saint Gaudens and the race, which two days later is scheduled to finish at Sanremo on the Ligurian coast in Italy, will be truncated: that stage will stop short of the border, in Menton.

A

Stopping before the border was a neat solution to a sporting crisis, but zoom out from that afternoon in 1950 and the national rivalries only become more complicated. Menton may then have seemed to Jacques Goddet a safe haven, but seven years earlier it had been under Italian occupation. And a century before that it had been an Italian town through and through; as had Nice, Saint Étienne de Tinée, Bousiéyas – almost all the places I've been writing about in this book.

Until 1860 they belonged to the Kingdom of Sardinia, ruled by the House of Savoy, which had its seat in Turin. None of the countryside around Nice was French until Vittorio Emanuele II of the Savoy, during the birth traumas of the Italian nation, gave it to Napoleon III of France.

Confused? Don't worry. The history of the Alps is confusing, political and often counterintuitive. The Alps are shared between eight countries and are at once a natural barrier between languages and nations, a contested margin in which boundaries are constantly slipping, and a region unto themselves where neighbouring peoples either side of a borderline often have more in common with each other than with their distant capital cities. It may seem now, when escaping on a bike, that these mountains are remote from the world's concerns, that they are the sole preserve of pleasure-seeking tourists, hikers and cyclists. But for much of Europe's past they were central to the dramas that have shaped the continent.

Some of these dramas were peaceful – take, as an example, the more than 55,000 mules and their *muletiers* who facilitated the salt trade, working the *Via del Sale* between the Mediterranean and the Col de Tende, south-east of the Bonette, conveying the precious commodity up to the Savoy stronghold of Turin. In that case, the mountain roads we now cycle were originally mule tracks that navigated a route between directness and danger from the coast to the big towns in the north. Similarly, other road cols started life as time-honoured short cuts – the quickest way to get you, your donkey and your produce from one valley to the next (and beat your neighbour, who took the road down the valley, to market), even if you did have to battle gravity, bad weather and other hazards. The Col de l'Iseran, for example, which is now the highest paved pass in the Alps, started life as a mule track for cheese producers in the Beaufortain region (who make cheeses including

Beaufort itself and also the delightful Reblochon) towards Piemonte. They were also important routes for smugglers and contraband.

A lot of the roads through the mountains, however – most of the ones we now know and love – owe their development to a long history of paranoia, distrust and violence.

The first famous military crossing of the Alps is undoubtedly Hannibal's, but the mystery of which pass the Carthaginian warrior took on his march towards Rome in 218 BC has puzzled people since ancient times, with heavyweights like Napoleon Bonaparte (who was sometimes called the 'Modern Hannibal', as well as 'the Horse Thief of Berlin, 'the Nightmare of Europe' and 'Old Puss in Boots' among many less flattering things) and Julius Caesar, both well practised in taking armies over mountains, weighing in with opinions. There are enough clues in accounts contemporary or near contemporary to Hannibal's life to narrow down the selection. Polybius and Livy, the two main sources, talk of encounters with various barbarian tribes and say that the ascent was gentle but the path down into Italy steep, with a significant rockfall to overcome. There was space enough near the top for 25,000 men and animals to camp for a couple of days and it was high enough for there to be snow in October. It had views over the Po Valley and was three days' march from Turin. The relatively easy Montgenèvre, Mont Cenis and Little Saint Bernard passes have all at some point been front runners, and two high, difficult cols – Clapier and Traversette, rank outsiders – have lagged behind. However, no physical proof of his passage had ever been found.

In the 1950s a Cambridge engineering student called John Hoyte became interested in the debate; so much so, he borrowed an elephant from Turin zoo and got an expedition together to prove that Hannibal's feat was actually possible.

The elephant was a female, weighing 2.6 tons, and the group tried to name her 'Hannibella', but she did not respond to the new name so they had to stick with Jumbo.[1] Jumbo was a former circus animal, which, John Hoyte told a Stanford University lecture audience in 2007, 'delighted us. She had a great sense of balance. She could walk on a row of pilings about 18 inches diameter like a cat walks along the top of a wall. She was the right elephant for us.' Her balance was not good enough, however, for the British Alpine Hannibal Expedition to follow their intended route. They had determined that the Col de Clapier was Hannibal's most likely passage, but a rockfall on the climb towards it forced them to turn

---

1 Thus recalling the old joke: where does a one-ton gorilla sleep? Wherever it wants . . .

back; instead they crossed the Col du Mont Cenis and, upon successfully invading Susa in Italy, Jumbo ate 'special elephant cake' and drank a magnum bottle of Chianti wine.

In 2016, some evidence of where Hannibal did pass finally was found. Digging into a peat bog next to a pond at 2,580 metres, under the 2,947-metre Col de la Traversette, a Canadian research team found clostridia bacteria in ancient animal dung, and a significant amount of churn and disruption to the soil record over the whole site. The dung was carbon-dated to around 200 BC – very close to Hannibal's time – suggesting that a large number of people and animals walked, rested, ate, drank and, yes, evacuated on that spot around 2,200 years ago. Clostridia microbes are characteristic of the mammalian gut, and horses in particular, and, there is the hope, if that is the right word, that distinctive elephant tapeworm eggs might still survive somewhere in the frosty ground.

It is said that the past is a mirror into which a man may gaze and see only himself. Julius Caesar was a believer in Hannibal crossing the Montgenèvre, but that may be because it was his preferred route when he was going to survey his territories in Gaul. Napoleon Bonaparte thought that Hannibal followed the Isère river valley and therefore crossed the Mont Cenis, and he reportedly carved his name under Hannibal's when he found it inscribed in the rocks. During his rule, Napoleon would build proper roads over both the Montgenèvre and Mont Cenis. 'You wish to know Napoleon's treasures?' wrote the Comte de Las Cases, his friend and hagiographer. 'They are immense, it is true, but they are there for all to see: namely, the Simplon and Mont Cenis, the Mont Genevre and Corniche passages that open the Alps to the four points of the compass. These passages surpass in grandeur, art and endeavour all the works of the Romans.' Bonaparte's rationale for improving the passes in the early 1800s was to be able to move troops into northern Italy, where France regularly had to oppose the Austrians. The success of the Napoleonic Wars was such that at the height of his empire his influence extended over large parts of Italy, Spain, Germany and into what is now Poland.

Fast-forward 50 years or so and the situation had drastically changed. Napoleon III was the nephew of Napoleon I, and he had started his leadership as an elected president; however, the constitution did not allow for a second term, and it was at that point that he organised a *coup d'état* and appointed himself emperor. Although the first years of his reign were characterised by censorship and repression, there was also a keen intelligence at work. With Baron Haussmann's help he reconstructed Paris, making it the city of grand avenues and imposing buildings we know today, but he also undertook civic works in the far-flung regions – in part as a kind of political PR tactic, to foster loyalty to Paris. He began to improve the road networks in the Alps, and built the refuges on the Col d'Izoard and the Col de Vars that are still there to this day, and his relationship with Italy was cordial.

Italy was in a tumultuous transition from diverse city states into the recognisable modern nation. Napoleon III supported Vittorio Emanuele II's drive towards unification, and in return the territorial settlement the two powers reached seemed generous. In 1860, the County of Nice and what we now know as the Savoie region became French. In return, the French emperor allowed Vittorio Emanuele II continued possession of some of his favourite hunting grounds in the mountainous Niçois backcountry, and the new border was drawn.[2] Almost immediately, Napoleon III pledged to make

---

2 Not all of Italy's unification went so smoothly. At the other end of the country, in Sicily, there was fierce fighting between the (Nice-born) Giuseppe Garibaldi and

the Col de Restefond route (what we now usually call the Bonette) a *route impériale*. Nice and the region had been under more or less continuous Savoy control since the 14th century, and the Restefond road would be strategically important, lassoing the remote lands into France and helping guarantee their protection in case of attack.[3] It too can be filed under canny PR: one of the factors behind the County's vote to join France was that the Italians had left the peasants of the interior isolated and without much infrastructure. A new road would be a crowd-pleaser.

So far, so consensual. However, as Italy consolidated it became bolder and increasingly irredentist – covetous of lands that were once its own, or that might be considered in some way 'Italian'. And that left the French with a problem. On top of a problem. In 1870 they suffered a quick and hugely humiliating defeat to the Prussians in the Franco-Prussian War. Napoleon III was deposed and the new Third French Republic found itself shorn of its beloved Alsace and Lorraine regions in the north-east and also paying heavy reparations to the Germans. One – but by no means the only – failure that had beset the French in the Franco-Prussian War was that the Germans had comprehensively outmanoeuvred them, efficiently moving men, weapons and supplies behind the front line. That meant that in the mid-1870s almost the entire

---

the French House of Bourbon. Nice, Garibaldis, Bourbons – possibly the best stand-off in the history of biscuits.

3 The Passo dello Stelvio has a similarly interesting history. The pass was used as far back as the Bronze Age to get from what is now the Tyrol to Italy. But after the Napoleonic Wars, the northern region of Italy was given to the Hapsburgs, who ruled the Austro-Hungarian Empire. But in between the Hapsburgs and this new, rebellious territory lay the Alps, so the Austrians planned a road through – first in 1813 and then successfully in 1820. In only five years 2,000 workers under a master engineer called Carlo Donegani built this miracle. The north side, famously, has 48 hairpins, and there are 75 in all. During the First World War it marked the westernmost point of the *Guerra Bianca*, the 'white war' in the mountains between Italy and Austro-Hungary, but it is now completely in Italian territory.

length of France's eastern flank was a relatively new, undefended border. The Italian part of this stretched from the Mont Blanc massif to Menton on the coast: 1,200 kilometres through 13 separate valleys separated by some of the Alps's highest mountains.

Politically, Italy was moving closer and closer to the great powers of central Europe. In 1882 it would sign the Triple Alliance with Germany and the Austro-Hungarian Empire, a secret alliance that promised non-aggression and also mutual support in the face of attacks from any other major power. To the east, beyond the Vosges and the Alps, were massing unknown numbers of enemies, all malignly plotting against France. What France needed was not improved east–west roads. Far from it: Napoleon Bonaparte's mountain highways now led directly towards an increasingly capable and acquisitive foe. They were something France could do without. What it now needed was a backbone of *routes stratégiques* running through the Alps from north to south, as close as possible to the high ridges near the border, to help it defend and mobilise against Italy if – or, as seemed more likely when – the time came.

The most northerly of the really famous cycling cols to owe its existence to the construction of these *routes stratégiques* is the Col du Galibier, which marks the border of the Hautes Alpes and the Savoie. Long a passage for travellers, merchants and animal herders, it was improved and opened as the catchily titled '*Route de Grande Communication no. 14*' in 1879. In the mid-1880s, work began on a tunnel at 2,556 metres, to make the passage easier.[4] The work was overseen by General Baron Berge, an army man who had distinguished himself in

---

4 This tunnel, which was opened in 1891, was for many years the sole way across and the highest point of the col. Only in the 1970s, when the tunnel was in a state of dangerous disrepair, was the road over the top made passable. Thus bike racers suddenly found the Galibier about a kilometre longer and significantly more difficult.

Alpins en manoeuvres — Montée de canons au Col de Fours (Queyras) 2309 m
Papeterie des Alpes Eug. Robert, Grenoble

the Crimea and been a prisoner of war of the Germans. As the military governor of Lyon and commander of the Army of the Alps, his vision was to 'open on the Alpine border a number of strategic routes, so that heavy convoys of the modern army are no longer the prisoners of the valleys and can climb into the mountains, crossing the cols.'

After Galibier, the general turned to the Col d'Izoard, the Col des Aravis, Col de Vars, Col du Parpaillon (don't know it? We'll come back to this . . .), Col d'Allos, Col des Champs and Col de la Cayolle – creating an Alpine spine along which the military could easily move. Though some of the contractors were civilian, the majority of the work was carried out by the Alpine infantry, who would eventually be christened the *Chasseurs Alpins*, the 'Alpine Hunters'. These were elite French mountain infantry brigades, which had been created in response to Italy's *Alpini* – 45,000 specialist troops highly trained in the art of mountain warfare, the majority of whom were installed just the other side of the border. Even though traces of their presence can still be seen, on both sides, it is difficult to imagine them all up there, festooning the peaks.

It must have been difficult to move without bumping into a soldier or two. Building roads gave the *Chasseurs Alpins* something to do, and helped give them pride in the remote places where they were stationed and which they would be called upon to defend. They wore short breeches and short jackets, for ease of movement on the slopes, and an oversized beret with a trumpet logo on it. Apart from the trumpet, which was yellow, everything else was blue. And that was how they got their nickname, *les Diables Bleus* – the Blue Devils.

Most of our famous Alpine roadways, those repositories of cycling legends and receptacles of sweat and swearwords, have a Blue Devil in their history somewhere. They toiled with spades, picks and explosives to widen and flatten the goat tracks, and build the bridges and retaining walls so that

CHASSEUR ALPIN (*Les Diables bleus*)

heavy artillery could pass. While the north–south route is surprisingly similar to what we know today, asphalting wasn't part of the Blue Devils' work. That didn't come until later. The cutting edge of road engineering at the time consisted of crushed stone of various sizes layered to provide good drainage and a smoothish surface. Tour riders in the early days might have expected, in more cosmopolitan areas, a fast-rolling raised roadway of crushed stone, and maybe even a camber for drainage. Stray from well-peopled areas and things were different – and the mountains, as we already know, were another world.

Today, most major passes in the French and Italian mountains have enviably smooth surfaces as if, despite the battering they take during the months of snow, it is a point of honour (and indeed public safety) that cyclists can whizz down them free of worry.[5] Even the Col de la Bonette, which for many years had a terrible surface (and even for a while had an illegal tollbooth at its foot, in a desperate attempt to raise funds for its maintenance) is now pretty flawless.

You can still find the Blue Devils' work in its natural state, here and there, if you go looking hard enough, and a good place to start is the Col du Parpaillon. Parpaillon is a secret col much cherished by French *cyclotouristes* and Audaxers, those hardy socks-and-sandals tourers and long-distance cyclists who tend to be a little wider of tyre and baggier of clothing than your average road cycling fan, and yet are still able to smash out incredible distances without a second thought. It lies south of the Col d'Izoard, somewhere in the folds of

---

5 Tarmacadam, using tar to bind the surface, was patented in 1901 in England, and only with the rise of fast-moving motor vehicles which sucked particles up, creating dust clouds and degrading unsealed surfaces, did these kind of roads slowly spread. It's a fair certainty that no roads in the first Tours were tarmacked.

the high mountains between the Queyras and the Ubaye valleys, above the ski resort of Risoul (which was favoured with a Tour finish just a few years ago and will be the Giro's summit finish the day before the Bonette). The top of the Parpaillon is at 2,637 metres and it was modernised by the Blue Devils essentially as emergency back-up for the Col de Vars, which is very near the border and was considered especially vulnerable. For many years the Parpaillon was the highest road in France, but eventually, being higher and steeper and more problematic than the Vars, and yet connecting the same two valleys, the decision was taken not to modernise it further and asphalt it, and so it fell into disuse. Today it is still a registered 'D' road on the national road network, but it is a very rough track, the preserve of 4 × 4 enthusiasts, adventure motorcyclists and, one day, of me and a couple of my friends.

Some rides that you take on are safe and predictable: you switch on your GPS device, switch off your brain, count the lamp posts as they pass and let your stomach think about what you'll have for lunch. Some of them, well ... I think we knew that day that we were potentially biting off more than we could chew. The plan had been to climb the Parpaillon, about 17 kilometres at 7 per cent, descend the other side and then loop around via the Col de Vars. Up via history's dead end, you might say, and back along the path of progress. To make the task even more difficult the previous day had delivered a large storm, which had soaked us to the bone in freezing rain, and furnished the peaks around the pretty town of Barcelonette with a dusting of fresh snow in late June.

Heading up a back road to a mud-and-gravel track after a snowstorm did not seem propitious, but we had a goal: we wanted to see the tunnel in the sky. At the top of the Parpaillon, marooned in a landscape of nothing like the lamp post in the Narnian wood, is a perfect, painstakingly constructed brick tunnel, big enough for a single vehicle to drive through, with large iron doors that are closed in winter – to keep what in, and what out, I'm not quite sure. It was built by Berge's Blue Devils using pickaxes alone, and wheelbarrows to transport out the quarried rock. At 466 metres long, was a considerable engineering feat for the day. It took 10 years to build and opened in 1901, and for many years there was a refuge at the tunnel's mouth, but the several hundred troops stationed on both sides chose to site their encampments further down, as the weather at 2,600 metres could be bitter, even in summer. There is an old postcard showing the entrance to the tunnel one July under – it is claimed – five metres of snow. It is, actually, rather a small dump of fresh snow on top of some very large drifts, but still the tunnel is obscured, men are passing with difficulty and the white canvas bell tents disappear into the blanket.

We were hoping for less than five metres, and a weak sun was shining through the mist as we pedalled up the main valley road and turned off to begin the climb. Quickly the

Parpaillon (3000 m) en Juillet, 5 mètres de neige, en face apperont le col de Girabeau, le Pic St André (2560 m), la montagne de Meaille (2922 m) et...
1879 Louvet, édit. à Gap

asphalt became broken and rutted and then, past a spring and a small chapel, it turned into a dirt track shaded by dark pines. The first few tightly pinned switchbacks led us deeper into the forest, the air thick and warm with moisture and the trees bearing down upon us, crowding our vision so that we could not tell if the forest simply went on and on without end. But then we rounded a corner and it opened out into a stunning glacial valley with acid-green grass, guarded by a hikers' refuge, a small stream and a bridge.

Ahead, the path narrowed and climbed steadily up and the brightness of the Alpine meadows shaded into white. Beyond the bridge the track steepened and the stones grew larger, and the combination suddenly made the going tough. Mud began to stick to our tyres and brake callipers, making every turn of the pedals a huge effort whose reward was only a few centimetres progress, dizziness and a darkening of vision from oxygen depletion. At 2,300 metres, fresh snow began to impinge on the track, which had become a muddy meltwater stream tacking up the valley side. I stopped several times to

clear the clinging mud from my bike frame and stop the grit scoring circles into my wheel rims. At about 2,400 metres there were wolf tracks in the snow that now covered the path, and we were forced to dismount definitively, pushing our bikes towards the top of the col like the racers in the earliest days of the Tour. You may recall that only Gustave Garrigou made it to the top of the Tourmalet in 1910 without putting his foot down, and it was easy to see why. Though his bike would have had much thicker tyres, and so be more adapted to the rougher surfaces prevalent in 1910, it would also have been heavier – by a factor of two, maybe three – and it would only have had one so-called 'climbing' gear. The marmots that were playing with increasing insouciance all around us seemed to think that this valley belonged to them but, in the silence of the clouds on that wet stony track, it felt as if those heroes of bygone days might still be out there on the road. That the mud and spray raised by their passing had just settled

and that they were just out of sight around the corner, or over the col diving down towards the finish in the valley far below.

Around 80 metres below the col, just underneath the final switchback, a sort of muffled, anaesthetised calm descended. Our everything shrank into whiteness and it began to snow gently. Although we had hoped to pass through the tunnel, really we had climbed just to see it, fully aware the iron doors would probably be stuck shut. And, for an hour or two, we had believed we would get there. But now, as the temperature dropped in the grey clouds, we accepted we were not going to make it, and turned around and walked and freewheeled down again. Not victorious but, somehow not defeated. We had ridden up a track as if riding back in time, into one of the most beautiful valleys on earth and, finally, that was enough. Confronting the tunnel would have been an exercise in 'pataphysics: an imaginary solution to a problem that did not exist.

One of my companions that day has since gone back, but later in the year, and he tells me just how close we were to

making it. He also tells me that the journey through the iron doors into the icy blackness and towards the pinprick of far-away light was just as dark and thrilling as we'd hoped. An ocean without a monster lurking in the deep would be like sleep without dreams – and without dreams we would be but cows in a field. I am sure that tunnel is there, I will go back. I know that I will see it one day.

Napoleon III never got round to fulfilling his pledge to build his *route impériale* over the Col de Restefond, aka de la Bonette. Even from very far away – which is mainly where Napoleon III was – it would have been a self-evidently big and expensive job, and one that could be punted down the list of priorities until a later date. And before he could get round to it he had his ass handed to him by the Prussians, and that was that. It was only later, during the Blue Devil dynasty, that anything got done, and they didn't, as I mentioned before, join the two valleys up completely. It was judged simply too difficult a route to defend from an Italian attack, and the Tinée valley on the

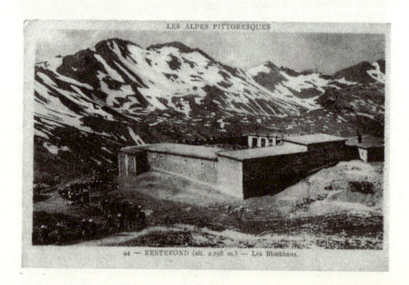

44 — RESTEFOND (alt. 2.798 m.) — Les Blockhaus.

south side was too difficult to supply and defend (the French were keen not to make that mistake again). Had the Restefond road been built, the *Alpini* could have come streaming in from the north, over the top and on a direct march to the coast. That would have been game over, and Nice would have become known as Nizza once again. So the Blue Devils took the road up to the main garrison, the imposing Caserne de Restefond, and then to the huddle of stone huts and bell tents of the Camp des Fourches barracks down the other side.

And that's where they stopped. The army lost interest. That's because, after more than 40 years of fortification and militarisation of the French–Italian border, the wind began to blow the other way, and the wider geopolitical situation changed. Remember the Triple Alliance, the secret non-aggression and cooperation pact between the Germans, Italians and the Austro-Hungarian Empire? It was maintained and renewed periodically every few years after 1882, but in 1902, only five months after signing up to the Alliance once more, Italy made another secret deal. This time it was an understanding with France that both countries would remain neutral in the event of an attack on the other. Both pacts seemed clear cut, but the growing tensions that would lead to the First World War also meant that both things could not simultaneously be true. Either Italy had to side with the British, Russians and French, therefore breaking its pact with Germany and Austria-Hungary; or it had to side with them, and support aggression against France.

Would France once again be at odds with its transalpine neighbour? When war broke out in 1914, Italy pledged to support Germany and Austria-Hungary, but months passed and it did not show its hand. Finally, in May 1915, Italy entered the war and sided with the Allies, and at a stroke all those barracks on Bonette, and at countless other positions the length of the border, were rendered irrelevant.

The other great force behind improving the roads was a happier one: tourism. As we saw, the bicycle can claim to have played a large role in this in the Pyrenees, but in the Alps the motorcar gave back to the bike. From as early as 1904 the Touring Club de France (a motoring organisation of the waxed-moustaches-and-dashing-tweeds ilk if ever there was one) had been pushing for a 'Route des Alpes' from Evian to Nice, linking the two biggest spa towns in France in summer and winter respectively. The project was born in the spirit of adventure and discovery, and out of a patriotic desire to show anyone who cared that France was the most beautiful country in the world. The Touring Club wrote that it would be higher and more spectacular than any other routes, and that it would 'skirt glaciers and precipices, wind along snowfields and surprise gushing rivers at their source'. Given the strategic aspects, the state poured in funds and the Blue Devils were again put to work. A caravan of vehicles carrying dignitaries assembled in Nice on 3 July 1911 for the inaugural voyage along the Route des Alpes. The itinerary took in quite a few cols that are now unknown or have fallen out of favour, but the Izoard and Galibier were there (just before the Galibier's first Tour de France appearance on 10 July that year) and gradually others came into service as they were modernised and deemed ready for motor traffic. By the time the Col de la Croix de Fer was added, in 1912, thousands of people were travelling the Route on a regular open-topped bus service. On 10 August 1914 – long after war had broken out in the Balkans, but before France's involvement – French President Raymond Poincaré took part in the inaugural voyage over the Col de la Cayolle.

The First World War stopped all this, of course; and afterwards, with the military impetus to defend against Italy gone, it took longer to get anything done. The 2,764-metre Col de l'Iseran wasn't opened until 1937, demoting the Passo dello Stelvio from its title of highest pass in the Alps. In 1970 the Cormet de Roseland road opened, and from then on the route was exactly that which many Alpine bicycle tours favour today. Finally, the whole thing was relaunched as the *Route des Grandes Alpes* in 1992.

You'll gather from the pictures and the descriptions that, Hannibal aside, it doesn't take long when you're cycling in the Alps to see evidence of the military history. In valleys and on ridges from north to south are medieval walled citadels, castles, lookout points, garrisons and forts, each one corresponding to the latest challenges thrown up by the evolution of war. The barracks on Bonette, the Fort du Télégraphe near the Galibier and the ring of forts around Briançon, to name just a few of the Third Republic forts from the late 19th century, were cutting edge for their time. Artillery had advanced so much in range, accuracy and frequency of fire that, rather than build a wall about a town and hide everyone inside, which was the classic medieval gambit, the best way to defend the civilian population was to engage the enemy several kilometres away, and draw the fire elsewhere. Some Alpine forts were even constructed from reinforced concrete, the first in all France to use this new technology. Still, defending a pass in the mountains is different from defending the flatlands – the pass funnels the enemy through one narrow point, and many of the forts you see standing duty in the mountains look recognisably like the sort of castles you might draw standing atop a hill.

And then there are the bunkers.

'Everybody will be entrenched in the next war. It will be a great war of entrenchments,' wrote Jan Bloch, a banker who devoted his private life to the study of modern warfare, in 1901. 'The spade will be as indispensable to a soldier as his rifle. The first thing every man will have to do, if he cares for his life at all, will be to dig a hole in the ground.' His book was called *Is War Now Impossible?*, and if the title was rather hopeful, then his prognostication, 15 years before the Somme, was only too accurate. However, even he failed to see the next logical step – or at least *a* next logical step – which was to bury the forts in the ground, an idea that would become the cornerstone of France's defensive strategy in the years leading up to the Second World War.

Its actual manifestation was championed by two French ministers, Paul Painlevé and André Maginot, in the 1920s and implemented by the latter. They proposed a line of concrete fortifications and artillery installations to extend the length of the borders of Switzerland, Luxembourg and Germany, and some of Belgium too. It would be called the Maginot Line and it would protect France from any further aggressions from the east. André Maginot himself called his Line a 'subterranean fleet'; the rest of the French called them *forts* or *ouvrages* ('works'), but in English we would call them bunkers because, like an iceberg, the vast majority of their bulk is unseen. Below ground out of sight are vast galleries, bunkrooms, kitchens and ammunition stores, sometimes requiring lift shafts up to five storeys deep and miniature underground railways to shift stores around. Hundreds of men lived inside, but up top all that typically could be seen were a few squat concrete cubes, soft geometric curves, the cyclopean glare of a gun position peering at you from a cupola. Years after the war, J. G. Ballard described his encounter with derelict bunkers (Nazi this time) on a beach in western France: 'Almost all had survived the war and seemed to be waiting for the next one,' he wrote, 'left behind by a race of warrior scientists obsessed with geometry and death.' Nowhere do his words ring more true than in the mountains where the concrete and steel structures, so different from the graceful peaks around them, resemble UFOs, alien craft that could take off again at any time.

The Alpine Extension of the Maginot Line is the last chapter in France's long history of recurrent paranoia, enmity and conflict with Italy in these mountains, and it stretches from near Bourg Saint Maurice to Roquebrune, right by the Italian border on the Mediterranean Sea.[6] They are surprisingly little

---

6 Italy has the *Vallo Alpino*, the 'Alpine Wall', as its defensive mirror to the Maginot, though the Alpine Wall actually protects the border with France, Switzerland, Austria and all the way to the former Yugoslavia.

known and undocumented, and even their construction was not initially a priority. In the 1920s the French were convinced (rightly, it would turn out) that the main future battlegrounds would be in the north-east. However, as Mussolini grew in power, he began to threaten, if only verbally, the Savoie region, Corsica and Nice. And so the schedule in the south was accelerated. It must have been hard work. On the flatlands, the bunker plans were fairly standardised, but in the mountains each had to respond to the particular properties of the steep terrain it was sited on, leading their architects to create some extravagant forms. Each of the *cloches* – the cast iron observation or gun emplacements – weighed more than a ton and sometimes had to be transported by horse and cart. Concrete was mixed on site with local aggregate, meaning that each bunker blended into its surroundings, and for the highest bunkers construction could only take place during the brief Alpine summers when the snow had melted. Many sites were unfinished when war broke out, others were downgraded to cut

costs, but the scale of what was achieved, in some of the most isolated and remote corners of Europe, remains impressive.

I discovered the bunkers over years of cycling the high roads of the southern Alps. The further I went, the more I realised how numerous they are and how they litter the landscape (there are four or five separate complexes on the main Col de la Bonette road alone, and a similar number on the Col de la Madone, just to pick a couple of examples). They helped me realise, after stumbling across a few bunkers and then researching their history, just how much these mountains are a military conundrum as well as a sporting playground. Whereas a road wraps like a ribbon around the contours of the hill, the bunkers are arranged according to other principles. Looking for them means approaching the terrain more laterally, thinking of axes and channels, weak points and redoubts, and sightlines to the passes, and when you come across one it is like an ambush. You are cycling along enjoying the view or concentrating on the climb and then, suddenly, you glimpse an incongruous shape. Above you, always above, a series of soft, regular curves on the prow of a hill (the rounded corners were designed not to cast stark shadows for observers looking from afar). A presence betrayed. And then you realise that you are under surveillance across time. There are dead eyes looking down, tracking you with murderous intent, and this road you are cycling is no longer innocent. It was originally built by the military and it too has played a part in this long-ago drama. Simply by being there you have been drawn into the conspiracy.

Mainly, though, what I have taken from these bunkers is a feeling of a great misplaced energy, and of waste, because the onslaught they were built to defend against never came. With the benefit of hindsight it is easy to wonder if Mussolini sending troops through the Alps was ever a serious threat to France's territorial integrity. One could charitably say that these sentinels standing watch over the passes were a crucial psychological deterrent, but, then again, nobody has successfully invaded over the Alps since Hannibal. It does seem, at best, like a 2,000-year-old tactic. It's just not modern warfare. The closest I can reach for is during the First World War, when Italy was forced to defend its borders against Austria-Hungary in the Dolomites, fighting from ice trenches and shelling enemy positions at 3,000 metres altitude, encampments and positions that are now being revealed for the first time in a hundred years as the glaciers recede and the ice melts. This so called *Guerra Bianca* or White War seems like a terrible, primitive throwback, and the figures bear this out: more than 150,000 men died fighting for this lonely high border, and it is estimated that a third of them perished from the cold, or ill health not directly attributable to the fighting.

Modern warfare happened in the Ardennes, far to the north of the Alps. In May 1940 a *Blitzkrieg* of German tanks came through the thick Belgian forests where there were no Maginot defences, circumventing and neutering the static defensive positions. Italy did not declare war on France until 10 June, and the Alpine front was very quiet until 21 June. The

Italians attacked only after the French had signed an armistice with the Germans (but before it came into force on 25 June). That seems sneaky, but all's fair in love and war, I suppose. Even then, the attacks were localised, and though the Italians took some towns and villages, none of the Alpine Maginot defences was breached. Thousands of men had been stationed here through harsh winters and glorious summers, waiting in these remote corners of the world for the actions of great men far away to have a catastrophic effect. Finally the decisive action took place, but elsewhere, and though a few of them fought valiantly, they had mainly waited in vain.

I became somewhat obsessed with these bunkers over the course of several years riding in these mountains. Over many separate rides I travelled further and wider, even as my targets became more focused, narrowed down to precise GPS coordinates, until I was carrying my bike over snowdrifts on unpaved tracks towards forts defending a border that no longer existed – Italian bunkers stranded in France thanks to a shift in the borders after 1945. And I thought I had seen enough to imagine, at least imagine, the bare outlines of the misery of living under the constant threat of bombardment, of fighting and dying in these holes; and to feel the contrast between the dark discomfort within and the glorious views without. But I never expected to find anyone alive who had lived within, or any testimony of what it was like. Then a shepherd led me to a time capsule, buried under a rock in the beautiful, peaceful meadow just where his sheep were grazing above the Camp des Fourches.

Like many of the old fortifications, the Camp des Fourches had been reoccupied during the Second World War. Its inhabitants, I can only suppose, emulated their predecessors, and during the winter months laid planks between the roofs of the barracks, creating a platform to hold the heavy snowfall and safe, dry walkways below. Above the old stone-built barracks a reinforced concrete bunker complex, the Avant Poste du Col des Fourches, was built. In all, 42 men and an officer were stationed there. The time capsule's creator, Jean-Marie Joseph Deroux, was one and, as an old man, he came back to the battleground to leave his testimony, written on paper and laminated and put in a preserving jar, where he served. On 23 June 1940, he writes:

At three in the morning a shell exploded close to my hut. In the blink of an eye we went back to our holes (three in each), but it was still night and the weather is set in . . . a fine mix of rain and snow, and by the end there must have been 20cm of snow covering us. With no shelter and in a dreadful din of shells, we lay there, our teeth chattering. Soaked in the snow that melted on our backs we stood guard so that the enemy couldn't take advantage of the bad weather and advance quickly. Towards the middle of the day, when it got brighter, the Italians were still a long way off. And this was their worst hour, because we massacred them. If we didn't get badly hit ourselves, it's because we didn't obey our captain, who had asked us to dig our holes 100m further to the left, when we'd already dug these ones! When he'd left we'd said, 'What's done is done!' Quite a few shells passed only a few metres above us, and lots of shells hit where we should have been! A few shot too short even fell on their soldiers (*the Alpinis*), increasing the destruction. There were about 250 dead or injured at this spot, not counting the prisoners.

Monday 24 June. The snow melts. The Italians take away their dead and injured, and we let them, as ceasefire is being called at 00h35 tomorrow. If we'd wanted, we could have shot all of them.

Tuesday 25 June. We went down to where we'd been shooting . . . and we felt sorry for the Italians who had been sent into this butcher's shop to attack us. We found a body lying on the path, searched it and saw that he was a husband and father. No words. So as not to leave any weapons for the enemy we destroyed them all.[7]

The message in a bottle is there still in the hole Deroux had dug and where he lay. If you're on Bonette, I can give you directions. Or pay attention, instead, to the bunkers themselves, which, though forlorn and crumbling into the landscape, stray facts from a future passed, keep vigil and are also a testimony of sorts – guilty reminders of these things we'd probably rather forget. Ask yourself, how, precisely, does one remove from the side of a mountain a structure with concrete walls almost three metres thick, which was literally designed to withstand massive explosions, and you'll realise that they'll be there much longer than us.

It is said that Gino Bartali helped to avoid a war, or at least a popular revolt. During the 1948 Tour de France, the leader of the Italian Communist Party, Palmiro Togliatti, was shot in the neck as he was leaving the chamber of deputies in Rome.

---

7 The fighting was mainly concentrated on the Italian border south of Bonette, and there wasn't much else in the Alps. Later, in occupied France, the Germans made Chamonix a major operational base. The great mountaineer, Lionel Terray, describes in his autobiography how he helped the fighters of the Resistance scale peaks the Germans thought impossible, and fire down on their heads:

> We had long realised the slight military value of all this fighting in the Alps. Life in the front line had ceased to be a patriotic mission so much as a big game of cowboys and Indians, made all the better by the fact that it was played out among our beloved mountains. On the patrols and raids for which we always volunteered we did not really set out to slaughter Germans or anything of that sort. What we enjoyed in this pointless and obsolete form of war was its resemblance to mountaineering. We sought adventures where courage, intelligence and strength might enable us to overcome apparently impossible obstacles; action in a world of grandeur and light which appeared different from that of grubs crawling around in the mud.

By a miracle, he survived, but the situation in post-fascist Cold War Italy became very tense. A general strike was called, Communists occupied factories and radio and TV stations, and an angry row in parliament almost came to blows. The Italian premier, recognising the danger, rang Bartali at his hotel and appealed to him to restore national unity by putting on a show. Bartali won three Alpine stages in a row, soloing over the Izoard, fighting on the Galibier and leading on the Croix de Fer. After that, he led the Tour by 14 minutes, an unassailable margin. With immaculate timing, Togliatti woke from his coma, received the news of Bartali and asked for the general strike to be called off.

In 1950, to return to where we started, rather than helping to avoid a war his actions almost caused one. I was going to make an analogy here, but it would be hyperbole, and writing even that makes me uneasy. To paraphrase one of the speakers in Don DeLillo's great sports novel *End Game*, I reject the notion of cycling as warfare. Warfare is warfare. We don't need substitutes because we've got the real thing. Too much of it, everywhere, and what we live with is the aftermath. The infrastructure and cockeyed logic of war. The roads, the crumbling concrete in the meadows, the forcing people to take sides, the scuffles on the ground between Bartali and Robic. Cycling is not warfare; it is a highly regulated form of competition in which tensions are played out and small supremacies established in ritualised and usually entirely safe ways. Cycling is where teammates and countrymen can stab each other in the back (metaphorically), and even the Swiss get hit – as Ferdi Kübler was, in the scuffles around Bartali and Robic that day. And yet at the end of the day – most days at least – everyone goes to bed, next to each other in the same hotels, and gets up to ride their bikes and tear chunks out of each other again in the morning.

However. Do not forget that in 1950 France had only been liberated for five years. And though the Italians had played no part in the fascist aggression after 1943, they had nevertheless been an occupying power. Many of the French standing on the sides of the road during the 1950 Tour would undoubtedly have fought against them. It's conceivable that some of the riders might have found themselves facing each other in combat. Now they were lining up with their bicycles. It was more than simply a bike race. Remembering this shadow play of history – the Tour and all that's beyond it – is part of the richness of riding in the mountains. These are not simply battles between riders, or internalised struggles between a rider, gravity and the mountain: the ground beneath our wheels has been won and lost, defended and fought over fiercely.

As for the main players in that bike race, it is surprising that Gino Bartali, known for his courage and strength, felt himself in physical danger and could not continue. There might well have been something else going on (one theory being that he couldn't bear to see Magni win). On the French side, everyone was very apologetic and conciliatory. Robic blamed Louison Bobet, as far as there was blame: all three of them had been hampered by a motorcycle that had been slowed in the dense crowds. Bobet tried to profit from it and jump away, there was a touch of wheels and down everyone went. Bobet explained that Bartali wasn't really working in the break, and so he had attacked. 'And for this I ask you to apologise to Robic, who might believe there was an ill-meaning gesture on my part,' Bobet said.

And with that, peace broke out; but the Italians were gone.

Chapter 8
GETTING HIGH

Or, sublime altitude and switchback aesthetics, why altitude
camps are not simple things to understand, and the hotel
at the beginning of the world ...

This was not specifically my intention but I'm on my way
back to the first mountain I ever climbed, and I find a sort
of serendipity in the idea that said mountain has now become
a top destination (no pun intended), a secret Mecca even,
for bike racers. I was probably five or six and my brother
was a toddler, and I wasn't on a bicycle, not even close. We
were on holiday with our mum on Tenerife, staying in a resort
on the south side of the island. Coincidentally, my grand-
parents were staying on the north side; in between us, the
3,718-metre-tall El Teide. I don't remember much else about
the holiday, but I do remember driving over to see them and
the hire car breaking down somewhere near the top of Teide.
I remember the hairdryer wind and standing there on the
side of a tiny winding road next to a duff Fiat Panda. My
mum, in her twenties, and two young kids; no mobile phones,
no GPS, helpless. Pine trees and pink rocks, sunlight and
the warm, warm wind. We were saved by a local who, in my
memory at least, wore Ray-Bans and looked like Freddie
Mercury. He drove us down in his Mini, forcing the little car
into the bends, my eyeline no higher than the low retaining
wall that would not stop us if, as seemed inevitable, he lost
control, overshot a hairpin and we careened down the scree
slopes into the cacti below. But we did not die, and almost

30 years later I am in a hire car on my way back up this mountain, cuing little flashbacks of that little Mini – as well as a few surprises, because Teide is like no other place I remember.

To take a short diversion into geology and plate tectonics, a long, long time ago all the continents were a single super-continent, Pangaea. In the Jurassic era this began to fragment, and the rift created by America and Africa drifting apart began to form the Atlantic Ocean. Over the course of millions of years, in fact, the African continental plate moved almost 1,000 kilometres to the north-east, forcing the oceanic crust downwards and causing whole oceans to disappear. Then, shortly before the dinosaurs died out (shortly in geological terms at least), the African continental plate collided with the Eurasian continental plate, a colossal pile-up that lifted rocks into gigantic ruches. All the great mountain ranges from the Atlas and the Rif in the west to the Hindu Kush and the Himalaya in the east are, broadly speaking, the product of tectonic collisions like this between the Eurasian plate and the neighbouring plates to the south; this great vertical push of matter towards the sky is why you can find, if you know what you're looking for, material from the seabed of the long-disappeared Piemont-Liguria Ocean high in the southern Alps. Essentially, these mountains are folds.[1]

El Teide, on the other hand, is a volcano – a great upwards splurge of molten rock, gas and ashes from a fissure in the

---

1 This is obviously a sweeping generalisation. Many of the granite massifs – Mont Blanc, the Argentera, the Mercantour – are 'autochthonous', i.e. they are still found where they were created. They are where the unstoppable northward force of the plate tectonics met the immovable object of this very hard rock, and geologists believe that they have risen as high as they have due to their buoyancy – their relative light-ness as a liquid magma. Similarly, there is volcanic material to be found in the Alps, but the basic opposition of tectonic to volcanic origin holds. Give the Shoumatoffs a read for more on the geology of the Alps, if you're interested. Details are in the Further Reading section at the end.

earth's crust that cooled and solidified to make land. The whole of Tenerife, in fact, is a volcano,[2] and not even an extinct one. Teide is still erupting, cooling and solidifying (most recently in 1909, and it is currently running behind schedule with its next), and the roads immediately south-west of the summit pass through black, spiky, barren lava fields that look like ancient landscapes but which are actually fresh apocalypse. And stranded in the caldera at 2,150 metres there is a hotel. Lower down, the red-rocked scenery resembles Arizona as you'd picture it in an old cowboy film. A little higher, it tends towards the extraterrestrial, and this desolate landscape is often isolated above a sea of clouds. The hotel at the end of the world, you might say; or, since this just-cooled-lava land is some of the newest rock on the planet, at its beginning.

The Parador Las Cañadas del Teide is a squat stucco building next to a squat stucco chapel, almost at the road's highest point but still far from the volcano's peak. Teide is on the same latitude as southern Morocco, yet in April the top is still spotted with snow. You can see it in pockets where the cable car drops sightseers at the zenith of this island, which even into the 18th century was thought by some to be the tallest peak in the world. These high, rocky slopes used to be used as pastures for sheep and goats, by beekeepers, and to procure sulphur, firewood, medicinal herbs and snow.[3] It seems an unlikely place to find the cream of cycling's talent,

---

2 All of the Canary Islands, little domes of land stuck in the middle of the Atlantic Ocean, are volcanic, and Teide is actually the third-largest volcanic structure on earth. That this is measured from the bottom of the ocean makes it less impressive (it rises 7,500 metres from the ocean floor). What makes it even less impressive is the Olympus Mons volcano on Mars, which is 624 kilometres in diameter and 25 kilometres tall, and is the largest known volcano in the solar system.

3 The Spanish word *cañadas*, which forms part of the name of this particular side of the volcano, can mean 'meadow'. It is also used to describe the shepherds' tracks used by men and livestock in the *transhumancias*.

yet here they are, a whole lot of them, crammed into one little hotel. It is three weeks before the Giro. Team Astana and Cannondale-Garmin are here, and two of the lottos – Team LottoNL-Jumbo's men and Lotto-Soudal's women – are in residence. Tinkoff were here last week (they've left bike boxes in the store) and Team Sky are on the premises too: Chris Froome, even though he is not riding the Giro, is getting an altitude top-up. Joe Dombrowski later observes to me that if by chance the volcano erupted at any point in the spring, the world's supply of Grand Tour riders would be seriously depleted and cycling's biggest races thrown wide open. There are a few other random, and to this untrained eye unnameable, elite endurance athletes staying, and then team staff, a couple of old French hikers and me. Literally two French hikers and me. It's nigh on impossible to book one of the 30-something rooms here between February and June there are so many cycling teams trying to squeeze in. Later, I hear from a rider that his team had been looking into buying a property on Teide (on top of the difficulty in securing a place at the hotel, it's not cheap), but couldn't, because Teide is a national park and development is prohibited. So for now, the Parador Las Cañadas del Teide is where it's at.

It would be impossible to imagine a bunch of football teams staying cheek by jowl in the same hotel to put the finishing touches to their World Cup prep. And, granted, bike training does not take place in the hotel: it is a closed thing, between a rider and his or her power meter or among teammates on a remote road. Nevertheless, all the teams convene in the same building every night, and the sombre green and beige upper corridors of the Parador (which, when empty, have something of the atmosphere of the Overlook Hotel from *The Shining*, only friendlier) begin to resemble a dorm hall. The restaurant does staged dinner times so rivals don't

collide over the buffet, and for posh teams there is even a private dining room available.

The food's OK, but it's not as if the Parador kitchen has a magic recipe for success. What is it, then, that packs them in like this?

A

The pursuit of altitude has been going on since . . . well, in truth, height has signified something special, and even spiritual or sacred, throughout human existence. The Tibetan name for Everest is *Chomolungma* or 'Goddess Mother of the Land'. Tibet's summits were revered as an abode of the gods, and local people would not, before Westerners came, climb them. The neighbouring Buddhist kingdom of Bhutan, meanwhile, is home to Gangkhar Puensum, which is thought to be the highest unclimbed mountain in the world. Gangkhar Puensum is 7,570 metres tall, and no climbing of mountains over 6,000 metres has been allowed in Bhutan since 1994, partly because of the lack of resources to deal with high-altitude emergencies (India has the closest), and partly to respect local customs. Gangkhar Puensum and similar peaks are thought to be the sacred homes of protective gods and spirits. The ancient Greeks believed the much lower Mount Olympus (altitude 2,918 metres) was home to Zeus and his warring family of deities. Mount Sinai in Egypt has a prominent place in the Jewish, Islamic and Christian traditions, and anyone riding through the Alps will be used to seeing chapels and monasteries perched on the highest points around – evidence that the Christian faith continued to associate height with spirituality long after Noah, and Moses receiving the Ten Commandments. The practice of placing a crucifix at the top of prominent peaks or ridges in the Alps dates back to the 13th century at least, and it boomed in the early 20th century, when such crosses would sometimes be adorned with scientific measuring equipment (although given the spots were chosen mainly to advertise God's magnificence to the maximum number of eyeballs, their scientific relevance was probably limited). Those who worshipped or lived in the numerous chapels and monasteries built in the high mountains shared a celestial vantage point and were, up in the heavens isolated from materiality, in many senses closer to God. Taking refuge from earthly temptations in the great solitary silences, they also showed a self-sacrificing devotion. The crucifix on the peak was a powerful symbol of omniscience, and also of piety, speaking as it did of the backbreaking effort needed to erect the cross. For religious communities on high, constructing the buildings and living up there were simply very difficult things to do.

A couple of hundred years ago these directly religious experiences of the peaks began to fade. Or rather the general population, which was becoming more secular, began to see them in another way, influenced by explorers and travellers, and

Romantic poets, writers and artists such as Casper David Friedrich. Think of his painting, *Wanderer above the Sea of Fog*, from 1818, that famous image of a young gent in a frock coat with his back to the painter and the viewer. He is standing on a rocky crag, left foot forward, as though vanquishing it. His reddish-blond hair is being whipped by a stiff wind, and in his right hand he brandishes a cane as he looks out over the clouds into a glorious expanse of nothingness. Only rocks and a distant mountain meet his view. He is gloriously alone in his contemplation. This is one expression of the feeling of the sublime, that semi-rapturous, dread-tinged feeling of the infinite being of the world and the nothingness of one's own existence, a shiver of fear and delight mixed into one, that people, from about the mid-18th century onwards, came to associate with mountains. These days we call a lot of things sublime – a tennis stroke, a bit of fancy footwork in a football match, even just a nice afternoon in the sun – but originally it described something extreme, beyond normal experience and perhaps beyond the grasp of human comprehension. Transcendence, the very pinnacle of existence in moral, aesthetic or spiritual terms, or something that is religious in effect though rarely explicitly so in meaning. 'Delightful horror', was one way the 18th-century philosopher Edmund Burke described it. In his *A Philosophical Enquiry into the Origin of Our Ideas of the Sublime and Beautiful* he said that delightful horror was 'the most genuine effect and truest test of the sublime'. 'Vastness' and 'magnificence' were two aspects of Burke's sublime. Magnificence, as in something awe-inspiring, was a quality people increasingly looked for in landscapes, art and music, and, so runs the theory, correspondingly less so in orthodox religion.

> It is no coincidence that the Western attraction to the sublime landscapes developed at precisely the moment when traditional beliefs in God began to wane. It is as if these landscapes allowed travellers to experience transcendent feelings that they no longer felt in cities and the cultivated countryside.

That's from *The Art of Travel* by writer and thinker Alain de Botton. And that book, along with Robert Macfarlane's excellent *Mountains of the Mind*, traces in much greater detail how our imagination began to be shaped to seek these experiences in the mountains. This is just a potted history, but enough, I hope, to suggest that the sublime – the tiny individual confronted with the vastness of the world, transcendent nature and of pleasure mixed with terror – is something that those who go cycling in the mountains will recognise. It's one factor, I think, which leads people to become unexpectedly emotional when cycling up mountains. Sooner or later everybody cries, and that's OK. It's OK to cry on a mountain. It is far easier to prepare for the physical hardships than for the unexpected mental journey. For when your thoughts slip into that gap between discomfort and concentration, and roam untethered around the subconscious before alighting, perhaps, on a wound you didn't know was there, or had forgotten. And then, in that unexpectedly vulnerable place, at the end of your physical resources, you take a look around, and the magnificence and awe of the world floods into that raw spot on your soul.

The other reason to mention the sublime here is to demonstrate that there is nothing innate or 'natural' in the attraction we have for these places. People haven't always striven for the heights, or found mountains beautiful. The art historian Michael Kimmelman wrote that the poet John Donne called them 'warts' upon the face of the earth, and that Daniel Defoe wrote about the 'inhospitable terror' of the Lake District fells. Victor Hugo, meanwhile, thought that the human brain struggled to deal with the sights of the high mountains, a derangement of the senses that in his opinion led to the Alpine regions being full of mentally deficient people. And even if people of old weren't repelled by the high peaks, they felt no need to go there. Gods and monsters aside, mountains are cold, wild and capricious environments, and since time immemorial people have avoided them simply because life was tough enough already. They still do. 'I think mountain climbing is a sign of degeneration in mankind. As long as people have to work hard to earn a living, to keep their houses warm, to work small fields like mountain folk have to, they don't think about climbing mountains,' Rheinhold Messner once said in a TV documentary. 'They're afraid of the mountains. Of avalanches and of the storms that come down from them and especially of the torrents that tear up the land. My neighbours, farmers in the mountains where I grew up, in Villnöss, still tell me it doesn't make sense to climb mountains, that it would be much smarter to use my energy for something else, and I'm not sure they're entirely wrong.'

The story of the modern appreciation of the mountains is generally said to begin with Petrarch, an Italian scholar who walked to the top of one of cycling's favourite summits, Mont Ventoux, on 26 April 1336. There are older accounts of climbing Ventoux, and Petrarch himself reports meeting a shepherd who claimed to have climbed it many years before, receiving only fatigue, repentance and torn clothing for his troubles (something that might sound familiar to cyclists). But Petrarch's is the most famous, and most detailed, and his ascent heralded a new way of thinking. He claimed to be the first since ancient times to climb a mountain purely for the pleasure of the view, and in that, his attitudes and motivations are recognisably modern. Petrarch gave us an aesthetics of altitude. These days, our natural impulse, when holidaying in a new city or surrounded by strange countryside, is to find the nearest tall thing, be that a spire, a campanile, a mountain, a cliff or a hill, and see what we can see. Even glancing from the window of a descending aeroplane gives us a scrap of that knowledge and the pleasure it brings.

René Daumal was a French philosopher whose final, unfinished work, *Mount Analogue*, is a parable of an expedition to find a mythical sacred mountain that rises so high it actually links the world of the divine to the human. In the notes he left towards its completion, he writes: You cannot stay on the summit forever; you have to come down again. So why bother in the first place? Just this: What is above knows what is below, but what is below does not know what is above. One climbs, one sees. One descends, one sees no longer, but one has seen. There is an art of conducting oneself in the lower regions by the memory of what one saw higher up. When one can no longer see, one can at least still know.

Upon reaching the summit, Petrarch took out his volume of Augustine's *Confessions*, which fell open, or so he reports, at these words: 'People are moved to wonder by mountain peaks, by vast waves of the sea, by broad waterfalls on rivers, by the all-embracing extent of the ocean, by the revolutions of the stars. But in themselves they are uninterested.' This caused Petrarch to look inward, and this introspection, when faced with such awe-inspiring views, massive space and natural beauty, is recognisable too.

Wanderer above the Sea of Fog, for all its uncanny wonder and characteristic mixture of the internal and external, has become a cliché, and Alpine scenes easily slip into the hackneyed stuff of chocolate boxes, postcards and Instagram. Yet the sublime fascination with picturing mountains is enduring. Two examples, more or less connected to cycling: first, this old postcard of the famous *Diables Bleus*, here stationed at the Col du Parpaillon in the 1890s or early 1900s. They are at camp, it is supper time, and the mood is one of cheerful relaxation (note the soldier in the wheelbarrow), but twinned with the semi-formal posing for the camera you sometimes see in vintage photos. A kind of awkwardness in which it's

Col du Parpaillon - L'heure de la soupe dans un campement de chasseurs alpins

clear that people didn't quite yet know what to do when a camera appeared, and probably also the product of having to hold still for ages while the shutter clicked and the chemical magic took place. Behind some skeletal trees in the background rises a Fuji-like mountain, almost perfectly echoing the shape of the white canvas bell tents. It should go without saying that no such conical peak exists in the Alps, and especially one that towers so far above a high-altitude camp. It is an invention of the postcard maker, purely, one surmises, to increase the rugged romance of the scene. The reality of the mountains, of life under canvas doing backbreaking work tunnelling under a ridge, was somehow insufficient for a public hooked on the sublime spectacle of the peaks. Not mountainous enough, it needed more mountains. It had to be sexed up and given more mountain appeal.

Second, this picture postcard of the switchbacks of the Col de Braus, a 1,000-metre climb located between the Bonette and the Côte d'Azur. Search for 'Col de Braus' online and you will see hundreds of pictures taken mainly by cyclists at this exact spot. The photo op comes after a short section of road where the gradient tips into double figures, and, as the vista opens beneath you to your right, you can forgive yourself for pretending it is solely the marvellous view of the switchbacks scaling the side of the valley, and not the steep slopes that come after almost 10 kilometres of climbing, that compel you to stop to catch your breath. Sorry, I mean take a photo. Because for road cyclists (and drivers and motorcyclists too, though maybe less so), there is nothing that improves a mountain view more than a nice bit of squiggly road going up it. The impulse to record scenes like this is deep rooted. People have been stopping here on Braus as long as the road has existed, just as they have on the Stelvio in Italy (which looks in some aerial photos like a child has

taken a biro and scribbled all over a picture of a mountain), on the beautiful cobbled curves of the Gotthardpass in Switzerland and on the tightly bunched switchbacks of the Lacets de Montvernier further north in the French Alps. These roads are all impressive feats of civil engineering, but that's not why they speak to us – or at least, not why they speak to most of us. There is something in the way the stacked hairpins replay, as we look back, our progress across the landscape; or, if we're looking up, render visible the task in front of us. Switchbacks like this gather the ascent into a coiled pile, make effort visible. Combine that with something incredibly beautiful, and the achievement is worth recording. You'll notice that I'm only talking about the up. The impulse to record and, let's be frank, boast, has become abnormally enlarged in the age of social media, but this postcard, printed in 1905 and widely reproduced, comfortably beats Instagram by at least a hundred years.

Cycling, more than many others, is an aesthetic sport. In Grand Tours, the majestic, rotating helicopter shots of the peloton ascending a pass tantalise from the TV, and the switchbacks dramatise the riders' exertion. Even down on the flats, where in our own rides there is often less to see, pro bike racing presents us with the hypercolour dash of the peloton and the smooth fluid dynamics as it parts to navigate a roundabout. And for many people when riding a bike there is, I think, a double consciousness: some of the thrill of the ride is a pleasure taken in picturing ourselves passing through these majestic landscapes.

Incidentally, the Col de Braus, you may remember, is where René Vietto's ashes were scattered, and where he made his winning break in his first road race and in his home stage of the 1934 Tour de France.

Impossible, once you know that, to imagine it happening anywhere other than with those hairpins as backdrop, isn't it?

As for sport and altitude, that's a completely different story, one that's first and foremost about physiology and physics. Physics because of Newton's law of gravitation and Boyle's law governing the pressure of gases: as we climb a mountain we move further from the centre of the Earth and the gravitational pull weakens. There is less mass of air pressing down from above and consequently the air is less dense. Oxygen is still present in the air in more or less the same concentration as it is lower down – around 21 per cent – but there are simply fewer oxygen molecules to breathe, which makes oxygen-intensive endurance sports like cycling a whole lot more difficult.[4] The physiology comes in because in hypoxic (oxygen-poor) environments the body adapts to this lack and begins to produce more red blood

4 At real altitude, there is just less air. Less of all of the constituent parts – less nitrogen, oxygen, argon, carbon dioxide, etc. Altitude simulators that are not hypobaric – i.e. that do not reduce the total air pressure – simply remove some of the oxygen from the air so that it is present at a lower concentration. Altitude tents, which some cyclists sleep in when they're at low altitudes, and which are becoming increasingly popular, are an example of this method. According to the experts I spoke to, the physiological effects of this are subtly different to really being at altitude.

cells. The more red cells there are in the blood, the more oxygen can be transported to muscles, improving efficiency, threshold performance and also recovery.

You can work harder, and longer, and then do it again better the next day. Almost like magic, no?

'If you're interested in hypoxic training, there's probably more than one reason it works. The main reason that people do it, you understand, is as a way of legally blood doping.' That's Professor Hugh Montgomery, being characteristically forthright. He has come to meet me straight from a night shift on the intensive care wards of University College Hospital in central London, just down the street at the Institute for Sport, Exercise and Health where he is director of research. 'Sometimes science is the excuse for exploration,' said George Mallory I in that fateful interview with the *New York Times*, and Hugh has taken that to heart more than most. He has led several expeditions to Everest and other 8,000-metre peaks to investigate the physiological effects of altitude and hypoxia. Over 25 years he has become a world authority: for one thing, because he is himself a climber and ultra runner, and is deeply interested in the cutting edge of sports science; for another, because looking at how healthy bodies function in low-oxygen conditions is seriously useful in understanding how to help critically ill patients – including cancer patients or those in intensive care – deal with hypoxia, which can be one of the biggest challenges to their survival they face.

We go to sit in the shiny white kitchen, where he makes tea and rubs his eyes, and we chat. At one point the sound of Daft Punk's 'Harder, Better, Faster, Stronger' playing far away floats tinnily through the open door. It seems apt. Endurance performance, Hugh says, is in large part about convective delivery – getting oxygen from the environment to the relevant cells. And everyone's concentrated on red cell mass because a lot of the other aspects governing convective delivery (what biologists call 'rate-limiting steps') are genetic, so you can't do much about them. For example, says Hugh, 'if you look at rowers, one of the prime determinants of success is just the size of their chest, because if they've got small lungs it's not ever going to work. You then need a bloody good heart,' he continues. 'Look at racehorses, and the classic rate-limiting step is the heart. Because if everything else has been optimised and you've got a bigger pump that can maintain a high rate, it just delivers more oxygen and the horse will run faster.' Moving down the size scale, you need big, healthy blood vessels, and plentiful mitochondria in the muscle cells to suck up the oxygen and put it to use. The final piece in the puzzle of convective delivery is red cell mass. The importance of red cells was overlooked for a long time, Hugh says, because when you measured the concentration of red cells in the blood of a top cyclist it could well be the same as that of a couch potato. Then doctors started measuring red cell mass, and found that elite cyclists and runners have at least a third more by weight: 'The watery part of the blood goes up by a third as well . . . so actually trained athletes have got a third more circulating volume of blood in total, delivering a higher total haemoglobin mass.'

Right, then. Increasing red cell mass is the main goal of hypoxic training – or, at least, the main goal that most athletes currently use it to achieve (cyclists are slightly different, but we'll come to that). It's also, as Hugh was implying, the main goal of doping with EPO. EPO, of course, is the illegal blood-thickening drug that increases the percentage of red blood cells relative to the other constituent parts of the blood. At one point WADA, the World Anti-Doping Agency, considered banning altitude tents, but then decided against it. So altitude tents, and altitude camps, are OK. But that still doesn't explain the cyclists' preference for the volcano.

The history of altitude camps starts, more or less, with the Mexico Olympics in 1968. That year, times fell considerably short of Olympic records in endurance events and many big nations underperformed. Conversely, many of the sprint track events saw outstanding performances and records beaten. Why was this? The Olympic Stadium in Mexico City is at a height of 2,240 metres. In the sprint events people moved faster through the thin air, and because it was anaerobic anyway, oxygen availability wasn't an issue. In the aerobic events it was simple: if you weren't used to performing at high altitude, you were not getting enough air and were at a big disadvantage. For many nations, this was a prompt to begin a voyage of discovery that would lead, ultimately, to Colorado, Kenya or Teide.

But not all big nations underperformed. When France won a solitary gold – in showjumping – at the previous Olympics, the 1964 Tokyo Games, it was a national embarrassment, and President Charles de Gaulle charged Maurice Herzog, his sports minister, with making sure such a national loss of face was not repeated. Herzog knew something about challenges at altitude: he was a celebrated alpinist, and part of the expedition that conquered Annapurna, the first 8,000-metre-plus peak ever scaled, in 1950. He chose a Pyrenean ski resort called Font Romeu to be the site of the new National Altitude Training Centre (abbreviated in French to CNEA). Font Romeu shares a similar altitude to Mexico City,[5] it is blessed with a warm microclimate and plentiful sun, and is almost as far south as it is possible to go in France. All these factors made it a good bet. An architect, Roger Taillibert, was engaged,

---

5 It's actually around 1,850 metres, so almost 400 metres lower, but all altitudes are not the same: the Earth is not perfectly round, and is actually slightly egg-shaped. So sea level is a relative concept, and gravity's pull will affect matter differently in different spots: 1,850 metres on the tip of the egg is very different from 1,850 metres on its flatter aspects.

and construction went ahead. It opened in 1967; the following year, France won seven gold, three silver and five bronze, coming sixth in the medal table.[6]

CNEA is still there and is busier than ever, a regular haunt of runners including Paula Radcliffe and Mo Farah. That it has endured shows that, even though they didn't completely understand the science behind what they were doing, the French had landed upon something. Because the 50 years or so of altitude training research that followed has shown that there's a bit more to it than climbing up a mountain and sitting there. Altitude is not simply a proxy measure of good training. As Hugh explains: 'If I say, "Come on mate, we'll really shove your haemoglobin mass up," and I take you to Chinese base camp on Cho Oyu at 6,000 metres, yes, your haemoglobin concentrate will go winging up really quickly, but the convective delivery of oxygen is so limited by its environmental availability that you can't train. When people get to that altitude, taking a pee or having a crap, actually, is enough. They're written off straining at a stool, gasping for breath for 10 minutes.'

This dip in training potential happens, albeit moderately, even at the kind of altitude cyclists encounter at Font Romeu or Teide (which is officially 'medium' altitude). Spend too long up there and it has a detraining effect: there is not

---

6 1968 was the first year the GDR (Communist East Germany) was recognised as a state by the International Olympic Committee. It won 25 medals in total and came fifth – at least in part, we know now, thanks to a huge state-sponsored doping programme – probably a case of why bother about the marginal gains if these pills/injections/etc. produce a 10 per cent boost? Later in the GDR's history, perhaps because doping controls had become more stringent, it too would experiment with altitude. However, it built its facility deep underground in a secret depressurised bunker. Track and field stars, cyclists, kayakers and athletes from all disciplines would descend for weeks or even months at a time, to be given the best of the decadent West's pop music – principally Supertramp – and forced to exercise in air as thin as at 4,000 metres/13,000 feet. All in all, 'a form of torture', as described by a former athlete inhabitant.

enough oxygen to put in the big power efforts, and so muscles start to atrophy. Imagine your usual anaerobic threshold power is 400W. At 2,000 metres that might drop to 350W; spend too long training at 350W and when you get back down to sea level 400W will make your muscles scream. The lack of oxygen has limited your ability to train. In addition, recovery is slower at altitude, sleep quality drops and athletes risk getting dehydrated, which can lead to respiratory illnesses.[7] If you go too high, your body stops synthesising protein, which consumes a lot of oxygen, to reserve what oxygen is available for more critical tasks – brain and heart function, digestion, those kinds of things. Not only will it stop making new muscle, it will also start to break down existing muscles, which partly explains mountaineers on Everest routinely lose 10 per cent or more of their body weight.

All that said, Font Romeu is, according to many, neither too low nor too high, but just right. You can go higher up to train in even more oxygen-depleted environments, or you can drop down to levels where you can put a little more oomph in. However, some sportspeople and teams have started to follow a different philosophy. As Hugh summarises: 'People started saying, well, maybe live-high, train-high, sleep-high is not what you want to do. Maybe you want to live high and train low. This is the idea that you go up somewhere and you pulse: you come back down, train like buggery and then you go back up; then you drop back down again, train like buggery, and go back up to sleep. You can see that it makes a lot of sense, actually.'

It makes a lot of sense to cycling teams. The Parador Las Cañadas del Teide hotel is only 45 kilometres from the

---

7 Recall that Joe was billeted in a hotel at 1,825 metres for the Vuelta's rest day in Andorra. Some of his rivals were resting at 1,000 metres down in the main town – a fact that he wasn't all that pleased about.

seafront – a freewheel down and a long hot slog back up. That means teams can roam the island to train on the abundant beautiful roads and tough climbs nearer sea level, then return to altitude to recover. Live high, train low. There is also ample scope for training high thrown in, which is necessary for those looking to acclimatise before a big race. Acclimatisation – getting used to performing at altitude – is what the French built CNEA for, remember. And acclimatisation is the other important aspect to altitude training for Grand Tour cyclists, who will have to put in their best performances at altitudes of 2,000 metres or more (Radcliffe and Farah and the rest generally race at low altitudes, and therefore are looking principally for the boost to their red cell mass). In Michael Hutchinson's book *Faster*, Hutchinson reports a conversation with Team Sky's head of athlete performance, Tim Kerrison, in which Kerrison is very pro-acclimatisation and fairly dismissive of altitude as red cell boosting: 'It's just getting acclimatised to training at altitude,' Kerrison told Hutchinson, 'because the big Tours are decided in the mountains, and if you go straight to altitude you lose 7 per cent for every 1,000 metres up, and the highest finishes might be 2,500 metres. It's not really about looking for a haematological effect.'

Team Sky came to Teide in 2012 to prepare Bradley Wiggins for what would be a winning tilt at the Tour. As a destination for pro cyclists it was at that time out of favour. In the early 2000s, Lance Armstrong's US Postal (and then Discovery) squad would come, among others, and Dr Ferrari was a regular visitor with many of his clients. That died down around 2006, and the visits tailed off – perhaps the pure, high air of Teide seemed tainted by association. For cycling's continentals, who are used to being able to travel by land to most places if they need to, Tenerife can seem remote and hard to get to (perhaps this is why Ferrari liked it). For Brits, used to the idea of going on package holidays to the Canaries for winter sun, it probably seemed pretty handy. Gradually they came back: the Liquigas team started using it again, and then Wiggins came. Wiggins's preparation at the Parador was crucial. He spent weeks up there subjecting himself to the heat, the mountains and the altitude – three things identified by Kerrison that Team Sky needed to master for Tour success. The top section of the climb, Sky's head coach Shane Sutton told the photographer Michael Blann for his book *Mountains: Epic Cycling Climbs*, is 'what made him a winner'. Shane continued: 'Teide became our world for weeks at a time . . . Your whole life becomes about getting to the top as fast as you can. All you can do is ride, recover and sleep. I remember sitting there, one day, thinking that we'd found a place where we can go deeper.'

Exactly how effective is altitude training? This is the million-dollar question, and a very hard one to answer, Hugh tells me over that cup of tea. Partly this is because of the secrecy that surrounds it. 'The data to support it are thin, because most elite sportspeople who do this, their governments and countries, don't go publishing their data. Take Team Sky – I'm sure they'll have data on things like this, but they won't be revealing it,' he says. 'It's partly suck-it-and-see, and it's partly a non-science, because a lot of the data aren't actually out there. But we know everyone's doing it, right?' Lack of data aside there's yet more uncertainty for anyone on a quest for that magic combination of height, environment and training patterns that alchemically turns leaden efforts into gold: 'The second thing is, of course, the individualisation of it, because people's responses to altitude radically differ by their genetics. We don't really know much about why that is,' Hugh continues. Hugh has two partners with whom he conducts his high altitude research on Cho Oyu and other mountains. Physically, he says, they're almost the same: weights, heights, VO_2 maxes, all of that: 'We are so identical that we had only one dinner jacket and suit in the office, because when we were doing the show and tell and the meet and greet it didn't matter which one of us took it, it fitted.' However, their experiences at altitude couldn't have been more different. 'Matt absolutely cannot function at high altitude. Just can't do it. And I can ... I can get there. I plod my way up. But you watch Mike at altitude and it's like watching someone have a little potter in north Wales. He just wanders up and down hills at great speed, completely unworried.'

I ask Hugh to describe his gruelling training regime to prepare for the huge feats of high-altitude endurance he undertook during these expeditions: 'My personal training for high altitude doesn't involve long-distance running or whatever. I do 10 minutes on a stepping machine at the highest possible work rate until I cannot breathe, and I fall off it,' he says. 'I do that a couple of times and then I go and have a pint and go home. Because actually what I'm doing is telling my body: you'd better learn how to cope with no oxygen.'

Backed by an eminent professor no less, George Mallory II's secret weapon, stairwell-running, suddenly seems eminently reasonable.

∧∧∧

There is something rather monk-like, still, in the cyclists' pilgrimage to Teide. The hotel lobby is very quiet. Among the dark wooden fittings and the plush green carpets of the lounge, a kind of enervated calm reigns. Three Astana riders spread-eagle horizontally, long bodies across small chairs in the manner of bike racers in hotel lobbies everywhere, a position that emphasises the heaviness of limbs and the exhaustion of work done, smartphones poised above the head illuminating sun-darkened faces. The pose embodies the unimaginable ennui of waiting for red cells to multiply. You know I said that there was more to altitude training than just going up a mountain and sitting there? Well, yeah, all that is true; but also, it turns out, there's not much more to it than that, either. In between the training blocks, there really is nothing else to do other than sit around. I knew this already, having visited Isola 2000, the ski resort near Nice where Joe and his local friends sometimes go for altitude training when they have a gap in their schedules. There, the typical day was something like: go down the hill; train more or less hard depending on what the programme said; go back up the hill. Have a massage, if you're lucky, cook something simple and maybe watch a movie. Go to bed early and repeat.

It's not much different on Teide, and Joe, in the Parador, confirms it. The camp has been something of a smashfest, he says, a succession of six-hour rides, many of them finishing with a team attack up the road back to the barren volcano high above. Then they ride their bikes around to the back of the hotel, where they're stored ready for the next day, shower and eat and . . . 'And the rest of the time you literally just sit in bed and read books and watch series,' Joe finishes. 'There's nothing else going on in your life.'

This is the final team camp before the Giro, where he will be one of the key mountain players helping Rigoberto Urán, Cannondale-Garmin's designated leader in the 2016 race. Previously, Urán has won a Giro stage and the young rider's jersey, and finished second and seventh overall, and he is, according to Joe, in good climbing form. But it wouldn't be hard to believe that Urán has had something of a head start, climbing-wise: he is Colombian. The nation's cycling stars have benefited from a magic fusion of genetics and environment that has, since they first broke into the international peloton in the 1980s, helped to forge their reputation as fearsome climbers. Much of the cycling-mad country is mountainous or at high altitudes: Urán's home town is at an altitude of 1,830 metres; Nairo Quintana's, a thousand metres above that.

The first scientific studies into hypoxia, in the 19th century, took place in South America, and subsequent studies have shown that many individuals in populations that have long been living at high altitude, be that in the Himalaya or the Andes or the Ethiopian Highlands, have higher concentrations of haemoglobin in their blood than lowland natives. These high-altitude natives are more fertile and suffer less infant mortality, and if they have a higher red blood cell mass in their blood (i.e. their blood is consequently thicker), they are not as prone to heart attacks or strokes as lowlanders with the same increased viscosity. In the past decade there has been considerable interest from geneticists and, although the studies don't always agree (some say Andeans and Tibetans produce more red blood cells, others that Tibetans also breathe faster, and nobody's quite sure yet about the Ethiopians) it is clear that there are some specific genetic adaptations behind these observable advantages.

Basically, it means that Urán was on an altitude camp his whole childhood, and that everyone else on this two-week stint is just giving themselves whatever small environmental stimuli they can to catch up.

Joe, while not a native of the Andes – he's from Virginia – is lucky enough to be good at high altitudes. That leaves him in an interesting and specific situation: 'Most guys are the complete opposite to me. For them the question is, how do we get the weight down? How do we get as much O_2-carrying capacity as possible? [And the answer to that is], go to altitude. You know, there are guys that really don't deal well with it but sometimes they respond really well [to altitude training] and at sea level see a significant performance increase. And then other guys that are really good at altitude but they don't really see that much of a bump.'

Joe is the second of these hypothetical guys, and so this winter before the Giro his training has taken a different approach. Jonathan Vaughters, the Cannondale-Garmin team principal, took over his schedule and prescribed a programme full of weight sessions in the gym. 'I talked to JV and he said, yeah, if you want to continue being the best in the world at a three-hour-long uphill time trial, then you can do that. But the only time that really would pay is a high-altitude climbing race. Even on a 25-minute climb you don't quite have that pop, if it's at sea level, to follow all the accelerations, so you're kind of limiting yourself.'

It's here I remember that thing about training that the rest of us (who aren't striving to be the best) are apt to forget: specific work gives you specific results. Sometimes you have to do precisely the opposite of what you like doing and are good at to achieve your goals. Personally, I am probably up there with the best in the world at a nice, leisurely three-hour loop in the mountains at exactly my pace and with rigorous coffee stops and Instagram breaks, but nobody's going to give me a medal or an eyewear endorsement deal for that. And while being the best in the world at a three-hour-long uphill time trial sounds impressive and even desirable, Joe's objective isn't to get up a theoretical hill the fastest: Joe wants to win stages – and stage races. Hence the gym work, which is designed to keep him in contention in that crazy surge at the bottom of the climb, and also to improve his time trialling and performance in crosswinds on the flat. It's a fairly radical overhaul of his body.

I point out to him the suckiness of the fact that he has to spend all his winter in a gym working for this performance boost while his teammates just have to sit in a comfy hotel and eat fish and salad, but he is undeterred. He did some tests, he says, that showed his 15-second anaerobic max power – i.e. what he can do flat out for 15 seconds – has gone up by 60 per cent. And when someone tells you data like that, something you can grasp and that you know is going to be useful, you can build your confidence and your preparation around that. Aside from that, he says, 'It's been a cool project. In the off season I found it was nice too, as it's gave me a bit more of a chilled-out time, where I think before I've been a bit gung-ho, going out smashing rides in November.'

At the previous training camp, which was in Girona where most of the team is based, Joe had some very uncomfortable days. 'JV basically said at that camp, "You're going to finish some of these rides kind of bonky, because we've done all this anaerobic stuff and you've gotten your muscle fibres used to feeding on sugar all the time, doing all these short, punchy efforts,"' he says. 'I thought, OK, this isn't ideal, I'd like to not feel like shit at the end of the rides, but we set out to do something and we knew that that was a side effect, temporarily. It almost proves that what we set out to do actually worked.'

It's a failure that, perversely, could be a harbinger of potential success.

'Whether it works in the grand scheme . . . we don't know. We know that's what the plan was, and what we thought the outcome of the plan for the first phase was gonna be . . . Well, that was accurate.'

And so now Joe is sitting up here in the Parador honing his endurance form, burning off a bit of excess weight and doing, well, nothing. Apart from the intensive riding and the team-building, the other beneficial part of altitude training is the focus, something Joe thinks is often underestimated: 'It's the intangible part of altitude training,' he says. 'You can look at the physiological impact, or what you can do on the bike – you can get a lot of climbing done, or whatever. But also, how much of the improvement comes because you're somewhere where there's nothing else to do but ride your bike?

You're not utilising any energy towards anything else, it's just riding.' Eat well, sleep well, rest well. Follow your plan to the letter, don't even go to the shops, pay any bills, lift a finger to do the washing-up like everybody has to at home. In bed by 9.30 and then up for another day's dedication. It's a spot of time – a well of tranquillity, focus and belief that can be drawn upon in the struggles to come. I do not mention the grandstand finish on Bonette for my book because, while everything is relaxed, the atmosphere is intense and serious. There is something monk-like still in pro cyclists' pilgrimage to Teide.

I wake up the next day and, not having a bike, go for an early morning run. Outside, the air is cold and the sun is not quite up and Astana are lined up next to the hotel doing calisthenics in the blue dawn. I set off as they are finishing their star jumps and stride past them with purpose, hoping to make an athletic impression. Quickly this collapses. The sound of my breathing increases, takes over, becomes ragged, and before I'm out of sight what I am doing is visibly less of a run than a slow jog. Ten minutes later, on a slight incline on the trail I am following, I think about stopping. Five minutes after that, I stop for a breather. I am gasping. It's easy to underestimate the altitude effect because few of us get the chance to stay in places like this. Usually when I'm riding my bike at these lofty heights I've had to ascend from the valley below, so when I get to 2,000 metres I have, say, 10 kilometres uphill already under my belt and it's natural to be out of breath, which masks the altitude's effect. But when you start at 2,150 metres you can tell straight away that altitude is no joke. It increases my admiration for the guys currently showering or at the breakfast buffet. Doing anything up here is extremely hard. For those of us not used to it, even a slow shuffling jog is a smashfest. It gives me maybe a tiny glimpse of the form that is needed to race up here.

On that long straight road in the half dark the mountain is an echo chamber that amplifies and clarifies thought, and I think of the efforts all these riders are making – in the gym over the winter and here on Teide – and that old quote from Muhammad Ali comes to mind: 'The fight is won or lost far away from witnesses, behind the lines, in the gym, and out there on the road, long before I dance under those lights.'

The Parador experience has been slightly boring and strangely compelling and enlightening all at once, but the isolation is getting a bit much. My final day is Joe's rest day, and we had planned to take the cable car to the top of the volcano, like tourists. Though it doesn't take you right to the top of the cone, it would certainly be higher than the Cime de la Bonette's summit at 2,860 metres, and therefore definitely would be the highest place I have ever been. But Joe has been stranded on the island above the clouds for more than 10 days, and doesn't feel the need to get higher. So we decide to go down instead to a bodega in a local town, where we eat tapas – tuna-stuffed pickled peppers, chickpea and potato stew and thinly sliced local pork – and watch normal people, Spaniards, tourists, doing normal things in the sun. Then it's time for me to go, and I drive him back up to complete his altitude work. A mystic science that is oddly suited to this harsh, otherworldly desert. An act of faith that may only be repaid, weeks later, in the crucible of a Grand Tour ascent.

Chapter 9
COUNTING SHEEP

Or, mules and helicopters, thinking like a mountain and the
still point of the turning world

I went to the top of the Bonette once to watch the sun go
down, taking a hunk of bread and a large ripe tomato, which,
having no knife, I ate like a peach, leaning forward so the
juices did not fall on my jersey; plus some *saucisson* and
Comté cheese, all bought at the tiny shop in the village. I
went up there towards the end of summer, as the seasons
were shifting and the days shortening, just to watch the light
stealing from the world. A week hence it would be 10 minutes
earlier, and so decline until the equinox, the perfect balancing
of day and night. And then it would not be long until the
snows came. At 2,800 metres the snow does not disappear
until very late in the year, and a little can persist year-round
in pockets and hollows on the northernmost faces.[1] At those
altitudes time is elastic, the summer is compressed and the
seasons are out of sync, always being pulled forward or back
to midwinter. Spring tarries, is held back, back, back and
then is propelled in a shining rush through summer headlong
into autumn; no sooner has the snow cleared than winter
storms back in.

---

1 One of the traditional industries on Mont Ventoux used to be ice-making. Villagers
from Bédoin and Malaucène at the foot of the climb used to pile snow in cavities in
winter, cover it in branches and sell the resulting ice cubes in summer. The ice was
used in applications as diverse as sorbet-making and cooling cadavers. The trade was
tightly controlled and the ice was sold as far away as Marseille and Montpellier.

It is quiet at the top of the Cime when I arrive, and perfectly bare of snow, only a young couple there who soon leave. And then nobody, the odd solitary car far below, announced from afar by its headlights winding slowly up through the gathering gloom and then slowly winding down again. There is a clear view through 360° at the summit, and I sit on the painted panorama table that names the peaks and eat, and write, and watch the day end. There are no trees this high up, only sparse Alpine pastures and, where the land steepens, scree slopes that parabola into vertical rock faces. The clouds are soft as watercolours and are turning the colour of bruises, pink into purple into dark blue, final shafts of sunlight arrowing through the cracks. Soft, soft light touching the flanks of the mountains, a painted background to a Technicolor film. Distant reliefs fade, become silhouettes, and the pale concrete of the Second World War bunkers that litter the desolate ridges starts to shine. The silver thread of a stream picked out in the last rays. As the sun disappears it takes with it first the reds, then the pinks and yellows, leaving cold greens, dark blues, grey. Below, a van draws up and an old man gets out. He stands at the side of the road, surveying a flock of sheep in the steep bowl of the valley beneath the road, appears to talk a moment or two with the last of the travellers passing by. Marmot whistles float across the depths. The land darkens still, but where I am sitting, suspended between heavens and earth, shares the light of the sky, as if you have almost left the world behind and become celestial. It is incredibly peaceful. No shouting in the night but a vertigo, an unravelling of self in the face of the gigantic presence of the mountains below and the capacious vacuum all around. I think of a line from the British landscape writer Edward Thomas: 'The earth is like an exhausted cinder, cold, silent, dead, compared with the great act in the sky.'

Low baaing and the gentle tinkle of bells interrupt the silence. There are in fact, two herds, one of sheep, one of

sheep mixed in with goats, being driven down opposite sides of the col into the gloaming. The Bonette is a watershed: on the south side the Tinée falls into the Var and heads for the sea directly south at Nice, while water to the north heads almost to Gap, then into the Rhône and doesn't reach the Mediterranean before the salt marshes of the Camargue, the other side of Marseille. The flocks may as well be descending into different worlds. I leave my perch and climb down the mound to try to talk to the shepherd, but by the time I get there he is gone. Only the distant sound of bells and sheep droppings on the road remain. It is too cold now to stay high, and as I descend the earthly darkness accretes around me. Soon it is almost black, but underneath the abandoned barracks of the Camp des Fourches I see another shepherd. Rarely do you see them in the day, but now the tourists and cyclists have left, it is as if the old ways are reclaiming the mountain. He is guiding his sheep across the road, directing two small black dogs with a series of whistles. The sheep have passed, and taken water from, a series of log-hewn troughs, timeworn conduits for a small mountain stream made just for that purpose, which would be almost invisible if you didn't know what you were looking for. This I see as I have stopped my descent once again, leaving the car in the middle of the road, and take off on foot behind him, walking across an ancient landscape that is melting into the night.

When you leave the road you realise how narrow the experience is upon it. A road is a cut across the contours, a routing via the easiest passages to the top and over, and that is what we cyclists fix on. But the mountain is not linear, and – unlike cyclists – the shepherds' goal is not to overcome but to live on, and with, the mountain. And it may seem to be stating the obvious but you realise too that those spaces between the wet spaghetti of the tarmac aren't just 'there'. Almost all bear the imprints of people, and animals, and people and animals. The terraces stepping up the sides of the valleys, now mostly overgrown but formerly planted with kitchen gardens or chestnut trees; those moss-covered stones, the remnants of a wall, the once seemingly featureless slopes actually criss-crossed by irrigations and divagations, streams, troughs and animal paths. However wild they look, there is little that has not been touched in these wildernesses we cycle through.

I missed my shepherd that day. The sheep and dogs were moving quickly and my feet were not as sure as his, and I did not want to surprise him out of the night at this, the last testing moment of his day. I also felt out of place, and was wary of setting off on foot through the high mountain mead- ows, even though the road was shining in the moonlight and the hamlet of Bousiéyas twinkled security below. The shepherd melted into the night and was gone.

A

It was also at dusk, the dusk of an early summer in a previous year, that I first encountered the shepherds of the Bonette.

I was driving over the top in a rented car and was feeling apprehensive that the road, not long open, would be dangerous or frosty at its highest extremity, when I hit a large and improbable traffic jam. This was good in one sense. A solo drive up a cold mountain at dusk is disquieting, and at least now I was assured of companions on this road less travelled. It was also annoying. The evening rush hour brought to a standstill on a lonely mountain. Soon the cause became clear: a vast flock of sheep being herded up the road. It was the *transhumances*,[2] the age-old movement of livestock from the valleys and plains where they pass the winter to the mountainside pastures where they spend the summer.

Probably, if you've cycled in the Alps or the Pyrenees, you've encountered some of these flocks wandering over the roads too. Raising livestock has been one of the main ways of life in the mountains for centuries, and in most of the southern Alps and Provence, where much of the land is unsuitable for cows, this has principally meant sheep. Cheese and milk from those less nomadic flocks; and wool and, latterly, meat, for those that undertake the *transhumances*.[3] Alpine pastures and the fast-growing, seasonal grasses that thrive there can have as much nutritional goodness as the finest fields on the plains; they are a huge resource available for only a few months a year, and it has long been the shepherd's job to seek out the best pastures, to make the fattest, healthiest sheep – and the most money – wherever these pastures may be. Such is the importance of the trade that legal documents survive from the Middle Ages, scrupulously recording and controlling the industry. Towns and villages were born and grew rich on processing the wool, making and selling the cheese and hold-

---

2 From the Latin *trans* (across) and *humus* (earth, ground).

3 In addition to the *transhumances*, there have always been shepherds living year-round in the high mountains, and a very few of them still practise this way of life.

ing the fairs at which the sheep were bought and sold. Some of the sheep movements shared the roads with the salt trade (on the various *routes du sel* and *vie del sale*, depending on which side of the border you were), one of the complex interdependencies that has sustained life in these mountain regions for centuries. And some of this salt, in fact, was given to the sheep, since sheep in the mountains must have it added to their diet to survive. It is poured out onto flat rocks every day or so for them to lick up, and during the *estives*, the summer journey up to the high pastures, shepherds transport hundreds of kilos with them to the cabins that, for up to four months, will be their homes.

It's not only salt that's transported: there's also beans and pasta and cooking oil; firewood, gas bottles, batteries, troughs, anything they might need in this time, because once they are there they cannot leave the flocks for more than a few hours, if at all, and everyone down in the valleys will be busy making hay for the winter. The transport used to be solely by mule and it would take multiple trips to and fro to stock up fully. Now it's mainly achieved by helicopter drops, which are subsidised by the regional council, but there are still some mules employed, to take provisions from where the last 4 × 4 track ends or between huts as the grazing moves. Each shepherd knows his pastures, and travels between June and October (when the *hivernailles*, the winter descent, takes place) in a circular route from low to high and back down again, so that the sheep attack the juiciest grass first and give the most elevated pastures time to defrost completely and for the grass to grow.

The sheep get a lift up too. In olden times they would have been walked for several days along the roads from the coast, but the proliferation of dual carriageways and other non-sheep-friendly aspects of civilisation means that they now ride most of the way in trucks. For the final few kilometres

they are usually still driven in the traditional way, with dogs and by foot, and that's why we were waiting on Bonette. The sheep had been dropped at the bridge at the bottom and were heading up for their summer holidays. Eventually, we reached the hamlet of Le Pra, where the shepherds waved us down a side road that would let us all overtake, and we left the sheep and their *estives* behind.

A couple of years later and the flocks are again stopping traffic – it is a feature of life in the mountains – this time at the local shepherds' festival in Tende, a town made rich by salt some two valleys away from the Bonette. It is August and it is the saint's day of St Roch, patron saint of the local shepherds,[4] and the bells that presage the traffic-stopping begin pealing as I stand in front of a huge copper cauldron of milk heating over a wood fire, watching a strapping lady,

---

4 Wikipedia would have St Roch as the patron saint of ironmongers, suggesting instead St Geneviève (for shepherdesses) or even St Loup de Troyes. This latter seems laughable – *loup* is French for 'wolf', so I'm giving the Tende shepherds this one.

bicep-deep in the steaming vat, heap coagulated cheese curds onto what looks like a giant tambourine held by a boy next to her. It is not actually a tambourine, but a cheese cloth; however, musical accompaniment is provided by a band of men in traditional shepherd's attire of black waistcoats and elaborately ruffed shirts. One has a drum in the crook of his arm that he is hitting with a curved stick (the skin of the drum is presumably a sheep's), and the others pipe-and-bag instruments that look suspiciously like Scottish bagpipes. There are Celtic overtones and a certain amount of chaos, and the resulting mix of percussion and drone is something of a mash-up between a Highland fling and a free party circa 1999. A group of old ladies sit close by, seemingly unperturbed. They too are wearing traditional dress, white petticoats and long dresses with embroidered fronts, and they chat and laugh as they take raw wool from a big pile on the ground and spin it into yarn on wooden spinning wheels. There is cheese. Lots of cheese. And also clogs, other things fashioned out of olive wood, a fair amount of *porchetta* and pasta,[5] and that acme of typical mountain fayre, a giant paella.

Earlier in the day the Brotherhood of St Roch, which tends sheep and gives charitable help to local shepherds, had processed a statue of the saint through the streets, blessed it and then given thanks in a church service, but this is the main event. Even though it is August and the transhumant sheep are still in the high pastures, there are enough lowland dairy sheep and shepherds to make a ceremonial commotion. To the sound of 50 people ringing giant sheep bells on the flower-adorned balconies of the Italianate town hall, a small

---

5 Tende belonged to Italy for almost 90 years until it was taken back by the French in 1947. It sits below the Col de Tende, a historically important pass and is, confusingly for a French town, on the main road from the Italian Riviera to the Po Valley, Cuneo and Turin, in a little outpost of France left isolated by Napoleon III and Vittorio Emanuele II

herd is driven along the main road under the massed ranks of the houses that cling to the steep flank of the mountain. Behind the sheep, an oompah band and 20 dancers following the bobbing short-tailed behinds – men in waistcoats, white shirts and red sashes, and women in long dresses and colourful scarves, twirling up the road towards Italy. And behind them, behind a police escort, a large contingent of the San Remo Harley & Flowers motorbike gang. Big, squat men in half-helmets and shades on big, squat low riders. They advance at idle speed in front of the traffic and even at low revs almost drown out the band. The flock is directed down a side street, the dancers leave the road and the bikers open their throttles, and in a wave of noise and exhaust, the old-time celebrations are swept away.

Later that year I went to another shepherds' festival, in a village called Belvédère, one valley closer to the Bonette. This

one was more real, in a way, in that it was celebrating the return of the *bergers* from the high pastures.[6] But there was also more cheesemaking (and a lot more cheese) and more handicrafts, including a stall run by a former Parisian couturière who had left the City of Lights for the country and now made small models of shepherds' huts in her spare time. Each was presented on a slate, and, with their wells and little buckets, and mini fruit trees laden with tiny fruit, they were undeniably pleasing in a twee kind of way. Upon further inquiry it transpired that all the model huts were imaginary, save for one, the most detailed, which had been bought by the mayor and which depicted an actual hut in a valley above the village. That hut was iconic (for French people at least): it that had been used in the filming of *Belle et Sébastien.*

---

6 An awkward translation, 'herder': the French word *berger* doesn't always distinguish between the animals being looked after and can refer to cowherds, goatherds, shepherds etc., so keeping *berger* is probably simpler.

Belle et Sébastien, if you didn't know, was a famous TV series about an orphan who is rescued by a shepherd and who befriends a giant, shaggy white mountain dog called Belle. It begat a Japanese children's anime series in the 1980s, and a floppy-haired Scottish indie band in the '90s – either of which might ring more bells than the TV series – but mention the original to any French person of a certain age and it is a sure thing they will go misty eyed at the memory of the poor orphan and his faithful friend. But Pyrenean mountain dogs – or *patous*, as they are known by shepherds – have a serious side, as the mayor was about to explain. Despite his penchant for mountain kitsch, he too had a serious side. He passed through the crowd like a gangster, in an ill-fitting black suit, flanked by policemen with tall hats and big bellies overhanging their dress uniforms. 'We won't keep you long, the priority is to get to the *bergers*,' he said, before launching, with the help of some other regional officials, into a lengthy and wide-ranging elegiac discourse that lasted several tens of minutes.

He talked of the disappearing heart of the village, a community where once every family would own a few cattle, or a herd of goats or sheep, but where now there were no pastoral farmers living permanently inside its limits. Of how, on the first of June every year, all the cattle used to be led to the high valleys above the village for the summer, to be cared for by *lou pastre*, as he was known in the ancient Provençal language, who would spend the next four months with them. He spoke of the woodsman who would supply the firewood to heat the milk that was produced in the dairies on high, and the cheese that was transported down; and of the different pastures on the mountain, each of which with its own cabin where the *berger* would stay while the livestock were there, and how the different landowners and livestock owners would work together to survive. 'What remains of this

co-operative system?' he asked. He talked of the cowshed that had been destroyed by an avalanche two years ago and not rebuilt; of the four cabins that had fallen into disuse and disrepair, and how the state had intervened to help renovate one of the precious ones that still remained. Of the *héliportage* to the cabins which the state supported, but how the lowland infrastructure – the abattoirs and the local buyers – was disappearing. How all this threatened the shepherds' way of life, despite modernisation and new initiatives to sell their artisanal produce to tourists and in the cities. He spoke of the evolving role of the shepherd in the local communities, of their contributions to sustainable development, their care for the environment and for the mountain landscapes they lived upon. He called them out by name – the dairy farmers, the cheese makers, the beef and the lamb producers, and even the beekeepers – and asked for a round of applause for each.

But most urgently of all he spoke about wolves. How wolf

attacks were up 20 per cent on the previous year: 406 attacks in the first seven months of 2015, killing or injuring 1,800 animals, which represented in just this one small *département* 50 per cent of the attacks in all of France. (The actual number may be much higher: farmers can report and are compensated for carcasses, but many are never found, and distressed ewes often lose the lambs they are carrying, which again are not taken into account.) He spoke of the single wolf killed by the authorities in all this time, despite a government mandate to cull more than a hundred. He talked passionately about how the farmers had the right to live from their land free from this terror, and how he would be calling on the prefect to authorise the shooting of wolves from helicopters. And he talked of the *patous*, an increasingly indispensable presence for the protection of the sheep, but which also sometimes frighten or even injure walkers – who don't realise the white mountain dogs are there in the middle of the flock, or that walking through a herd and splitting it in two looks to the *patous* like a threat. For these dogs that live on the mountain and sleep within the flock have to stay aggressive, almost half wild, to face up to the attacks it is their job to confront.

Then it was time for the *bergers* to stand together and take a bow, including those freshly descended from a summer on the mountain. They contrasted strongly with the officials in their uniforms and shiny suits. If they had modern technical clothing, it was a fleece, but it was more than likely holed; they wore old T-shirts and jeans, and well-worn walking shoes. One was still holding his staff. With a full beard and moustache, a woollen cape and an old-style hat with a feather in it, this man, not old but not young, caught the eye particularly. He seemed, more than the others, to find this new sociability, this village square packed with people, difficult after four months on the mountain with mainly animals for company.

Although many of the cabins have been modernised, and often electrified with solar panels (and therefore have running water pumped in from a nearby spring), life up there is basic and hard, tiring and solitary. The guy seemed to be suffering from the culture shock and was, not to put too fine a point on it, simply pretty drunk. Later, he got involved in a long conversation with the policemen after an argument broke out. But that was not before another procession of animals, cows driven by the Corniglione brothers (introduced in the speech as beef and dairy farmers), and then a few sheep too, for good measure. Shouts and whistles and a lumbering through the village and the crowd parts, ripples out of the way and hides behind pillars, because oh-my-God the cows, which are Salers and bred for meat, look beefy enough in the fields but up close they're bloody big and moving fast; and the sheep have their heads down and are running in a dense pack through the square into the narrow – almost too narrow for the cows, let alone a car – old streets, shepherded by a serious-looking boy of about 11 with a staff and a canary-yellow T-shirt. And then the rumble's passed and there's a lot of shit left behind, great piles of it, except where one old man, immediately they are through, pops out to hose the passageway in front of his door clean, and also offers to wash the animal muck off people's shoes.

The Cornigliones own the last farm on the road up to the valley where the *Belle et Sébastien* cabin is, I learn as I walk with them driving the herd out of town. They reach a small steep field and begin to set up a temporary pen. One brother closes the gate while the other secures the perimeter of the bottom of the holding space with rope from his knapsack that he measures and cuts with a knife. There is some temporary electric fence to be rigged (cows are curious but they're not stupid, the Cornigliones tell me), and then a hose to be weighted with a rock, tied with string cut from a ball and then thrown into a bright blue plastic industrial barrel, which is left to fill with water. The Cornigliones in part sell their beef through their butcher's on the Avenue des Diables Bleus in Nice, and actually, says Louis, the more voluble of the two, their cows will be going back up to pasture for a few weeks more, where they will be tended by his brother, the silent one, until the snows really threaten.

But it was important, he says, to bring them down to participate in the driving through the streets, to keep the tradition alive.

It is difficult to comprehend the wolf problem from afar, but all the more powerful and affecting for that when seen up close. The theory about the resurgence of European wolves – or at least one of the theories – is that all the factors contributing to rural depopulation have affected remote mountain areas most, and that small, marginal farms and their farmers are disappearing from the uplands. This, coupled with the entirely laudable focus of the past quarter-century

on environmental and species conservation, means that large swathes of the continent are now becoming wolf territory once again. They are spreading back across Western Europe, pushing south into Greece and north into Norway, causing trouble in areas where they have not been seen for centuries. Murderous packs of wolves have naturally repopulated the Alpes-Maritimes from the Ligurian Alps over the Italian border, where isolated local populations remained. Certainly there is no need to suspect, as some locals whisper, they were deliberately reintroduced to the Mercantour National Park by environmentalists. The great wilderness was enough. And now they are spreading further down the mountains, south and west towards the lowlands and the coast. For an urban-living, mountain-visiting cyclist, this might seem a romantic notion. But if you're one of the diminishing number of shepherds on this increasingly dangerous frontier between the cultivated and the wild, whose job is being made even more difficult by these predators returning to fill a vacuum, not so much. It is causing many shepherds, contrary to their instincts and wishes, to leave the vocation altogether.

There is a powerful essay called 'Thinking like a Mountain' by Aldo Leopold, an American forester, writer and naturalist. It described his realisation, while working for the US Forest Service killing predators in the New Mexico mountains, that exterminating wolves had unexpected and unwelcome ramifications: 'I suspect that just as a deer herd lives in mortal fear of its wolves, so does a mountain live in mortal fear of its deer,' he wrote, of the damaging overgrazing he sees caused by large herds. 'And perhaps with better cause, for while a buck pulled down by wolves can be replaced in two or three years, a range pulled down by too many deer may fail of replacement in as many decades.' He continued: 'The cowman who cleans his range of wolves does not realize that he is taking over the wolf's job of trimming the herd to fit the range. He has not learnt to think like a mountain. Hence we have dustbowls, and rivers washing the future into the sea.'

Take a system that has evolved over time and remove an element suddenly and something else will overspill. Leopold's work was influential in the development of a modern environmental ethics, and ecologists now call this kind of imbalance caused by outside intervention a trophic cascade. Actually, the situation he describes is almost the opposite to the wolf problem in the Alps, which seems rather to be provoked by the curiously perverse and maybe defining conflict of our times: hypermodernity colliding with a kind of nostalgic atavism. Times have changed since 1949, when the essay was published, and maybe thinking like a mountain might now usefully (also) mean something else. For me, the shepherds' festivals were a glimpse of the interconnectedness of things, how the culture and the economy of the valleys and mountains is a real living thing; how if you change one thing in one place, something else shifts too, and probably not how you would want it to.

This is just one point of view on the wolf issue. There are many sane voices that support this rewilding. But on that first ascent up the Aspin, Aubisque and Tourmalet, in the Pyrenean ranges known as the Circle of Death, Desgrange's riders feared the bears; perhaps we modern-day cyclists should worry about wolves.

I eventually caught up with the shepherd I had been chasing through the twilight on the Bonette; or rather, he more or less came to me. I had been spending a few days at the *gîte d'étape* in Bousiéyas halfway up the mountain, sharing the bunkroom with a revolving cast of walkers on their way up or down the Alps via the famous GR5 hiking route, and I was sitting outside reading a book about shepherds and watching the usual suspects trail in. Two skinny French guys with huge

backpacks filling bottles up with water at the spring; a tall
Australian smothered in an emulsion of sunblock, wearing a
safari shirt and a floppy hat who, contrary to all regulations,
seemed to be intent on camping on somebody's vegetable patch
that night; Spanish road cyclists in technical-looking kit, eating pasta; Italian bikers. And then some unusual suspects. A
smartly dressed old woman who unsteadily gets out of the
car that delivers her, and sits under a parasol. An oldish man,
florid and pale, in black trousers and black shirt, a kind of
rustic Johnny Cash, who kisses her on both cheeks in greeting
and then disappears inside the refuge. He comes back out,
trips over the step and opens the small church across the
road with the keys he has just picked up. Then he rings the
bell vigorously. Over the next 20 minutes more people join
them. A woman in a wheelchair and a very old man, who
leans in close to the man in black to talk in his ear. The man
in black declines a coffee, decides on a beer instead, lights
a cigarette and laughs as he greets more arrivals. These earthly

pleasures done with, he gets up, trips over again, recovers, rings the bell and the congregation files in.

It is 15 August, Assumption Day. A Catholic mass is held in Bousiéyas each year to celebrate the Virgin Mary being taken into heaven, but this year it is also a memorial service for Gérard Brun, a shepherd from the hamlet who died over the winter at the age of just 58. It turns out that 'my' guy, whose name is Jean-Pierre Benoit, is the deceased man's nephew and is one of the churchgoers. Jean-Pierre is from a long line of shepherds and is also from Bousiéyas.[7] It was his family's sheep (and indeed his father checking up on them) that I had seen that night, from the panorama, in the bowl underneath the peak. Brun's flocks also spent the summer on the upper slopes of the mountain and Jean-Pierre had watched over them each year for 15 years, while Brun spent time making hay, assuring food for the flock over the winter.

Plainsong drifted from the open doors and mixed with the sound of spring water falling into its stone basin. After the service we were introduced, and I arranged to meet him the next day with the sheep.

I found him in an idyllic meadow cradled between two peaks, just above the Camp des Fourches at around 2,300 metres altitude, on the edge of a sheer drop into a cirque, the source of the Salso Moreno river.[8] While the lowlands were mostly privately owned, and the peaks were communal, grazing rights for each mountain pasture were rented from

---

7 Until 1962 Bousiéyas was lived in all year round. When the snows fell, people would retreat into the specially designed buildings, which housed the farmers' families, livestock, food stores, firewood and crops all within their walls. The final year-round resident was an old woman, who had the *Nice-Matin* newspaper delivered every day – which meant a daily snowshoe expedition for the local postie. When she died, the region decreed that the hamlet must be abandoned every year between October and April.

8 It was Jean-Pierre I have to thank for showing me the soldier's time capsule buried there.

the village council. Jean-Pierre was standing on a bluff on the ridge at the northern limit of his lands, his binoculars trained on some chamois on the other side of the river as his sheep cropped gently below him and his two dogs lazed at his feet. He was wearing an old hat with a floppy brim to keep the sun off, a T-shirt and a rucksack in which he kept, among other things, a woolly jumper for cold evenings and mornings, and in his hand he held a wooden staff. He was sturdy and moved in measured steps, and he was quiet, and when he spoke his words were gentle. In the clear days of high summer the sheep would graze contentedly in the morning, then gather together to spend the midday hours resting, he told me. The trick, he said, was to let the sheep feel like they were doing what they wanted and not to police the herd too much with the dogs. They remembered where they'd been and moved towards the untouched grass of their own accord, each day pushing a little further on. When things were quiet and calm, it was good to savour the peace of the mountains, because the weather could quickly become foul at any time of year. Clouds could envelope the slopes in only minutes, reducing visibility to almost nothing and drop the temperature by 20 degrees. Then the sheep would become nervous, start running, scatter into the fog and get lost or injure themselves; worst of all they hated hail, which could strike even in mid-summer. In the spring, perfect balmy periods alternated with days of bitter wind, when the sheep were agitated and quick to fright, and you wished you were still down below. No day was the same as the one before, but the best, he said, were often in September, when there was a freshness in the air, and the first night-time frosts were scorching the grass but the sun still shone; when the leaves were turning and the sheep, content after a summer's grazing and increasingly heavily pregnant, were calm.

Jean-Pierre did not pass his summers in a cabin. His house in Bousiéyas was close enough that he could return home after nightfall for dinner, sleep in his own bed and then drive back up to the *parc*, where the sheep were enclosed for the night, in the morning. There, he would check the flock and attend to any sheep that needed care; then it was an hour or more to walk them up to pasture, where he would lay some salt out for them on a rock. His sheep were pure-breds, either *Préalpes du Sud* or *Rouge de Guillaumes*, two local breeds that were well adapted to life on the mountain. Lambing happened in late October or November, when they'd come off the mountain, with a second round being born in the spring to ewes that had missed out. It was in June, just before the *estives*, that the autumn lambs were sold. Most of the females went to other shepherds, who crossed them with other breeds to produce chunky lambs suitable for eating, and therefore needed fresh pure-bred sheep every year to maintain their flocks; others were kept, to renew the herd; still others (including almost all of the males, save for the most perfect specimens, which were kept as studs) went straight to the butcher.

The sheep were intent on eating, the bells around their necks tinkling gently. It was a perfectly bucolic scene, but for Jean-Pierre it was tinged with sadness. The year was a strange one. For Jean-Pierre, 2,000 sheep were manageable in the summer, but after the *hivernailles* (the winter descent) he always returned to help his father with his own family's flock, which wintered some 250 kilometres distant, at Saint Martin de Crau near Arles. And for Brun's widow, Jean-Pierre's aunt, 2,000 were too many to handle alone over the winter. It is difficult to hire good shepherds – if a young shepherd is talented then he quickly establishes his own flock – so, after Gérard Brun's death, half of the herd had been sold and Brun's 2,000 had become 950. The fact that Brun's sheep

had been handed down to him, and so were actually Jean-Pierre's grandfather's flock, made it all the more poignant. 'I've got a lot of grass!' Jean-Pierre said. 'In other years, I'd have had to manage them, keep them tighter.' Next year, he said, he would look to take on the guardianship of another lowland farmer's sheep, to add to the summer flock so that his aunt's rented pastures weren't wasted: 'The same mountain and half the sheep, that's expensive. It's like buying three baguettes, eating one and then throwing away the other two. You're still paying for them.' With only half the flock, the pressure to move was less, and so he wasn't up to the highest pastures yet. Normally, by 15 August the flock would be at its zenith; Assumption Day was the still point of this turning world, the tipping into autumn. The fogs would start to rise up the valleys, early in the morning and in the afternoon, and the sheep, which had been so eager to gain the high ground in the spring, would become reluctant, knowing, by the dwindling hours of daylight perhaps, that it was time to begin the arc downwards again.

Jean-Pierre showed me the cliffs above the pasture where his father used to pick *génépi*, the local strain of wormwood that is made into a bright-green absinthe-style liqueur, and told me how the National Park authorities were only just now letting locals collect it again. The park had literally been created around the local residents, and they had found themselves subject to restrictions on renovating their houses, bans on hunting, and on mushroom and herb picking. (On the positive side, it also protected the pastures, banned 4 × 4s, and banned any dogs except working dogs within its perimeter.) The conversation inevitably came back round to wolves. They had long been on this high, remote sector, and were not more numerous these days, he said, but perhaps they were extending their territories down to where they were more of a noticeable blight. Yet he also described their increasing

boldness and cunning: how they could take a straggling sheep
in bad weather without the shepherd or even the rest of the
flock realising. And how last year the local village mayor's
sheep were attacked by two wolves at once, one of them
drawing the *patous* away while the other waited downwind
for the dogs to chase into the distance and the flock to be
vulnerable. Jean-Pierre was resisting getting *patous*. Although
they protected the sheep they could also cause problems and
stress within the flock, not to mention the occasional incident
with unwary hikers. As long as the electrified enclosure at
the *parc* was effective, he would not own such dogs, he said,
but if the wolves got in, he'd have to think again.

Without *patous*, however, he could never be completely at
ease, even on open ground in broad daylight. In the past he
had been able to leave the sheep for an hour or two in the
static period in the middle of the day, confident they'd be in
the same place when he returned. But now he was forced to
stay with them, and watching a flock of sheep have a siesta
was not the most edifying part of his work. If he needed to
leave for more than a few minutes, he had to take them down
to the *parc*, which disrupted their rhythms and drew out the
working day if one wanted, as he did, to give them maximum
grazing time. Before the electric fence they could roam more
freely. Now, they were safe but also exposed: if the wind blew
a certain way they might not be able to find a windbreak
to huddle against, and if the rain came they were stuck. It
pained him. It also pained him that the twice-daily passage
of 4,000 cloven feet over the same paths destroyed the mountainside. This did not fit how he wanted to exist on the land,
where the impact of the flocks, though great, should be more
nourishing than destructive. A thousand sheep can consume
five tons of alpine plants a day – that is 500 tons in the
season – but without these thousands of living lawnmowers,
the Alpine meadows would not be as clear and inviting as we

know them. Neither would the mountain forests: larch forests in particular need grazing to lighten the cover beneath the mature trees and make space for saplings to grow. There would be more brambles, fewer paths and bigger risks of both wild fires and avalanches. And the villages in the valleys would lose precious inhabitants, making our passage on two wheels through these cultured landscapes more difficult, less interesting and less rewarding.

Early October. The shoulder of the year; an in-between time when human life has more or less deserted the high mountains. All the summer's tourists are gone, there are no cyclists left, and yet the ski lifts still hang motionless above green meadows. The wooded hillsides are a riot of reds, oranges and yellows, and the mountain meadows above them grey from a light dusting of snow on the ochre grasses. It is the first snow of the year and the Bonette road is officially closed for the first time. I have this liminal space to myself, time to play, and to attempt one final ride up into the cold wind. First, the curious thrill of cycling past the 'Road Closed' sign, of snatching the improbable from the jaws of the impossible, and then the ascent into the advancing winter up high. At Bousiéyas, where the *gîte* appears closed, it is 3°C. Above there, the mists obscure first the other side of the valley, then the valley too, and finally almost the road itself. Near the top, a couple of ibex with huge curved horns crash out of the clouds and across my path not 20 metres in front of me. Rocks are scattered across the road – how quickly it is reclaimed – and the only other thing to pass is a solitary police car, emerging out of the nothingness and disappearing just as quickly, completely inattentive to my presence.

At the top the col is open, and dry, but Jean-Marie and his road-clearing team have ceded the Cime loop to the elements for another year. The steep, precipitous asphalt is now part covered in thin trails of slick run-off-turned-ice, and pebbledash frozen snow that is deepening into ruts. I had been promising myself all the way that however far I got I would not waste time at the top. It is not a place to hang around, but there is a bleak and monochrome soft-focus beauty to the fogged-in scene that is too magical to leave. By the time I am ready to descend a subzero chill has set in almost to the bone.

Those kilometres downhill through the gloom are the coldest moments I have ever spent on the bike. I descend at a snail's pace, racked by shivers, hands too cold either to curl or uncurl on the brakes. Cold that causes pain in my fingers like I've never felt, and dizziness when I get off the bike at the *gîte*. I bother the proprietors for a cup of hot chocolate with two sugars and an espresso mixed in, and then another. They only start the process of returning life to fingers and toes, but are perhaps the most delicious things I have ever drunk.

Somewhat restored, I freewheel to the bottom, and am stopped at the Pont Haut by two pick-ups, a livestock truck and temporary fencing. Two *patous* patrol the junction as three farmers herd sheep into the fences funnelling them into the transporter. They are packing up for the season, they say, and heading down to the plains of the Var at the sea's edge, and it occurs to me that I have seen these shepherds before. Years ago, the first time I ever rode up the Bonette, they were here. It had been early October too, but sunnier and a little less cold. We had seen them at the bridge with the same truck, but we had frozen so badly on the descent that by the bottom my companion's lips had turned a rather special shade of blue. So instead of stopping to observe them we headed down to the village to an Alpine-style restaurant for hot chocolate espressos with two sugars and, it would turn out, the best pizza in the world. A pizza with the thinnest base you could possibly imagine – a result, just maybe, of the thin, high-altitude air into which the dough had been thrown; a pizza with goat's cheese from the herds grazing by the rushing Tinée river and cured ham; a pizza at least 15 inches

across that spilled decadently over the edges of the 12-inch plate it was served on; a pizza to savour, and to turn you from an ice lolly into a human again.

There is something about riding in the mountains that elevates simple things – pizza and hot chocolate, hot and even cold – and gives back to them their true value. But more than that. I knew if I came back just before the snows next year, or the year after, these farmers would be parked up here at the bridge, taking the flocks back down. Riding up there was a connection to the seasons and to these natural rhythms, a connection to the old balances and old ways. This time, instead of rushing down for pizza, I stopped to have a chat. Maybe unwelcomely, as most of the ewes were in the loading pen or on the truck itself, but the bellwether had just been separated and needed dealing with. The bellwether is the castrated ram that leads the flock – a wether with a bell around its neck to help the shepherd keep track of where the herd is heading. Locally it is called the *floucat*, and the tradition is to cut its fleece into distinctive, often funny and demeaning, shapes. He was bulky and strong, and not entirely willing to be manhandled into the back of the pick-up. It took four people while I somewhat awkwardly looked on. But once he was lifted and loaded and locked in, the shepherds showed me some lambs born overnight, the beginning of a new cycle.

In all probability these little guys would not be here this time next year – these farmers bred their lambs for slaughter – but that was part of it all too, and I knew that there would be more.

Chapter 10

IL GIRO

Or, time to dance under those lights

The twenty-eighth of May. It is as if reality has been binned in favour of a script stolen from the desk of a writer of melodramas. Actually, nobody would have dared write the Giro thus: even in a *telenovela* this script would have been chucked out for lacking verisimilitude. But it seems to be happening regardless. The twenty-eighth of May, the day of the final real stage of the Giro d'Italia 2016, from Guillestre to Isola 2000, and the entire race is hanging in the balance. Yesterday, on the descent of the Col Agnel into France, the race leader, Steven Kruijswijk, a Dutchman riding for LottoNL-Jumbo, through misjudgement or fatigue drifted wide on a left-hand bend, hit the bank of snow bordering the road and somersaulted over his handlebars. Those he was descending with – Vincenzo Nibali and Esteban Chaves – were those who had most to gain from the crash, and to make matters worse Alejandro Valverde, a veteran racer also high up in the standings, passed him too. Kruijswijk dusted the snow off and remounted, but his bicycle needed attention from a mechanic and by the bottom his *maglia rosa* was hanging in the balance. Valverde, Nibali and Chaves pushed the pace ahead of him on the final climb to Risoul and the Dutchman cracked, losing minutes to them all. 'I've lost the Giro, I've fucked up everything,' Kruijswijk said in Dutch to the media that followed him to the hotel.

For Vincenzo Nibali it was a remarkable resurrection. The

Italian had been the pre-race favourite but in the first two weeks he had looked a no-hoper. In the big Dolomites stage to Corvara he had lost 37 seconds. The following stage, a 10.8-kilometre uphill time trial, his chain came off, but even accounting for that his performance was poor and he lost around two minutes to Kruijswijk, Chaves and Valverde, the other pink jersey contenders. A further loss of one minute, 47 seconds on the relatively easy mountain stage to Andalo, after the rest day, confirmed something was up. He was a long way off top form and the team sent him for blood tests (later, it would be revealed that he had been suffering from stomach problems). But Nibali had not thrown in the towel and had kept riding. And now, thanks to a spectacular and costly mistake by his main rival, he was back in it. The Italian media were breathlessly talking about legendary comebacks by Fausto Coppi and Charly Gaul, and the Giro was again within his reach. Before the race, Michele Acquarone had predicted a Nibali win and he had kept the faith through the first two weeks, despite being ribbed by a journalist friend for his choice: 'After the first week, she said, "What about it?"' he told me. 'I said, "I think that Nibali will win at the end because he's the strongest. No Valverde or Dutch rider can compete with Nibali." After the second week she rang and said, "Can he still do it?" I said, "Sure, because the Giro can be completely crazy. Even if you lose minutes in the first and the second week, there's always the third week. And then the two final stages where anything can happen."

'I lived the Giro and I know that it's always like that. The weather, the craziness, people get tired. It's a very tough race.'

For his comeback to be complete, today Nibali has to win back 44 seconds from Chaves, Orica-GreenEdge's cheerful, pint-sized Colombian who is wearing the *maglia rosa* that fell from Kruiswijk's shoulders in the crash. Kruijswijk is in third, another 19 seconds back, though nobody knows how badly injured he is. Behind him lurks Valverde, a tenacious, experienced racer with a knack of being in exactly the right place at the right time.

Elsewhere in the myriad battles that comprise the race, Team Sky's Mikel Nieve took second place in the stage yesterday behind Nibali. That puts him in prime position for the mountains classification jersey, so that will also be decided today on the stage over the Bonette. And then there is Joe. Back on the top of Teide, five weeks earlier in Tenerife, the Cannondale-Garmin Giro squad had been in good spirits. Joe had been looking forward to riding for Rigoberto Urán, an easygoing but committed rider who already had two Giro second places under his belt. 'He may be the key guy in Rigo's run for the win,' Jonathan Vaughters, the team boss, had said to the CyclingTips website. Urán had been in good form too. The team had navigated the windy, tricky opening flat stages in the Netherlands without hitting any problems, but after the race transferred to southern Italy for the long and bumpy haul back to the finish line at Turin, the plan seemed to falter. On Stage 6, which was the first uphill finish and which happened to be on Joe's birthday, Urán had not been at the front of the dwindling peloton on the 17-kilometre road towards the summit. The team had had to work hard to bring him back to the favourites when Tom Dumoulin of Giant-Alpecin attacked and the bunch exploded. Then Urán had a bad time trial – not the uphill one where Nibali struggled, but 40 kilometres in the rolling hills of Chianti on Stage 9. An illness was putting paid to his GC ambitions. However, in a minor echo of Nibali's tenacity, Urán had also gritted his teeth and kept going, and on the eve of the stage over the Col de la Bonette he was sitting in a creditable eighth position overall. That's bike racing, as they say.

As a climbing *domestique*, Joe had had licence to go easy on the flat days and had kept a low profile in the first week.

Then, with Urán fading, he'd had the opportunity to ride a little for himself. Mauro Vegni, the race director, had told me to watch out for Stage 13, in the Friuli region right on Italy's border with Slovenia, since it was much harder than it looked on the route profile and had the potential to spring a surprise. In a small act of industrial espionage I had passed this insider tip on to Joe, figuring all is fair in love and war and bike racing. Joe chose that stage to get in the break, and then, with Mikel Nieve, to ride right off the front for a bit. And although he could not quite stick with Nieve, the eventual stage winner, and finished minutes back, everything augured well. He repeated the escapade in Stage 16, making the selection with Steven Kruijswijk, but was frustrated when he was gapped on the flat and the chance for a stage win slipped away. It was exciting to watch from the sofa as he repeatedly found himself in contention when the final move was made. And Joe had told me after the Vuelta that he'd learnt that the third week of a Grand Tour would present him with some opportunities: 'Honestly, the first week of the Vuelta I was getting blown out. But then, by the third week, I could just move around and do what I wanted, it was awesome,' he said. 'I realised that those guys who can smash it sprinting out of every corner and can ride in the wind every day are the same guys that are in the *grupetto* every day in week two and three, and they're not going to be in your way any more. OK, you're going to be really tired and not feel good, but nobody feels good: everybody is tired and everyone has a cough and nobody's sleeping well. But if you're strong, then in the third week you see who's really there and who's not.'

The signs were good, the head was good, the legs were good, Joe was repeatedly in the right place at almost the right time. But time was running out. Three more mountains for him to make his mark. His home roads, his parents coming from the States to cheer him on, my mountain to climb (although my joke that I was expecting big things from him on the Bonette was really wearing thin). Plus Mikel Nieve bidding for King of the Mountains, and the GC for the taking after an encounter with a snowdrift.

3,166 kilometres raced, 297 to go. How had it come to this?

A

I arrived in Saint Étienne de Tinée a few days before the stage to see the final preparations for the race's passage, just after a spring snowstorm had closed the pass. There had been weather problems at one of the Giro's lead-up races, the early-season Tirreno–Adriatico, which had caused Nibali to threaten not to race the Giro. His point was that Tirreno had been materially affected as a race by the cancellation of a mountain stage due to bad weather: why should he, as a climber and a GC contender, commit to the Giro if the stages where he might make his talents count might be nixed at short notice? Briefly, in Saint Étienne, his diva moment seemed to be justified. There was consternation in the local press, but it was short lived. Acquarone believed, he had told me, that climbing through big walls of snow was integral to the magic of the highest climbs, but he acknowledged the jeopardy: 'That's how cycling legends are created,' he had said. 'Of course if you are in July you can wear shorts, get tanned and have fun, it's great. But the race can be a little bit boring. The weather can do something magic. That's why I love the Giro in May. It's totally unpredictable.'

Almost the first person I saw in Saint Étienne was Aurelien, the snow-clearer. He was on his way home from work, near the subdivision headquarters on the one road in and out of town. He had cut his hair. It was looking trim, much better. 'The work keeps going, that's all,' was all he had to say about the snowstorm. It had, in fact, also snowed the previous day, and because of the wind everything had become blocked again. But it was all OK now. 'You see, it falls and you just have to keep working,' he explained, a Sisyphus of the snows.

The forecast was set fair now, if a little gloomy and cold for race day. The Giro organisers had played Russian roulette with the weather over ten 2,000-metre-plus passes, and it looked like the gamble would pay off, and the race would come out unscathed the other side.

The next day I rode up the col. All around was evidence of activity. Where the surface had cracked near the bottom were deposits of fresh black asphalt to smooth it over. Hay bales were piled against protruding retaining walls, the road-side bushes and trees were being trimmed, and further up a truck was descending, sweeping away any last pebbles and thorns. It was past the customary clocking-off time when I reached the highest slopes, but the ballet of the snow-moving machines was continuing, Bernard and Aurelien cutting and chopping and tipping the snow from the sides of the road to make more room for spectators.

After two days in the village I meet my friends at the walkers' *gîte* at Bousiéyas, the night before the race. The plan is to stay here, halfway up the mountain, and ride up the next day over the top, so that we watch the riders climb rather than the Technicolor blur of the descent. That evening a group of park rangers stop by for an aperitif, and they proceed to pour cold water over my excitement about the next day's stage even as they pour cold water over their Ricard. There will be no caravan, they say. No garish commercial sideshow chucking trinkets and product samples to whip grannies and toddlers into a frenzy before the riders come – not a single vehicle even crossed the border. And no helicopters. Or rather, the high-altitude aircraft that serve as relays for the signals from the TV *motos* will fly, but the park's rule forbidding (wildlife-disturbing) overflying at less than 1,000 metres above the ground will stand. The Giro had been fighting the park police, but it had not prevailed. 'They didn't understand that they don't have the same privileges. Only the Tour de France,' one of the rangers said. Riders will be warned not to litter, and they are not even allowed to take 'natural breaks' while in the park. An overreaction? Do wolves shit in the woods? In addition there will be no parking allowed outside of certain designated bays (this is a sensible precaution given the narrow, precipitous road), with the closest to the top still three kilometres away. There has also been widespread confusion about when the road will open or close. Perhaps the road below us is already closed to traffic, perhaps not. One of the beauties of the mountain in the evening is when the daily traffic stops and peace descends, but tonight it is preternaturally still. The park police leave and we stand in the middle of the road, scanning the mountainside opposite for herds of deer. Tomorrow will be quiet, almost silent in Grand Tour terms. No *Apocalypse Now*-style helicopters advancing up the valleys below, no glorious sweeping aerial shots of riders snaking up and down the road, no tourist advertisements for the barren beauty of the Cime de la Bonette and the surrounding peaks, as Jean-Marie-André Fabron had hoped. It is as if the race is on manoeuvre in enemy territory.

The twenty-eighth of May. I am on my mountain staring down into the void towards the Caserne de Restefond and beyond, where, somewhere as yet unseen, the Giro dramas are being teed up, played out or resolved. I have no phone reception and am consequently completely in the dark about what is happening. For all I know the race has been abandoned due to Nibali being abducted by aliens live on TV. A fat and opinionated Dutchman standing next to me is no help. I sip some brandy from the hip flask I carried up in my jersey pocket. This is not even the decisive climb of the day. A cold wind is blowing and dark clouds sit in ranks across the infinite sky. I am very happy and terribly, terribly nervous. This is the only place I could be.

We had set off in the morning and slowly climbed the 12 kilometres to the top. It is still and quiet, the deer are still in the valleys. Barely a motorhome anywhere. Further up we meet the first of a steady stream of race vehicles coming the other way. Technical vehicles, team cars, sponsors' vans and then press cars, some of whose occupants I recognise, from the atomised global community of writers and photographers spinning centripetally in the maelstrom of the pro cycling circus. They stop to say hi, and suddenly the incongruity of seeing them, friendly faces in beautiful places, of the race and the world coming to the mountain, of the enormity of what is about to happen, makes a lump rise in my throat. I'm nervous for Joe; nervous, weirdly, for myself, pinning everything on a stupid race on a road on a big hill in the south of France. There is nothing to do but keep going.

At the top there is a lone figure standing on the ridge above the col. An Italian flag flies from the bunker, which seems like a provocation. Among the handful of people waiting at the narrow defile of the col are Aurelien and the park police. They are standing behind a metal barrier where six weeks

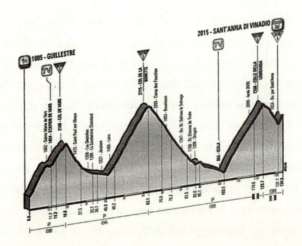

earlier was the blue portacabin. We say hi, put on our down jackets and beanies, and then freewheel down to take up our position. Staring down into the void towards the Caserne de Restefond. Are they coming yet? Is that them? When in doubt, brandy. I sip from my hip flask and squint at the snow and wait.

Is that them? The first tiny dot appearing on the road far below. It's not a group, it's a single rider. Is that him? It inches past the barracks and, preceded by motorbikes and followed by a car, slowly takes the right-hand bend. A minute, two minutes pass. The wind blows but otherwise it is still here on high. They reappear. A Team Sky car. So not Joe. It's Nieve. He must be pushing on to secure the King of the Mountains points. As if by magic, my phone vibrates into life. There is a break behind, it's been away since the gun, and Joe has been in it. BMC's Darwin Atapuma just rode away from it and Joe has ridden back to him, Giovanni Visconti too. The break from the break. They are a few minutes behind Nieve, I can see them now, zigging and zagging left and right on the distant switchbacks, then Nieve suddenly appears close to, on the road nearby. He is not inching as it had seemed but riding strongly, pedalling smoothly, very composed. Then he is gone. Joe's group behind him seems to reach us faster and too soon Joe is swooshing past. There are six of them. I scream and scream my support. I have sun cream in my eyes, they start to water, that is the only explanation. He gives us a small wave, and I remember something he said, no doubt when we were eating fish and salad in the sun: 'It's interesting when your friends come to mountain stages because it's slowed down enough sometimes in your periphery you see them. You never forget when it happens. You'll be on a finishing climb and you hear your name and you glance over for just a second, and then it's back to what you're doing. My friends back home, they were at Cali last year and when we finished on the Baldy stage there's a picture of me and one of them running next to me in a banana suit. It's just priceless.'

I curse that I forgot the banana costume.

Shouting, hoarse, three seconds, an eternity. And then they're gone. Joe looked comfortable. He definitely saw us. And I saw he was comfortable and within himself. (I later find out that with this ride he takes the Strava KoM for the climb.) I saw six riders and controlled effort and racecraft and calculation and I knew that the stage winner would come from this group. I had not expected a glorious solo break over two mountains – I don't know what I'd dared to expect from those contesting the stage – but seeing the break pass like

this made the battle real. Obviously Joe will be waiting for the next climb past Isola to attack, but the break had had to go early or else they would have been caught in the fireworks that will happen on the GC. He is waiting for a real chance at the stage, racing cleverly. I wonder if he's thinking of his parents up the road, waiting in their turn, and the hope and expectation and delight that racing past them near the front, maybe in front, will bring.

The road is quiet once again. Nine minutes later the peloton comes past, grim-faced and lined out, passing within millimetres of the edge of the tarmac on the racing line, followed by the support cars. Maybe 10 minutes later the *grupetto* and the cars and race vehicles behind. Finally, after a straggler or two, the broom wagon and the breakdown truck and the official van that marks the end of the race cordon. I get on my bike and race to and hug the back bumper. I need to get back down. I pass over the col and glimpse the race disappearing into the distance, fight through the exhaust fumes, past the fire trucks and the ambulances and I descend as fast as I can, shadowing the racers arcing gracefully through the distant hairpins, many kilometres away and hundreds of vertical metres below.

I try to imagine what's going on, what they'll be thinking in the break. The group of them will have no trouble catching up with Nieve and then the stage will be anyone's for the taking. Joe had told me about the final short climb to the sanctuary of Sant'Anna, where the finish line lay, which is past the border after an eight-kilometre descent, but it was the Col de la Lombarde, the 22-kilometre climb to the frontier sign, that had him excited. 'I'm pumped,' he had told me. 'I've been up Lombarde a hundred times. When you're training at Isola you have to go up and down every day. Knowing it starts hard, that it's really steep the first few kilometres and then it evens out a bit, I think that's really valuable.

Particularly with positioning and stuff, knowing where you can move up, that kind of thing. It should be epic,' he added. Followed by a pause and then: 'EPIC.'

At Bousiéyas I chuck my bike against the wall, grab my iPad and sit down on the floor of the dormitory in my cycling kit. My girlfriend has been sending me text updates; now she has found me a live stream to watch. We are watching the break. Sean Kelly is commentating and explaining that he expects attacks. Nieve loses the wheel. Now they are seven. Twenty-one kilometres before the top. The sun is shining as they follow Visconti up. The pace slows, they are looking around at each other. It is steep. And this is where Joe attacks. Joe is leading the race. He is on his own. They are slow to react, but Atapuma chases through the tight hairpins and is the first and only one to make it over to him. The texts from my girlfriend get more frequent and excited. She doesn't follow cycling much but has briefly met Joe, and this – a recognisable face leading the race – is the catalyst for her excitement. As for me, I am glued to the glitchy pixelated figures on my tiny screen.

He keeps going. There is a big no man's land now between Joe and Atapuma and the shattered remains of the break, Visconti floundering in between. Back in the valley in the main group Nibali is looking cool, but Chaves is not yet showing signs of the great fatigue the commentators say he is carrying from his efforts the previous day. Chaves looks OK, but nothing is happening, yet. Soon somebody will try something.

Now it's Visconti, Atapuma and Joe. Visconti is choosing to do very little work, but that's to be expected since he is probably riding with half his mind on Valverde, his teammate, who started the day sitting in fourth place in the GC, just off the overall podium, and who is no doubt lurking on Chaves's wheel, his hyena breath loud in Chaves's ear. The peloton is at the bottom of the climb now and Nibali's team-mates take to the front. There is a sense of foreboding, of barely concealed conspiracy, a mob assassination about to take place. Ten and a half minutes ahead are Joe, Atapuma and Visconti working well, climbing through the forests. Joe is still looking good; Atapuma, tenacious and also comfortable. Visconti is sandbagging, or maybe he is faking weakness and riding a clever race. Is Joe the strongest or is he doing too much work? Is he the strongest and *also* doing too much work? I cannot know. It is getting unbearable. I am glued to the screen. So is my girlfriend, who is starving but cannot tear herself away to make lunch. 'Fucking shitballs,' she texts.

Behind Joe's trio are Tanel Kangert, Rein Taaramäe and Alexander Foliforov, and Nieve, who has made it back. Nieve looks knackered but the two Estonians and the Russian, though on different teams, have formed a post-Soviet alliance and they are motoring on. Joe's group pass under the Italian bunkers that guard the old border, so they still have at least 10 kilometres to go to the top. They are caught by Taaramäe and Kangert. Nieve and Foliforov are gone. Now they are five. Joe is at the back. This is either bad or good. Or neither. It is very possible I am second-guessing too much. (Am I second guessing whether I am second guessing?) They are through the avalanche tunnels now, which I know are just below the ski resort. The road is long and straight.

The camera cuts back to the *maglia rosa* group, where Michele Scarponi, Nibali's right-hand man, has attacked. Immediately Nibali bridges, as does Chaves, but Chaves has no teammates, only Rigoberto Urán, a compatriot who has said he'll do a pull for his diminutive friend. Chaves's mirrored glasses hide his eyes, but his face is set in a rictus. Nibali bites into an energy gel. The atmosphere is ominous. There are only a dozen of them left and Nibali's Astana are firmly in charge. Valverde hunches his shoulders, gets on the radio to his team. Everyone is making plans. The knives will soon be out. There are no spectators around, nobody to jostle them like Bartali and Robic, there will be no mistakes. It will be clinical. This will be assassination caught on CCTV.

Joe's group is now at the ski station, so there's about five kilometres left on this climb. They take a left-hand hairpin and Joe leaps. The Estonians are dropped, but Taaramäe comes back. Kangert, a teammate of Nibali, has let go. He has been told not to burn all his matches. He is soft-pedalling next to a team car. The camera cuts away, cuts back, and Taaramäe has pulled away. He has drifted ahead and has a significant gap. Joe and Atapuma are following, but maybe they don't realise the threat because they seem to be attacking each other rather than chasing together. Come on, Joe. The trees are thinning out, the road is very beautiful and deserted. Taaramäe is away, and though there are no time splits yet being shown to measure the effectiveness of his attack, I'm sure he has won the race.

Joe has 12 kilometres to go – two kilometres up, eight down and then two more up – when Nibali attacks the pink jersey group. Chaves is with him. Valverde makes it. Kruijswijk, with his grazes and his broken ribs, does not. So that's that. Nibali must distance Chaves by 44 seconds to steal the GC lead. Out comes the knife. He attacks again. Chaves cannot follow the shark. Chaves is distanced. Nibali is in high-cadence, rock-solid locomotion, his trademark. Legs like pistons. Valverde attacks too. It would be massively advantageous to Chaves if Valverde would work to his pace, but Valverde knows he only has to gain 43 seconds on the stricken Kruijswijk to win a podium place and he is riding hard. They are working together in a fashion, but instead of nursing Chaves through Valverde is almost goading him to give what he has, and then to dig deeper. He *might* be helping him, but an equally persuasive reading of it is that he is sitting behind, making him work, then sprinting, getting a gap, working him over. Fucking shitballs indeed. Nibali looks to have exhausted his initial momentum, but here is Tanel Kangert waiting for him, and Nibali can sit on his wheel and recover while Kangert does a suicide pull – a superhuman effort that will, should Nibali win the *maglia rosa*, as now looks highly likely, no doubt be extremely well rewarded. Astana are so far playing their hand to perfection. We cut to Taaramäe who is going over the top of the climb alone, just a descent and one final uphill from glory. 'This is a beautiful race,' says the commentator, as the helicopter camera sweeps over snow-capped peaks.

Where is Joe? Unfortunately for me, Joe's battle is comparatively minor in all of this – and especially for the Italian broadcasters controlling our international TV feed. The camera has not been with him for minutes. We know that he is behind Taaramäe, somewhere, with Atapuma and Visconti there or thereabouts. We also know that not so long ago Nibali was still eight or nine minutes behind Joe, six at the very least, and so should not threaten the stage's podium positions. More than that, who knows? The broadcast is glued to Nibali and Chaves. 'Pedalling squares' is a cliché of exhaustion but I cannot remember anyone who looked closer to pedalling squares than Chaves right now.

Urán arrives in the picture for the final two kilometres of this climb. Finally Chaves has a friend. Valverde is still pushing on. Visconti, we see briefly, is still with Joe. Surely he will drop back for Valverde. Surely. Kruijswijk is slowly slipping off the podium, at least if Valverde has his way, but it is unclear which of Chaves and Kruijswijk is feeling worse. Kangert peels off, he is blown, but Nibali now has 30 seconds of the 44 he needs to win. He is looking strong again and he is also a very fast descender. *Les jeux sont faits*, I think. It is agonising. Chaves can no longer hold Urán's wheel and Urán floats away without seeming to mean to. Valverde knows a sinking ship when he sees one and departs, and Chaves is alone, wearing that pink jersey for a few minutes more. He is losing the Giro d'Italia just as Kruijswijk did the previous day. The hill goes on.

For a second or two we see Joe, and he is with Visconti. No Atapuma. Does that mean Atapuma has cracked, or has he left the other two behind? From the way he looked earlier, I think Atapuma may have jumped. Fifteen minutes ago Joe was leading the race and now, if Atapuma is ahead and Visconti is still in contention, there's a real chance he won't be on the podium, it seems, which would be totally wrong, just wrong. There is no more brandy.

By the time Chaves reaches Italy – the border is at the top of the col – he has lost the pink jersey. Nibali is flying down the valley on the narrow, narrow road, 55 seconds ahead and counting.

Taaramäe is now on the final climb. Atapuma, it seems, is chasing behind him in second. There are no time gaps being shown, but I don't think he will steal it. Where Joe is I have no idea. More importantly, where is Visconti? Has he dropped back? Is he ahead of Joe? That would be devastating. Their last known positions were third and fourth. I can't bear it. All we are being shown is the turquoise streak of Nibali descending through larch forests, twisting the knife.

My girlfriend's web stream in London is ahead of mine and I cannot hear from her what she is seeing and then watch it a minute later, so with 1.6 kilometres to go I ask her not to tell me anything more. I will suffer this alone.

The camera is now with Taaramäe, who is within the barriers close to the finish. Now the final 200 metres. He will win the stage. He wins the stage. Atapuma is approaching the line . . . and there is Joe! He is in the barriers too. He must be third. Must be. The camera cuts to Visconti, who, as I had hoped, is back with Valverde.

Atapuma has taken second. And there is Joe, still climbing, another 15 or so seconds back.

He has his podium place. 'Joe Dombrowski, a name to watch in Grand Tour racing,' says the commentator.

Epilogue
TIME PASSES

Stop me if you've heard this one, but I want to tell you about a memorial to a fallen cyclist. It's on Mont Ventoux, to the right of the road about a kilometre from the top. Just above the one to Tom Simpson, the British cyclist who collapsed here chasing his dream of winning the 1967 Tour de France, which was disappearing up the road ahead of him.

Oh, you thought I meant *that* memorial. Sorry.

Those slopes are pitiless, and Simpson's tragic tale is well known: the pressure he was under to perform well in the Tour; the combination of heatstroke and exhaustion and drugs that killed him somewhere near where the stone now stands; his last words, 'Put me back on the bike.' But only a short scramble across the bare white limestone is this other stone on a plinth, one that few people visit or even are aware of. I've sat at its base and watched 50 cyclists pass without breaking their contemplation of their stem.

Its story is much less well known. The inscription on it reads: '*En mémoire du Gaulois P. Kraemer décédé an Ventoux le 2.4.1983. L'Union des Audax Français*'. ('In memory of the Gaul, P. Kraemer, who died on Ventoux 2.4.1983.') The Gaul Pierre Kraemer takes us away from the pros and into the amateur ranks again, and I know it's late in the day, but I wanted to introduce him here because his life and death tell a different story to Tom Simpson's – both about Ventoux and about cycling itself.

Pierre Kraemer was not a famous man, but he was a celebrated and much-loved member of the French Audax Union, the brotherhood of amateur long-distance cyclists who participate in, among other events, the historic 1,200-kilometre Paris–Brest–Paris 'brevet' ride. Pierre had completed the PBP multiple times, as well as many of the other classic long-distance brevets, some of them over distances of more than a thousand kilometres. They are undertaken not for glory but for camaraderie and the love of cycling, and this seems to have summed Pierre up. He was known for his generosity to less-experienced riders, his cheerfulness and his work as a ride captain – organising groups and making sure everyone was on the right road at Audax events. There's a photo of him as an older man floating around on the web. He is still blond, and it's easy to see from his Asterix-like handlebar moustache why he is nicknamed 'the Gaul'. Compact and stocky, he is wearing a blue short-sleeved jersey. In his oily hand he holds a glass litre bottle of milk, half drunk, which he rests on his leather saddle. Another rider, mostly out of shot, has his arm round him. It is sunny and Pierre is smiling.

At the age of 56 – not all that long after that photo, perhaps – Kraemer was told he had an incurable cancer. In April 1983 he decided to climb Ventoux one last time. And there, near the top, where the road ran into a snowdrift, he got off his bike, sat down and let the cold take him away. They found him later, buried under a metre of snow. Or that, from the tributes I found to him on the internet, from Audax friends who clearly knew him well, was what I thought happened. I wrote a small article telling the story and paying respect, I thought, to an extraordinary but little-known cyclist who deserved remembering. And that was that. Six months later, I was contacted out of the blue by a member of his family. That's a lovely piece you wrote, ran the email, but were you a friend? The family knew nothing of his cancer . . .

I was horrified. The last thing I had wanted to do was spread misinformation through the echo chamber of the internet. However, there were enough tributes to Pierre that I had assumed it was both common knowledge and true. We corresponded, I showed his niece what I had found, and we talked about taking the article down. She said that the family had never understood why Pierre had climbed Ventoux that Easter, because he had been warned about the bad weather. They had believed his death had been a tragic misadventure.

She filled me in with scraps and details of his life. How Pierre was a one-off and a non-conformist, a man who would think nothing of answering his front door in a Paris suburb – and then cooking and eating a meal – only wearing pants. The model of him riding his bicycle made for him out of sugar by the local *pâtisserie* owner. His Tour de France *Randonneur*, a solo, self-supported trip of 4,800 kilometres and 23 days, and she sent me the account he wrote of this odyssey around France, in which he described sleeping out at night under the stars in the mountains as much because he enjoyed it as because it meant not wasting hours finding a hotel or queuing at the breakfast buffet in the morning. She also told me that Pierre was the kind of man who might have hidden an illness from his family. 'He had the death he would have wanted,' she said.

Pierre loved the mountains. Over a lifetime of riding a bike up and down and around and around his country, he knew them well, and had a special feeling for them. Ventoux above all. I wanted to include his story here – both the stories, actually, and I present them equally – because it spoke to me, deeply and in a way that I could not pin down, about what mountains can represent to cyclists. It also seemed important to me to record that the memorial exists, literally side by side up there on Ventoux, with another intense and profound, and yet darker, tale of man's encounter with mountain. I had thought that there was a kind of duality in Simpson's and Kraemer's stories, and that Pierre as a figure was a counterpoint to Tom. Kraemer, with his two stories, complicates that somewhat, but I don't think it makes it any less true. The top of Ventoux can be a miserable and desolate place. The final footage of Tom Simpson's last ride shows a man being propelled jaggedly into a desperate, lonely oblivion. Whereas Pierre's stories speak of a love. A harsh and inhuman love, as hot as the sun on the white rocks and as cold as the snow and the wind. Dangerous and capricious, but a love, nevertheless.

A

After the Bonette Giro stage had finished and the race had passed, I found myself sitting in the *gîte*, alone in the calm. I should have been going back down to Nice, but after the ride up and down and the iPad finale I was a puddle on the floor. I was exhausted and I didn't make it off the mountain that night, so I took single occupancy of the 16-person dormitory and awoke in the sunshine on the empty mountain.

Usually, a mountain the day after a race is a strange place. All the animation and life – all Michele Acquarone's parties with the *tifosi* – have gone, and there is a peculiar hiatus while the natural tranquillity re-establishes itself. But there hadn't been much of a party here for the Giro. No crowds. It had all happened on the road, and that had not disappointed. The mountains had given us everything. On the penultimate climb of the penultimate day of the Giro the battle had been lost and won. There had been the final fight for the King of the Mountains jersey. The breakaway for the stage composed of first-class climbers, and then the multiple attacks that whittled them down to just a handful vying for the stage. Astana and Movistar, meanwhile, playing tactically perfect games in the GC battle. The down-and-out champion who rose again to claim his crown. Nibali's joy, Italy's joy.

Kruijswijk's suffering and the slow-motion heartbreak for Chaves who, at his absolute limit, had to watch as centimetre by centimetre Nibali pulled away and won the race. Astana had waited and waited to attack, it had come right down to the wire. We may not live in those gilded days of Vietto and Bahamontes and Coppi and their like, but here had been derring-do and endeavour and panache, and an indication that there may yet be new myths to be made. That the mountains will keep on giving.

And then there had been my own personal race – by which I mean Joe's. For me, there had been a sense of inevitability to some of what had happened. Not that I'd been presumptuous enough to think anybody could be a dead cert for a podium, or even a good showing, on a stage of the Giro. But everything had been leading to this, the stars had been aligning, it was going to be a culmination. Everything I had seen and I had found out in that past year, everything he had shown in the race to that point demonstrated the preparation, the focus, the plan and the ability to execute it. And then almost – but not quite – making the world conform to your will. And it would be unfair to burden anyone with comparisons to legendary performances by cycling greats, but something that Giro, that day, had changed for Joe. Soon, he might be calling the shots on these highest mountains; soon, on this showing, he might be the marked one, the one people would follow.

But what was it that happened in that maelstrom on the mountain that we TV spectators did not see?

'It wasn't particularly civilised in the break,' Joe tells me on Skype, a month or two later. He was luxuriating in a bit of off-season time at home in the US. I was still in France. 'Nieve was up ahead and Atapuma was attacking on Bonette, which seemed a little bit, I don't know, stupid. It was pretty windy and there was so far to go, I didn't understand the point of it, but nobody really wanted to let him completely ride off. I don't know why we couldn't have ridden in a civilised fashion, because ultimately it was going to come down to the final climb. We had quite a bit of leash and even if we were messing around, it was quite obvious we weren't going to get taken back unless we were really crawling.'

Joe hadn't been worried about Nieve taking the stage solo, since he knew the valley road between Bonette and Lombarde so well that he knew there would be headwind, and that a single rider would struggle to keep an advantage over the break working together. They all hit the Lombarde together.

'Visconti started riding a stiff tempo and I was on his wheel, we rode pretty hard for about five minutes. It was pretty steep, and I was thinking, this climb gets easier as we get to the top, so to me it makes sense to make a selection here where it's steep. When it gets flatter it can turn into a tactical thing and guys start jumping around. If you think you're the strongest just go when it's hard and don't look back.

'So I went pretty early and for a while I was alone,' Joe continues. 'Atapuma started coming across and eventually he made it, but the problem was I couldn't get him to pull. I was trying to tell him, "You and I are the strongest here, if we work together we're not going to come back, and the worst-case scenario is you'll be second. But you might win! But if we don't work together and we mess around then we have to deal with six guys ... and it turns into a bit more of a lottery."

'I couldn't get him to pull and he was just sitting on, and I didn't just want to pull him into the headwind. Looking at it retrospectively, and a couple of people said this to me, if you think you're the strongest there – and it looked like you were – you should just keep riding and eventually he'll probably get dropped.

'Ultimately, if I could do it again I would have done it

differently. Taaramäe came back, and because he was dropped early on, you think, oh well, he's not that strong, we don't have to worry about him in this instant. Then Atapuma and I were so focused on each other Taaramäe chipped off the front. There was a moment's hesitation, and that was the gap. He had a little gap and went over the top, we continued to jump around behind and that was it.'

When Visconti did make good on his promise and dropped back to help Valverde it left Joe safely in third position: 'I remember coming down the Italian side of Lombarde, and maybe this sounds weird, but I was actually just taking it all in. This was the last few kilometres of my first Giro, this is one of my favourite roads, I think it's one of the most beautiful roads I've ever ridden. My parents are at a kilometre to go, I'm a few kilometres away from them. I know I'm not going to win the stage but I'm also not going to get caught. I'm third, it's going to be what it's going to be. I'm going to enjoy this. Have fun on this descent then smash it up the last little climb to the finish.'

In a post-race interview Joe described losing the stage as 'heartbreaking', and as we talk he expands on that immediate feeling: 'Man, I honestly felt like I was the strongest guy, and it seems like on a stage like that, if you're the strongest, to not win is a real loss. You ask yourself, what did I do to lose the stage? It was really weird, I remember my head was spinning.'

It was one of a number of close calls with glory in that Giro, he says, but I put it to him that a podium at the Giro, even a third place, has proved something. It shows he's shifted gears. 'I think so,' he replies, 'And to be honest, looking at that specifically, at my Giro as a whole and even the season as a whole, I look at it positively because with any season there's always ups and downs. There's ups and downs within a race, there's ups and downs in a stage, even in one climb!

'I didn't end up getting my stage win, but since I changed teams it's been a steady build. Last year at the Vuelta the plan was to get through it and get the experience of doing a three-week race. There were times I was kind of there in the Vuelta, but I remember in the [Giro in the] Dolomites, I think it was the first time I could consistently follow the best six, seven, eight guys. It seemed like on the mountain stages I was always the last guy there who wasn't on GC.' He continues: 'It was the first time I was like, wow, I'm there. You sort of see over three weeks where you are in the pecking order. It's easy to overlook that [looking in from the outside] because a lot of times that never shows up in the results, but when you're in the race you see where you fall more, and I think I'd made a lot of progress. Looking at last year, I could never really be up there, and this year I was there consistently. So if you build on that, maybe next year you target a top 10.'

Calm and thoughtful, as he's always been in our chats. And he is on an upwards trajectory, which seems fitting.

⌃⌃

There's only one place this book can end, and that's on top of the Bonette, and so here I am at its foot. Writing this book has meant, as books do, a lot of stillness and a lot of time in the library. Plenty of time in the mountains, yes, but hiking and driving and writing and comparatively little riding, and I have lost much of my fitness, that feeling of grace riding uphill you only get when you have ridden hard and lots and beyond what is reasonable for a long time. But I have explored further and dug deeper and seen more, and that feels good.

Besides, there is still time for one final climb this year. At the Pont Haut the 'Col Closed' sign is up, but the barrier is not lowered and there is light enough to make it to the top. I ride up away from the grids and the lines of the civilised

world and up into the glorious empty spaces and freedom above. The road is covered with fallen leaves and spiky chestnut shells, as if it has been abandoned much longer than a few days, and rounding a corner I surprise a chamois standing in my path. Up past the waterfall and towards Le Pra, where a 4 × 4 containing two park rangers drives past me, but does not question my right to ride up. Each pedal stroke higher is liberating. A little fragment of being, breathed in and lived to the full, at my own speed. The larch forests are on fire with colour. At Bousiéyas I break into the unblinking sun, a crystalline light so piercing I wonder if it is actually this and not the wind that is chilling me to the bone. Work harder and a quickening of the senses, the exertion connecting me to the world below and the sky above.

At the Camp des Fourches, where the road narrows to the old soldiers' path, there is metal creaking in the wind somewhere around the roofless huts, and I greet the bunkers peering down on me like old friends. I wonder if the physio from the village below has made his final ascent and if this year he has beaten his rival. Higher, higher and there are stones on the road now, and winter is creeping over. Where just eight weeks ago sheep were grazing in the cirque under the peak, the ground is now covered with hoar frost that will not move for six months. The Cime will be unpassable now until May, when Aurelien and the rest of the team will come back. Up into the barren lunar heights and a final hard push. Peace within effort, freedom within restrictions. Chasing the shouting wind, soaring into the void, a small moment of forgetting, of holding hands with the infinite. Then a little zigzag between the icy tracks to make it to the col. If only to prove that, in this world where you're always being told not to do things – that getting there is not possible, normal people take the train or drive in a car, don't do that it's dangerous – you are still a force, a self-determined being in the world. This is my place, all this grandeur and splendour, it is mine. Silence.

It will only take one flake of snow, a single one upon billions, to tip the balance and for this world to be shut off for another year. The moon will rise and sink, and there will be a downpouring of immense whiteness through the dark between the cathedral spires of the peaks, swallowing up trees, snapping branches, confounding rocks, and every single thing will become one. Night will succeed winter night, the shining blanket below reflecting the moon above. The marmots come out to play. Wolves pass, ibex stand above where the road once was. The stars and planets rotate slowly through the sky. The wind blows and blows and another blizzard brings soft oblivion, mute destruction, an avalanche and a rockfall. Nobody will think of this, as they ride their bikes through the fields, on the lanes, on their turbo trainers in their garages down below. But as the mornings and evenings draw further apart, something again will stir in the mind, a memory or a

dream, or a memory of a dream of riding near these peaks. The thaw will begin and spread upwards. Renewal, regrowth and reopening, and another season will begin and the cyclists will come.

But all that is in the future. Time now for the descent.

GLOSSARY

À bloc: Full gas.

Autobus: The French-language term for the group of slower riders, mainly sprinters and *domestiques*, who band together in the mountains to make sure that nobody misses the time cut. In Italian, *grupetto*.

Cuite: French term for bonking, cracking, hitting the wall. Literally 'cooked'.

Directeur sportif: The sporting director, who makes a team's strategic and tactical decisions, and looks after its performance. Can encompass anything from a manager and mastermind combined in one man to simply the guy who's in charge in the team car on the road that day.

Domestique: A supporting rider, working in the service of one of his teammates. In Italian, *gregano*.

En danseuse: Standing on the pedals. Literally, shorthand for something, like in a dancer's position.

Faire le métier: An expression that denotes learning the trade of a professional bike rider. The rituals and etiquette of riding in the peloton; the lifestyle and practices of someone committed to that path. Back when being initiated into doping was part of one's passage into professional life, it had sinister overtones.

Gregario: See *domestique*.

Grupetto: See *autobus*.

Maglia rosa: Italian for the pink jersey worn by the leader of the Giro d'Italia.

Maillot jaune: French for the yellow jersey of the Tour de France leader. Most histories say it was first awarded in 1919 and that Eugène Christophe was the first to wear yellow.

Musette: Small cotton bag used to pass food to cyclists during races.

Palmarès: The roll call of a cyclist's race wins and achievements.

Parcours: A fancy French way of saying 'route' – though it encompasses the race's ups and downs as well as its lefts and rights.

Soigneur: Team helper with multifarious roles. Everything from masseur to rider's confidant, adviser, healer and spiritual guide. Helps riders learn to ***faire le métier***. May also hand out food and drink on the road and undertake general dogsbodying. In the old days often an unofficial pharmacist, the guy who sorted out a rider's ***soins***.

Soins: Literally 'care' or 'treatment'. Euphemistically, pills and drugs.

ACKNOWLEDGEMENTS

The thoughts and experiences that make up this book are ones that have preoccupied me for a long time, and to an extent everything I've worked on for years has added something to this book. But there are a few specific magazines to thank. First, *Rouleur*, who commissioned me to go and find René Vietto's toe, thank you for letting me retell that story here. Similarly, I first wrote about Everesting for the *Ride Journal*, and there are bits of that article in the mix in that chapter. I wrote something very different about Everesting for Strava, but it's for sending me to Andorra that I must thank them; and *Meter* sent me to Font Romeu to write about running, something that helped me explore the peculiar science of altitude. Thanks to Antton Miettinen, Camille McMillan and Andy Waterman for certain of the photos I've included.

And now to the main event: a thousand thank yous to Joe Dombrowski. If at any point I sound like a bit of a fanboy, that's because I am, and I am in awe of what he and other professional riders do. It was an exciting privilege to get to know him and spend time on the inside of a Grand Tour preparation, at such an interesting and important time in his career. Also top of my list to thank is George Mallory for his enthusiastic response when I emailed, and for taking so much time to chat when he was on holiday in Europe. It was a pleasure and an inspiration to spend a day or two with him. Then many thanks to everyone else I talked to or met, roughly in order of appearance: Jean-Marie-André Fabron of the Nice roads department, and Aurelien, Didier, Éric and Bernard,

the road-clearing crew; Jean Vietto, Jean Bertrand and Federico Bahamontes; Michael Horvath and Davis Kitchel of
Strava; Mauro Vegni and Michele Acquarone; Dr Hugh Montgomery; and Jean-Pierre Benoit.

In addition, I'd like to thank Claude and Laurence Albert
at the Gîte d'Étape de Bousiéyas for their hospitality and
advice. Steve Jones for some interesting conversations, and
for once again letting me make his writing retreat temporarily
mine. Rémi and Ali for taking me to the Giro and sharing my
love of these roads, as well as indulging my obsession with
shepherds' festivals. And Laura Meseguer, Hannah Troop and
Sergi Munyoz for translating and helping with all things Spanish. Oliver Glackin, James Fairbank, Paul Duffy and Ross
Hallard all at some point read bits of the draft and gave valuable feedback.

On the publishing side, thank you to my agent, Jon Elek,
and big thanks to Matt Phillips, the editor who was enthusiastic enough to commission this when it was only a vague
idea; then also to Tim Broughton, who took over the reins
and very thoughtfully edited and helped it across the finish
line. And to Fran Jessop, Mia Quibell-Smith and Bethan Jones
and everybody at Yellow Jersey for all the work they do.

Some of the last things to happen in the production process
were also some of the most important. Big thanks to both
Mattieu Lifschitz, Monvelle.cc, and The Handmade Cyclist
for their illustrated contributions – a beautiful map and amazing cover respectively.

Finally, thanks to Claire and Anton and John, for that first
mad ride up the Bonette just before the snow fell in 2011.

FURTHER READING

Here's a short list of some of the books I drew on when writing this, or ones that I have enjoyed and which have added to my understanding of cycling, the mountains, or both.

Aldo, Leopold	*A Sand Country Almanac*
Barnes, Simon	*The Meaning of Sport*
Blann, Michael	*Mountains: Epic Cycling Climbs*
Bonatti, Walter	*The Mountains of My Life*
Chany, Pierre	*La fabuleuse histoire du Tour de France*
de Botton, Alain	*The Art of Travel*
DeLillo, Don	*End Game*
Écomusée du pays de la Roudoule	*Route des Grandes Alpes*
Fignon, Laurent	*We Were Young and Carefree* (translated by William Fotheringham)
Fotheringham, Alasdair	*The Eagle of Toledo: The Life and Times of Federico Bahamontes*
Friebe, Daniel	*Mountain High: Europe's 50 Greatest Cycle Climbs*
Gourdon, Michel and Marie-Louise	*Berger d'en haut*
Hutchinson, Michael	*Faster*
Kimmelman, Michael	*The Accidental Masterpiece: On the Art of Life and Vice Versa*

Macfarlane, Robert	*Mountains of the Mind: A History of a Fascination*
McGann, Bill and Carol	*The Story of the Tour de France*
Murakami, Haruki	*What I Talk About When I Talk About Running*
Shepherd, Nan	*The Living Mountain: A Celebration of the Cairngorm Mountains of Scotland*
Shoumatoff, Nicholas and Nina	*The Alps: Europe's Mountain Heart*
Terray, Lionel	*Conquistadors of the Useless: From the Alps to Annapurna*

LIST OF ILLUSTRATIONS

Photos in the text are the author's own snaps, or old postcards from his collection, except where indicated.

INDEX

Page references in *italics* indicate photographs and illustrations.